THE EYE OF THE WIND

PETER SCOTT

THE EYE OF THE WIND

HODDER AND STOUGHTON

Revised Edition © 1966 by Peter Scott

First published 1961
Fifth impression 1963
Hodder Paperback edition (revised) 1966

*Printed in Great Britain
for Hodder and Stoughton Limited,
St. Paul's House, Warwick Lane, London E.C.4
by Richard Clay (The Chaucer Press), Ltd.,
Bungay, Suffolk*

TO
PHILIPPA

Eye of the wind, whose bearing in
A changeful sky the sage
Birds are never wrong about
And mariners must gauge—

The drift of flight, the fluttered jib
Are what we knew it by:
Seafarers cannot hold or sight
The wind's elusive eye.

That eye, whose shifting moods inspire
The sail and trim the sheet,
Commands me, though I can but steer
Obliquely towards it.

C. DAY LEWIS

CONTENTS

1. THE WINDOW

I am without question the luckiest, and I believe the happiest, man I know. I think I am lucky because I love, and am loved by, the woman to whom this book is dedicated, because I can spend my time and earn my living doing the things I most enjoy, because I have had extraordinarily good health and because I was born with a happy disposition.

Not that I have known no misery or discouragement or despair. No one knows better than my family how much I am given to moods. But they do not last long, because life is too short to let them spoil my enjoyment; and I think of that enjoyment as a glorious bonus—not as something I am entitled to as of right. My enjoyment is positive—a delight in being alive and sharing my enthusiasms with others, and particularly a delight in the natural world around me.

All animals have interested me, and birds more than others, but wild geese have an almost mystical importance. Long ago I decided that my home must always be within sight and sound of the winter wild geese. In only a small number of places in Britain, from one spot, can one be sure of seeing and hearing wild geese daily through the winter months, and on such a spot, close to the estuary of the River Severn, stands the house in which I live with my family. In winter-time the White-fronted Geese feed in the fields all around us; at dawn they stream over us on their morning flight, and under the full

11

moon the night echoes with their wild cries. It is just as I planned it long ago.

As I write, I am sitting in the window of my studio. It is no ordinary window; it is ten feet across and eight feet high, and it looks out upon water and birds and the green fields of Gloucestershire. A pool with islands reflects a flash of the setting sun in the ripples made by the ducks and geese that are swimming on it. The water comes to within six feet of where I sit, and clustered before me is a great crowd of birds, 300 or more, of many different kinds from all over the world. Many of them are tame, brought from distant countries to live together here in the Vale of Berkeley—Ringed Teal from Brazil, Barrow's Goldeneyes from Iceland, Ruddy Ducks from North America, Ne-ne Geese from Hawaii . . . But many, too, are wild ones from far-away breeding grounds which have chosen to spend their winter at the Wildfowl Trust on the Severn Estuary, and to come in to feed in front of my window—Pintails, Wigeon, Shovelers, Pochard, Tufted Ducks, Coots . . .

There is a grey ruffle on the far water from the light wind, which is coming from just a touch north of west. The precise wind direction, the very eye of the wind, has always been important in my life for the activities which have depended on it: the study of birds, sailing, soaring, all depend at one point or another upon the eye of the wind and an appreciation of its precise bearing.

The light has almost gone now, but still very dimly I can see the birds moving about on the dark-blue water and the black shapes of them as they fly against the dark-blue sky.

A pair of ducks circles round over the pond, out over the pollard willows until the two black specks are lost against the loom of the elm trees beyond and in the red reflection on the glass of the lamp-shade behind me. The wild Whitefronts of the Severn Estuary have gone east on the first stage of the long migration which will take them to their breeding grounds in Arctic Russia; only a few weeks ago we were out under those elms in the rain-soaked dusk, setting a net to catch the geese in order to mark them with rings on their legs; and before daylight on the following morning we were back again putting the finishing touches to our work before the geese should come.

A single goose called out of the darkness and then passed low over the field, only just visible against the sky. He was the mysterious and still unexplained scout, the forerunner of the great skeins, who flies yelping over the feeding-ground in the early gloom a few minutes before the main flocks arrive. Then we heard the first clamour of the main flight. We ran to the hedge, and stood there half hidden by it, as wave after wave of geese passed low over our heads. It was too dark for them to see us through the thin hawthorn branches, and to us the birds were no more than black silhouettes against the low grey clouds.

To each of the five of us watching they meant something different. To one a quarry species for the wildfowler, to another the raw material of a biologist's work. To me they were the single continuing passionate interest of my life, as a painter, and as a naturalist—just as exciting and moving as they had been thirty years before when I first fell under their spell. Familiarity had done nothing to lessen the thrill; the tingle still ran down my spine at the sheer beauty of the sight and sound. But, then, there was additional enjoyment that stemmed from this very familiarity itself. The first geese had landed just where I expected. From long experience I was able to forecast and explain their movements.

In the twilight of the dawn the geese had landed in the next field but one to our nets because it was still too dark for them to see the stuffed decoy birds which we had set out. Wild geese have surprisingly poor vision when they are flying in the half light. Once the first geese were down, the great flock began to build up in a thick mass in the centre of the grass field they had chosen.

When the whole flock was assembled—3,000 strong—and the daylight had come, I knew that my appearance at a precise point in the field beyond them would lift the whole mass and send the bulk of it in a great clamouring wave over the field in

13

which our nets were set: and this, in fact, they did exactly as I hoped, so that we had a great crowd of geese in our field. The geese, in combination with the weather, finally beat us and we never released our nets, but my thoughts for most of that day were those of a White-fronted Goose. Yet there were also things I did not fully understand, the things that nobody knew, the challenge of discoveries still to be made. What was the true explanation of the single scout before dawn? Why, when I flushed the geese from their first field, did two small lots go off into the distance instead of yielding to the powerful mechanisms which hold the flock together? Small mysteries these, leading up to the much larger mysteries of migration and navigation and the evolution of the traditions which order the life of a wild goose. To a naturalist these were signposts on a road whose end was far over the horizon; and I had been a naturalist ever since I could remember, for I had become a naturalist by the design of my parents.

A few days before he died in his tent in the Antarctic on 29th March, 1912, my father wrote to my mother:

'Make the boy interested in Natural History. It is better than games. They encourage it at some schools ... Above all he must guard, and you must guard him, against indolence. Make him a strenuous man; I had to force myself into being strenuous as you know, had always an inclination to be idle.'

But my father had made himself strenuous and my mother was always strenuous too, so 'idleness' in the accepted sense was not, for me, the most serious danger. The direction of strenuousness and enthusiasm into the right channels was much more difficult.

I was two and a half years old when my father wrote that injunction, and I cannot remember a time when I have not been interested in Natural History.

This interest has given my life its form, and led me very early on to the conclusion that the pursuit of beauty and truth are the two most exciting aspirations of the human spirit. So I

14

am a painter by profession and an amateur scientist. I paint mainly because I enjoy it. I am a scientist because I believe that adding to knowledge is worth doing for its own sake. The application of it to the material welfare of human beings is merely a useful by-product, but the main object of science is something much more important and majestic—the search for truth.

So my aims in life are to use such talents as I was born with, and such skills as I have acquired, to enrich the lives of other people during my own lifetime, and if possible after I am dead. I have an itch to create, and my life is too short for all the things I want to make.

Then there's courage. Ever since I can remember I have admired the brave, but always I have been obsessed with the fear that I myself shall not come up to my own standards, or to Service standards in the Navy, or to the family tradition. (In the war my mother once said, 'Your father would have been pleased about that.') Many times in my life I have been superlatively frightened. I cannot prevent myself from imagining what will happen if things go wrong. I can see in my mind blood and pain and death, and with them comes the near-panic of fear which I must challenge myself to beat. This was perhaps the main theme of the full-length story of my life that I wrote several years ago; it is perhaps the main theme, too, of this new and shorter version of the same story.

But kindness and tolerance are rarer and more important than courage, though it took me a long time to discover it.

2. AT AN EARLY AGE

I was born and brought up in a small Victorian terrace house
—No. 174 Buckingham Palace Road—which overlooked
Victoria Station, with its vista of railway engines. In spite of
this the commonest youthful ambition of that day—to be an
engine driver—was never mine.

I must have been quite young when my mother found herself sitting one night at a dinner next to Lord Baden-Powell,
the Chief Scout. He was ambidextrous and showed her the
advantages of being able to write and draw with both hands. It
would be nice, she thought, if her son, too, was ambidextrous;
so from then onwards she started taking the pencil out of my
right hand when I was drawing and putting it into my left.
This might have achieved what she intended had she not
slightly overdone it, so that I have been left-handed ever since.
That is the story she used to tell, although privately I think I
might have been left-handed anyway.

I suppose I was a slow developer as a child and certainly I
was late in learning to read and write. Even now I read so
slowly that I read very little—perhaps on the average no more
than two books a year, and this I greatly regret.

But if I learned to read late I began to draw early. I can
remember enjoying drawing in a positive sort of way at a very
early age, but the results in those days were sadly lacking in
artistic merit. Like so many children I was obsessed with

minute detail and accuracy—a fascination from which I have never been able to escape completely.

For holidays we had a tiny coast-guard's cottage near Sandwich, called 'Shingle End'; it stood in a small group of cottages among the dunes at the far end of Princes Golf Course. The striped curtains in the cottage smelled of damp, the rush mats were full of sand and there was an earth closet at the bottom of the garden. There was no road to the coast-guard station and we had to walk more than a mile along a sandy path among the golf bunkers, carrying all stores and provisions.

Around the group of cottages ran a grey brick wall covered with yellow lichen. The turf lay against the bottom of the wall, and if in summer you worked your way along it searching in the crack between grass and bricks, you could find, if you were lucky, the Common or Viviparous Lizard. These were the first lizards with which I ever became acquainted—the first of a long line of lizards which I have counted among my friends (among the latest in the line are the Marine Iguanas of the Galapagos Islands and the Chamaeleons of Kenya).

The turf around our cottage was rich in pink Rest Harrow flowers, and yellow Birdsfoot Trefoil on which the caterpillars of the Six-spot Burnet used to feed, and at times the sand dunes were alive with the glossy black and red moths as they hatched from their strange papery cocoons on the grass stems.

Here I first became conscious of the song of the Skylark. At Shingle End there was always a lark overhead. There were sea birds too, especially waders, and ducks ... and once Brent Geese—perhaps forty of them formed into a V with unequal arms and they flew low over the sea. As they passed the afternoon sun shone full on their bright white sterns. I did not know what they were at the time, but I carried the picture in my mind until long afterwards when I realised without doubt what I had seen—my very first wild geese.

In the front drawing-room of our house in London was a grand piano which was also a pianola. It used paper rolls longitudinally perforated. I was allowed to operate this machine from the time my feet would reach the pedals. It was an instrument ideally suited for the creation of an interest in music, for to any child it was an irresistible toy. We had a limited number of rolls which lived inside the piano stool. All were of famous music, which soon became well known to me. Many were special piano renderings of orchestral, even operatic, works. I can remember every one of them today; the G minor Ballade and the Polonaise Militaire of Chopin, a Liszt Hungarian Rhapsody, plenty of Beethoven—the Moonlight and Kreutzer Sonatas, the 1st Piano Concerto and the 4th; the Eroica and 5th Symphonies; Schubert's Rosamunda and the Unfinished; the Overtures and principal melodies from *The Magic Flute* and *Cosi Fan Tutte*; Rossini's music used in *Boutique Fantasque* and one or two more.

I shall never forget the thrill of hearing these works for the first time in the concert hall. To know the tunes intimately and then suddenly to discover what it was really supposed to sound like made a tremendous impact. I never learned to play any musical instrument, but music has led me to some of the most intense enjoyments of my life.

My wife once told me that when she was a child she had imagined me as a dark-eyed tragic little boy living under the perpetual shadow of my father's death in the Antarctic. But it was not like that at all. My father had left on his last expedition when I was one and a half years old. Never having known him I was brought up without any sense of loss. My mother who was one of the gayest people I have ever known, could never have tolerated any kind of continuing tragedy. She was a professional sculptor who had studied her art in Paris and had been a pupil of the great French sculptor Rodin. She was immensely energetic and in my early childhood she was already well known as an artist, especially for her vigorous portraits. Her larger-than-life statues of my father were in place in London and in Christchurch, New Zealand; her small statuettes, often including delightful babies, were exhibited regularly at the Academy and at the Salon in Paris; but in particular the distinguished men of the times came to her studio, and many of them became her lifelong friends.

During the First World War my mother accepted a job in the Embassy in Paris and took me with her. In those days there were roundabouts at various places along the Champs Elysées. These were my special delight, for as you took your seat on the wooden horse you were given a spike with a wooden handle and each time as you whizzed round you tried to collect on your spike one of a row of little rings which hung from a board. If you succeeded, another ring dropped down into the place of the one you had spiked. There were normally ten revolutions per ride, and if at the end you had ten rings on your spike you were given a free ride again. I must have been the despair of the roundabout proprietors, for in the end I became proficient enough to ride all afternoon for the original fee.

While we were in Paris the war was going badly; at one time the front line was less than forty miles from the city and the taxi-cabs were requisitioned for troop movements. There was also Big Bertha, the huge German long-range gun which fired into Paris. I can well remember the day it opened up. There was clear blue sky and it was very hot. Quite early in the morning the shells began to fall on the city and continued with an extraordinary regularity about every half-hour. A good deal of panic arose, and together with the rest of my school I spent the whole day in the cellar. For a long time it was believed that an 'invisible aeroplane' was operating, and a young pilot, who had been dining with my mother the night before, was sent off in his aeroplane to look for it. His mission was unsuccessful, of course, for there was no ghost bomber to find, but I remember a few nights later sitting in my pyjamas in our hotel sitting-room with my eyes popping out of my head while he told us about it. Twice during the day he had climbed high into the cloudless sky, creeping laboriously up to the maximum ceiling of his aircraft. He made it sound so exciting and so beautiful that aeroplanes immediately became wonderful, romantic things whose only object was to climb as high as possible into a clear blue sky.

Because of the Antarctic story I was, even as a small child, regarded as 'fair game' by the press photographers and reporters. At an early age I was frequently recognised in the street—a state of affairs which, as I have discovered more recently in a different context, has its advantages and disadvantages. During my childhood, my mother made great and, on the whole, successful efforts to protect me from the effects of this notoriety, but it was inescapably one manifestation of being my father's son. There were others; the people who said, 'Well, my little man! Are you going to follow in your father's footsteps when you grow up?' Or the ones who genuinely admired my father and expected me to be like him. All these things have had specific effects on my life. First of all, being the son of a national hero set me a standard. Whether or not I could live up to it, it was at least there (like Everest). Secondly, it provided an incentive to succeed in some quite different direction entirely on my own unaided effort; and thirdly, it inoculated me, to some extent, against the Antarctic story with which I grew up. This meant, and still means, that I know rather less about the intimate details of my father's explorations than many of my contemporaries. Of course, my mother read the story to me as a child, but I did not set out regularly to re-read it and so the details were gradually forgotten. Thus when I am asked about those more technical parts of the expeditions which I am naturally expected to have at my finger-tips, I find myself at a loss.

In polar exploration my father had achieved a position to which I could not possibly aspire. I could obviously never be more than a pale shadow desperately trying to emulate him, to be dogged all my life by direct and unfavourable comparison. If I was not to live in reflected glory only, I must strike out on a line of my own. I could not follow in my father's footsteps; but to follow his wish that I should be interested in Natural History was something quite different. About this my mother was very ingenious, for she did not thrust the subject down my

21

throat, but instead put me most subtly into the way of naturalists and biologists of all kinds, many of them famous men who were prepared to give time to me because of the passage in my father's letter.

A more romantic approach to animals came from the books of Ernest Thompson Seton. My copies of *Lives of the Hunted* and *Wild Animals I Have Known* had previously belonged to my father. They are inscribed with his signature and 'Discovery Winter Quarters, February 1903'. They and the others —*The Trail of the Sandhill Stag, Rolf in the Woods* and *Wild Animal Ways*—must have influenced me considerably and even lastingly. My favourite story was 'Tito, the Coyote that learned how'. At six years old I knew it more or less by heart.

These books were a part of my life: they were without question classics: every aspiring naturalist had obviously read them. Only now, looking again at the worn and dilapidated volumes and re-reading the stories, do I fully realise Thompson Seton's genius. In the days before animal behaviour became an exact science, he was a good enough naturalist to avoid making his animals think like humans, he was tender and sad, and simple enough for children, without ever being sentimental. It seems possible that Thompson Seton's achievement in introducing thousands of children to the wild woods will be increasingly valued by future generations of mankind.

My two godfathers were Admiral Sir Clements Markham, President of the Royal Geographical Society at the time of my father's first expedition (it was for him that I was christened with the middle name of Markham), and the Scottish playwright Sir James Barrie.

For all the time that I knew him, Barrie lived on the top floor of Adelphi Terrace House, overlooking the river. As a very small boy I used to go there for tea, sometimes with my mother, sometimes alone and feeling very independent. There is no doubt that Barrie knew all about how to get on with children. Although there were often long silences I cannot ever remember feeling shy in his company. He used to write me delightful comic letters, often in rhyme, and always full of invention.

Barrie himself first took me to *Peter Pan*, I when was four and a half. I have seen it several times since, and cannot remember what impression it made on me that first time. But Barrie always described how he asked me in the taxi on the way home which part I had enjoyed most. 'I think,' I am supposed to have said, after some deliberation, 'that I enjoyed it most when I dropped the programme on the fat lady's head in the interval.'

3. NO CLOTHES

My mother believed that hardiness could be induced by habit and training—cold baths and not too many clothes. I was always a thickset little boy, inclined to be podgy, and before going to school I had worn clothes which are more or less standard dress for children now—shirt and shorts, or just the shorts, in summer, and a jersey in winter. This has led people to comment, 'Of course I used to know you when you were a little boy; you wore no clothes.' This was relative rather than literal, for out of doors my contemporaries tended to wear overcoats, scarves, gloves and buttoned gaiters. A press report of the time even records with shocked amazement that I was usually *bare-headed*.

I was ten years old when I was sent to West Downs, a Preparatory School near Winchester, where, under Kenneth Tindall's headmastership, my Natural History interests were well served. Butterflies and moths, and especially their caterpillars, swam for the first time into my ken. One of the masters knew about 'bug-hunting', and under his encouragement I found my first Poplar Hawk Moth caterpillars on the leaves of the young poplar trees in the neighbouring nursery garden. My first Lime Hawk caterpillar was found in the row of limes above the cricket field; my first Puss Moths slept like black and green kittens on the leaves of the willows at the back of the miniature rifle range.

By this time I was deeply committed to Natural History,

and one day when I was going down to Sandwich by train I made an astonishing and useful discovery. I was standing in the corridor looking at a map on the swing door that divided the second- from the third-class carriages when the door, against which I was leaning, was suddenly opened from the other side. I put out my left hand and gripped the door-post for support. The door swung back on my thumb. I felt very little, but when I looked at my hand I saw that the flesh of the whole top of my left thumb was removed from the bone and hung like half a plum separated from its stone. Apparently I ran back into the carriage saying in matter-of-fact tones, 'Look, Mummy, my thumb's come off.'

Later, when the numbness wore off, it hurt terribly. We got off the train at Tonbridge Wells, where I was treated by a doctor. As it was being dressed my mother said, 'Think of the nicest thing you can think of.' At that moment the nicest thing I could think of was a fully grown Privet Hawk Moth caterpillar and I thought hard of its glorious velvety greenness, the purple and white diagonal stripes and the curved shiny black and yellow horn on its tail; above all, I thought of the satisfying bigness and fatness of it. I concentrated fiercely on this image and suddenly no pain remained in my thumb.

I had to return to London for final treatment. 'He will have no feeling in that thumb,' said the surgeon cheerfully, 'and will probably never be able to bend it again.' But in due course the only after-effects proved to be an inconspicuous scar and a slight malformation of the thumb-nail. Much more important was the discovery that concentration of thought could so strikingly affect physical pain. I seemed to have a sort of safety curtain which I could lower between my imagination and reality. It has been a useful standby many times since then.

At West Downs I made two discoveries which were unexpected: I could swim faster than most, and I had what was considered to be a reasonably good soprano voice. No doubt the swimming originated from visits to the swimming baths at a very early age. My mother had been determined that I should swim before I could walk. I may well have swum at a year old. Certainly I can remember swimming 'dog-paddle' quite happily and successfully at a very early age. I also remember a curious period of a year or two—at about the age of five—when I lost confidence and could no longer swim. But then suddenly the confidence returned.

The fact that I was unbeaten over the 'six lengths' distance in the school swimming baths went some way to offset my undistinguished performances on the cricket and football fields. Neither here nor at public school was my heart ever in organised games. With an acceptable treble voice, and a capacity to sing in tune, I soon found myself singing the solos in chapel and taking part regularly in all the concerts, at which term after term, year after year, I used to sing 'Polly Wolly Doodle all the Day', and I wonder whether the audience got more bored with the song than I did.

About half-way through my time at West Downs a new character appeared in my life—Edward Hilton Young, who was later to become 'Bill', my stepfather, a Cabinet Minister, and Lord Kennet of the Dene. I liked him at once and immensely. He was a naval hero of the war; he had lost his right arm in the Zeebrugge raid; he had commanded an armoured train in Russia; he had won a D.S.O. and a D.S.C.; he had written a book about the war, he was a Member of Parliament. He was quiet and brave and he knew about birds. What more could there be? It was some time before I realised that my mother was going to marry him, but when I did I was completely delighted. So far as I was concerned it was all a splendid idea, and this it remained ever after.

The three of us went to Tunisia for a holiday. Tunis is chiefly memorable because it led to my first ride on a camel (outside London Zoo). We went south from Sfax to Gabes, and rode in a caravan of camels westwards into the desert. The camel is not perhaps a particularly difficult animal to ride, but I still remember the glow of pleasure when I was first allowed to take my camel away from camp on my own, to go looking for animals. In a shallow pool at a small oasis one evening I found a terrapin. I slid down to catch it and had a difficult time thereafter trying to persuade the camel to kneel down again for me to remount! I had visions of having to return ignominiously to camp leading the beast behind me; and then suddenly and most unexpectedly it knelt, and in a moment I was up on its back. There was nothing now to mar my triumphant return—complete with terrapin.

At West Downs I became a Scout, and along with all my brother Scouts I set out optimistically to pass as many badges as possible.

The stalker's badge involved taking twenty photos of wild creatures so that they were recognisable in the photo, but although I began it, I do not think I ever achieved this badge.

The naturalist's badge, on the other hand, involved being able to identify a certain number of birds from pictures in a book. I had a copy of T. A. Coward's *British Birds*, a famous book which I often carried about with me, jammed into the slightly split pocket of my blazer. I knew all the pictures by heart, and for the test I laboriously covered the names by sticking stamp-paper over them. When the time came, the Scoutmaster very sensibly made me do it from some other book. To my surprise I found that I knew most of the birds, anyway.

I went in for my entertainer's badge by giving a lantern lecture on prehistoric reptiles. It was my first lecture on prehistoric reptiles. It was my first attempt at public speaking and I was dry in the mouth with fright, but hoped I was managing to conceal it. Those who heard me said they would not have known that I was nervous, but they had to admit that it was rather a boring lecture, though the slides, which I had acquired from an outside source, were, they said, quite good. They gave me the badge. The lecture, they said, had meat in it, but not enough humour. I can well believe it. I am still unhappy when speaking in public, and nervous before I go on.

My interest in butterflies and moths at school led to a delightful friendship with Miss Evelyn Cheeseman, the distinguished entomologist, who was Curator of Insects at the London Zoo at the time. She invited me to make a drawing of a Privet Hawk Moth caterpillar for an insect book on which

28

she was then working. This was the first of my drawings ever to be reproduced in a book.

My Zoo visits had long been regular, for I had been made a Life Fellow of the Zoological Society of London as a christening present, and this had enabled me to sign in my nannie with a cross even before I could write my name. At one of the Zoo's stormy General Meetings in 1958 I was able to put forward my point of view as the senior Fellow in the room, with forty-nine years of Fellowship behind me!

It seems from my letters home from West Downs that birds were already becoming especially important in my life. As ever, I was optimistic, particularly in listing the extreme rarities which I believed I had seen. I wrote to my step-father-to-be:

'My dear Hilton,

'We have seen such nice things. A Spotted Flycatcher's nest with four eggs, two Willow-Wrens' nests and a Chiff-chaff's, and a Cole Tit's. We saw a Wall Creeper, a grey-backed shrike, and a Pied Flycatcher, as well as a Spotted Flycatcher and a Long-tailed Tit, a pair of Goldfinches and a Nut-hatch going into its hole. My only reason for believing that the Wall Creeper was genuine is that it was rather like a Tree Creeper only it was climbing up a wall. It had a slightly longer beak than a Tree Creeper and was more curved. Yesterday we saw a family of Gold Crests in a fir tree and a pair of Bullfinches.'

When I was eleven, my mother decided our summer holiday should be spent in France. She went there to see a villa named La Solitude, which she planned to take on the island of Noirmoutier off the mouth of the Loire, and she wrote to me describing it glowingly.

When later we arrived at Noirmoutier it was as wonderful a place as she had said, and it became our summer holiday home for the next two years.

La Solitude was a small villa set in the pinewoods perhaps fifty yards from an uncrowded beach. The sand was smooth and white—a perfect beach with a rocky outcrop at one end. There were boats drawn up on the sand at the other end of the beach in front of a holiday hotel called the Beau Rivage. The sand dunes and the pinewoods were full of lizards and my cup was full.

I wrote again to my stepfather-to-be, who was at that time Financial Secretary to the Treasury:

> 'You absolutely must come here, it's too divine—fishes, birds, lizards, butterflies, sea, woods and everything.
> 'We have caught 4 kinds of lizards
> > Sand lizards
> > Green lizards
> > Common lizards
> > Wall lizards
>
> 'It's hot all the time and gorgeous.
>
> Pete.'

The letter was adorned with drawings of the lizards.

For the young, one of the objects of a holiday abroad is to learn the language. For an hour each morning Mademoiselle Herbulin, an elderly spinster, used to come to La Solitude to teach me French. She did not care for frogs or toads or lizards or caterpillars, but she told me she knew of a little animal called a Cochon d'Indes. I had no idea what this could be. I listened most carefully to the description, but somehow it never occurred to me that she was simply describing a guinea-pig. I was fascinated; I thought this must be the most rare and wonderful animal—something between a Bushbaby and a Kinkajou. 'And you can keep them as pets, too,' she said. 'I will bring you one tomorrow morning.' Excitement ran high, as may be imagined, until the guinea-pig arrived. Deep disappointment followed. It was, curiously enough, my first guinea-pig and inevitably it was not long before it laid strong claim to my affections. Without doubt it was a delightful pet; and yet it was some time before my faith in Mlle Herbulin was entirely restored.

But more important than Mlle Herbulin were the caterpillars. Two species are indelibly imprinted on my mind. One was an adult Pine Hawk Moth larva which I found walking across the sand just outside the door of our villa, looking for somewhere to pupate. It was the first of these that I had ever seen, it was beautiful and rare (at least in England), and it was an incomparable prize. It finally buried itself in a box of sandy earth which I provided for it, and in due course failed, so far as I recall, to hatch out. The other was a whole colony—some dozens—of the caterpillars of the Humming Bird Hawk Moth which I found feeding on bedstraw in the sand dunes just behind the beach. These adult caterpillars were of two colours, some green and some purplish brown. They had longitudinal stripes and carried on their tails the characteristic Hawk Moth spike. Again they were the first of their kind I had ever seen and each new one that I found was a new excitement; for the whole day on which I discovered this colony I was in a seventh heaven of delight.

Forty years later, when I took my own family to Noirmoutier we found Humming Bird Hawk caterpillars again—though in other ways the place was much changed.

Noirmoutier was (and still is) reached from the mainland across a causeway at low tide. In both directions from the causeway the road led through salt-pans, and salt-marshes and low-lying meadows in which there were always Yellow Wagtails.

Boats figured, too, in the delights of Noirmoutier. There was a small class of double-ended dories, with coloured lug sails and steered with an oar—fishing dories converted for racing. I was never allowed to sail in these boats during a race, but I can remember going out fishing in one and watching dolphins leaping ten feet out of the water and falling back with a splash to be heard half a mile away.

At the rocky end of the beach there was a fish trap which consisted of a rough wall of weed-covered rocks with a couple of grids. At low spring tides the area enclosed by the wall was almost dry and the small pool was full of large Wrasse and quantities of flat fish. As the tide went down there was tremendous excitement trying to determine what fish had been caught inside.

The summers at Noirmoutier are still a kaleidoscope of bright pictures; even by the next term at West Downs I was full of nostalgia in a letter to my mother:

'My dear,

'How nice it is to think of La Solitude, picking black-berries and catching lizards on the last day, and how good the cakes were from the patisserie, and that evening in the woods, our bathe by moonlight, the thunderstorms; all to be repeated next summer. Those lovely starfish; the fisher-woman's horn; walking round the walls of St Malo.'

These delectable memories, however, did not prevent me from enjoying the school term that followed.

But however successfully or unsuccessfully a school may provide 'the happiest days of one's life', holiday memories are likely to stand out most plainly. Many of our holidays were spent with the Austen Chamberlain family. Joe was a little older than me, Diane a year younger (and I was determined to marry her) and Lawrence younger still. I remember a simple and sad little story of deflation which happened when both our families were staying in the village of Trebeurden in Britanny. We children had been ranging over the gorse-covered hill look-ing for Dartford Warblers and we thought it must be nearly lunch-time. Approaching us was a Frenchman who looked as though he would have a watch; but who was to ask him the time? Was it not I who spoke French like a native—and why not? Had I not been to school in Paris and spent summer holidays in Noirmoutier?

I stepped into the road. 'Pardon, m'sieur,' in the faultless accent of the parrot. 'Est-ce que vous pouvez me dire le temps?' There was a giggle from behind me. 'Please can you tell me the weather?' How could I possibly have made such an elementary error? I can still remember the hot shame of it; and Diane is happily married to someone else.

When our house in Buckingham Palace Road was scheduled

for demolition to make way for the Green Line Coach Station, we moved to Bayswater Road. On the corner of Leinster Terrace, overlooking Kensington Gardens, stands a two-storey semi-detached house with an oval window in its side wall, a small garden in front and a larger one behind. At the far end of the back garden, which has a small formal pond and fountain, was a building which my mother converted into a studio for her sculpture. In it Barrie had written Peter Pan.

This new house was much nicer than the old. Like any house which has served a family for thirty-five years, its memories cover the full scale of emotions, but for me it is overwhelmingly a happy place. My half-brother Wayland now lives there with his large family. He had been born at Buckingham Palace Road in 1923 and was three years old when we first moved into Leinster Corner.

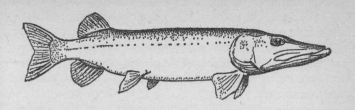

4. 'COME ON, OUNDLE'

In the autumn of 1923 I was sent to Oundle School which was principally renowned for its enlightened attitude to science and technology. Engineering was its special line, but the natural sciences were well served. For zoology, it seemed, I could hardly do better.

I arrived at the school in company with Michael Dilke, the son of an old friend of my mother. He was a keen ornithologist and had already been two terms at Oundle.

In the preceding Easter holidays, it was arranged that I should join a special course which went annually from Oundle School to the Marine Biological Association at Plymouth. It was here that I first met Bill Orton, a marine biologist of distinction. At Sandwich I had learnt a little about the animals of a sandy shore, and now Dr Orton showed me for the first time the animals of a rocky coast, and those which were brought up on to the deck of the Association's trawler *Salpa*, in the trawls and dredges from deeper water. But to me the greatest enjoyment of that first course was shore collecting at Wembury Bay. At low spring tides our party went far out on the rocky shore, each armed with a 'collecting basket' which contained one large jam jar, and a number of smaller ones. As we turned over the big stones, the profusion and variety of different animals we found underneath them was to me sheer delight. Rocklings, Blennies, Cornish Suckers and Butterfish; the beautiful carpet patterns of compound Ascidians, the delicate branching hydroids, the brittle stars and the quick-moving Polychete worms. With enthusiasm Dr Orton would talk of evolution, the struggle for existence, the range of variation within a single species, and suddenly I realised that there was more in zoology than putting a name to every animal you saw. All the time the beauty of shape and colour and the newness kept me enthralled. The course at Plymouth was a tremendous success.

We fished a great deal at Oundle, for the River Nene, which was near by, is famous for its coarse fish; and besides the river, there were near-by lakes and ponds well stocked with fish. According to local legend the ponds in Biggin Park were originally laid out by the monks. In one pond there were Roach and in another Rudd, while in a third there seemed to be a population of Roach–Rudd hybrids. There were also Bream, and in one of the ponds Rudd–Bream hybrids. All these peculiar fish interested me so much that I made detailed drawings of them which I took in due course to Dr Tate Regan at the Natural History Museum in London. The specimens from which I made these careful drawings were all caught on hook and line. It was exciting fishing, by the standards of those days—paste or gentles, or perhaps a red worm, on the smallest possible hook, a quill float, touch and timing.

Late one winter Sunday afternoon when ice was forming at the pond I hooked a much larger fish than usual. As I hauled it in, it suddenly clattered out on to the thin ice and I realised that my hook was no longer attached. There the great fish lay on the ice like an upturned carving dish, within easy slithering distance of the patch of open water through which I had been fishing. The ice was much too thin to bear my weight, so thin indeed that I expected the fish itself to break through at any moment. There seemed to be only one thing to do. I must jump into the two feet of water and grab the fish in my hands before it could make its escape. I can still see the fish slipping about on the ice in the cold, frosty winter's dusk. I got it to the shore and it proved to be a Rudd–Bream hybrid. It weighed, if I remember right, about two and a half pounds, and I kept it alive, as I often kept the larger and more interesting fish in those days. There was trouble about the sodden and creaseless pinstripe trousers of my Sunday suit.

The ponds in Biggin Park produced an even more dramatic encounter with a shoal of very large Perch. On one wonderful afternoon when I was fishing with a lob worm there was a great rush as I pulled in to recast. I tried again and a splendid Perch came after it, taking the bait as I paused to give it the chance. The fish weighed 2 lb. 10 oz. A few minutes later I hooked another in exactly the same way. By the end of the afternoon I had four Perch of over two pounds, and a fifth which weighed 3 lb. 2 oz. Two of the largest of these were sent some time later to the Aquarium at the London Zoo. For Perch they were exceptionally large.

I remember, too, from these days, a four-pound Tench caught with a noose as it cruised in the clear shallows of the lake at Blatherwyke, a fish which also went to the London Zoo.

But, apart from Pike, the largest fish we caught at Oundle were Bream. They were in larger schools and of larger size, so it seemed, in the river itself and they were most easily caught at night. The problem was to get out of school at night. It involved a certain amount of subterfuge and a certain amount of climbing, but it was fairly frequently achieved. On one particular night near Barnwell, on a bend of the Nene which was famous for its bream, two of us had three ledger lines down when the Bream shoal came past. Under each rod hung a loop of line with a small piece of paper folded over it. When the fish took the bait the paper jumped up, and this could easily be seen in the dark. As each of us played a great dish-sized Bream, I can still see the third piece of paper jumping up and remember the moment of panic; what do we do now? I forget how that particular panic was resolved. But I know that in half an hour we had caught a dozen splendid Bream, the largest $5\frac{1}{2}$ lb. We had to leave them out there that night in order to bring them back legitimately on the following afternoon.

Fishing was not always smiled upon at Oundle, particularly if it prevented attendance at football matches. I hated being made to watch other people playing football. I have never enjoyed watching other people doing anything so much as doing it myself. I could not bear standing on the touch-line shouting 'Come on, Ounder!' with a lot of equally bored contemporaries. In vain did they try to appeal to my community spirit. If it was a House Match, where was my pride in my house, if a School Match, where my loyalty to the school? Did I not mind how each of them fared on the football field? The sad thing was that I did not. Of course, there was a price to pay for this kind of delinquency, and finally it came down to corporal punishment. The first couple of times it was four strokes with the cane from the duty House Prefect, then six from the Head of the House, then six from the Housemaster and finally six from the Headmaster. This scale usually lasted me through the winter, for of course it was not every time that I got caught. On match-watching days I could be seen hobbling down the steps from School House with a stiff leg caused by the fishing rod hidden in my trouser-leg.

There were times when fishing was quite legitimate. I remember standing on the bridge which spans the River Nene near Oundle station, fishing for Chubb, when I saw the Headmaster approaching down the road. There was nothing illegal in fishing from there or at that particular time, but somehow I felt it would be best if the rod were concealed. Unfortunately at that precise moment the bait was taken by a goodly Chubb. As the Headmaster approached, deep in conversation with an assistant master, I turned my back on the bridge parapet and held the rod just below the edge. I could only use one hand for this, for the other would be occupied with taking off my straw hat to the Headmaster as he passed. He stopped suddenly when he was abreast of me. 'Well, Scott—not fishing today?' 'Well, sir, "Yes" and "No", sir.' 'Oh, well. Good luck!' and he was walking on again, while I returned to the problems of landing my Chubb.

The Headmaster was no discourager of enterprise and individuality, provided that it did not get out of hand. We were not supposed to go into the houses in the town because we might pick up epidemic diseases and spread them in the school. Nevertheless I had for some time kept a ferret which for the most part was boarded out at the home of one of the school employees. We caught many rabbits with this ferret and did not always have the necessary permission to do so. One afternoon I was returning from a sortie with the ferret, and was carrying over my arm, and concealed by my raincoat, two dead rabbits which had been caught in a dried-up culvert alongside the main road; rabbits which soon afterwards I should be presenting at the poulterer's shop in exchange for some welcome additional pocket money. I was about to turn into the little yard leading up to the ferret's home, when I chanced to look round and see the Headmaster walking in company with the assistant housemaster. They were twenty yards behind me and deep in conversation, but I thought that it would be unsafe to turn into the narrow yard, and the only alternative was to walk the full length of the High Street ahead of them. It was not until after I had left school and the Headmaster was a guest at my Lighthouse home, that I learned that three inches of the rabbit's ears had extended below the folded mackintosh and that he and the assistant housemaster had been discussing my lawlessness all the way along the High Street.

Not all the masters at Oundle gave so much latitude. There was, for example, John King the housemaster at New House, a magnificent and forthright character who did not believe in boys who did not conform to tradition. At some periods and especially immediately before a rabbiting excursion my ferret used to accompany me to the classrooms, living quietly in a makeshift 'poacher's pocket' which I had created by cutting a hole at the top of the lining of my coat. She was a small ferret and very tame, and normally she made very little trouble in class. But inevitably sooner or later the giggling or unexpected movements in my coat gave away her presence. Eventually I was hauled up for a stern rebuke. 'Supposing . . .,' said Mr

King, 'supposing 550 boys all kept ferrets in their pockets . . .' The absurdity of this classic argument against individuality made a deep impression on me. So much for the logical wisdom of my elders. My belief in the 'lone wolf' attitude was perhaps too greatly strengthened thereafter.

The chapel at Oundle had only just been finished when I went there. Some years before, my mother had made a nude bronze figure of a boy with upraised arm as a War Memorial for West Downs. Another cast of this statue was bought for Oundle and placed on a rather lonely and exposed site in front of the chapel. As legend under it, it carried the answer of Isaiah, 'Here am I, send me.' The model for this statue had been an Italian boy, the son of Fiorini, the caster who for many years cast all my mother's bronzes. I had never posed for it, and it was not at all like me, but it was useless to say so. It was (and I believe still is) widely held to be me. Only once have I ever been grateful for this assumption when I went back to the school to lecture after the war, and suggested that I had gone to the Admiralty at the beginning of the war with my right arm raised saying, 'Here am I, send me.' The lecture was a success!

If I have given the impression that I was not happy at school, this must immediately be remedied. On the whole the school gave great freedom to its boys and I managed to pursue my interests, which were almost entirely concerned with animals, with extraordinarily little interruption. By most present-day public school standards we were more limited in our range of operations because bicycles were not then allowed. In spite of this we managed to wander far and wide by devious means (often by the then little practised device of hitch-hiking).

Michael Dilke and I made a collection of the skins of British mammals. It was started when two dead badgers were brought to us, which had been run over on the railway line. Clearly they had been caught out on the far side of the line, had tried to get back to their setts when they heard the train coming and had been run down. To these skins we added a fox skin and later an otter's, and then we began in earnest to collect the skins of the smaller mammals, stoat, weasel, water rat, brown rat, black rat, the field voles, the wood mice and the shrews.

Collecting, of course, can become a mania, not only with children, and perhaps I was fortunate in not being much bitten by this particular bug. Michael Dilke, to be sure, had a modest collection of single eggs of British birds, and I was content to help him in the building of it. But apart from this and our mammal skins I was never a collector at school. Nevertheless a large number of pet animals figured prominently throughout my school years. Among these I particularly remember the bats which we found living in a colony behind two loose stones in the wall of the house. These stones were fitted into special holes intended to accommodate scaffolding in any future maintenance or repairs. The spaces behind the stones were each the home of half a dozen Pipistrelles—the smallest and commonest of the British bats. For the first twenty-four hours of captivity these bats always refused food, but after that they became so hungry that if offered a suitable fly they would take it from the hand. We had extensive fly-catching raids round all the school windows in order to keep them supplied. After a while they became extraordinarily tame. We designed a special box for them and made it in the school's wood workshop. The next stage was to give them their liberty again and yet keep them tame by hand feeding. We hung the box out on the wall near their original home and for a week or two the bats continued to use the box in preference to the hole behind the stone. The advantage of the box was that it could be opened, and food offered without actually dislodging and therefore disturbing the bats. But after a while they seemed to decide in favour of a little more privacy, and by the time the term ended only two bats were still living in the box.

Owls became a special line during my last two summers at Oundle. We had established a fairly extensive trap-line in connection with our mammal skin collection, and this provided a ready supply of food for owlets. We reared owls of the three common species, Tawny, Barn and Little. The Barn Owls were the most difficult, the Tawnies the nicest and the Little Owls the fiercest.

Then, of course, there were caterpillars. In summer-time the window-sill of my study was always lined with small dishes, muslin-topped jars and boxes, and larger breeding cages full to bursting with the caterpillars of British moths, especially the Hawk Moths, which I always thought of as the best.

I worked quite hard at school, and in due course found myself in the Biology VIth. I enjoyed the work as it had to do with animals, though too often dead ones, when the live ones were so much more exciting. I had a certain facility in drawing which enabled me to record neatly and tidily what I saw down my microscope, what I saw when I was dissecting my cockroach, my frog, my dog-fish or my rabbit (or my badger, for we dissected the badgers whose skins went into our collection). I was also able to make drawings of the birds I saw, and although they were the animals I enjoyed most, and enjoyed drawing most, I was left in no doubt that this was to be regarded as 'play'—it was certainly not biology.

Oundle School was noted for its music. During my four years there I took part in four great choral performances. In my first year I sang treble in Bach's B minor Mass; in the following year, in Bach's Christmas Oratorio I sang alto. The year after that I sang tenor in Handel's Messiah, and in my last year I was a bass in the B minor Mass again. Unfortunately these performances were never recorded, for recording in those days was a professional affair; but I have the feeling that they were rather important musical events. For a school of 550 boys to be going around for a whole term humming and whistling the tunes of Bach or Handel must surely have played a great part in the formation of their musical taste.

Kenneth Fisher, the Headmaster, was a keen ornithologist and from my earliest days at the school he used, from time to time, to take one or two of us to the flood-waters farther up the

42

River Nene at Lilford and Aldwincle—floods which in late winter stretched almost all the way to Thrapston.

On the flood-waters, which spread across the great meadows on either side of the old disused Lilford Decoy in its triangular wood, there were thousands of Wigeon, Mallard, Teal, a few Shovelers and a small number of Pintails which according to the books were 'rare inland'. To me the Pintails had a special appeal. They were so graceful, their plumage so perfect and the scientific name of their genus—*Dafila*—which was then still in standard use, sounded so pleasant when said; though I did not think then that I might one day use it to name one of my daughters!

But the most exciting things on the floods were the Grey Geese. These were the first Grey Geese I had ever seen, and we used to find their identification difficult. There were sometimes as many as 200, and nearly all of them, we finally decided, were White-fronted Geese, although there were small family parties of Pink-footed and Bean Geese. This then was my first acquaintance with the Whitefronts and Pinkfeet which were to play so important a part in my later life. Casting my mind back to those schooldays I can quite easily recapture the excitement with which we crept along the railway cutting to get a closer view of these wonderful birds. Already geese were to me more than just big birds. They had an atmosphere of romance and mystery around them.

Michael Dilke was also a regular member of the Headmaster's bird-watching parties to the winter floods, and to the lake at Blatherwyke eight miles from the school. We used to go in the Head's open Sunbeam car to watch Diving Ducks (among them an occasional Smew) and Bramblings (on a great heap of chaff) and to see the feral flock of Canada Geese and the single wild Greylag which lived with them. At this time Michael and I were working on a book; it was to be a book about birds in which I was to make the illustrations, while Michael provided the text. He came of a family with a tradition in writing and his own literary talent was already emerging. Our book was almost complete and rather secret when

John Brereton, a boy in the same house, somehow discovered about it and said that he could arrange for its publication: and so in due course 525 copies of the book were privately printed, under the title *Adventures Among Birds*, a title which had already been used, although we did not know it, by W. H. Hudson. The anonymous authors were described as 'Three Schoolboys'.

In my day Oundle had no swimming bath; we swam only in the river. I found, when I had the competition of 550 boys, instead of only eighty as at West Downs, that I was not so good as I had thought I was, though I swam every year for my house. In the summer I used to row on the river, rather than play cricket, which was the alternative. I rowed for the principal reason that it was possible to take a single-handed skiff and go down the river for the afternoon. This meant that I could troll a spoon bait on a pike line from the outrigger, and catch small Pike. I never caught a big one in this way. At rowing I finally stroked my House four, but I did not like it enough to go on with it at Cambridge.

Being a member of the O.T.C. was a dreary business, I thought, except for Camp at the end of the summer term, which was always rather enjoyable. It was during one of these camps at Tidworth that I had my first opportunity to fly. A party was to be taken over in a lorry to the aerodrome at Old Sarum. All members of the party had to have a signed paper from their parents to say that they were permitted to fly, but unfortunately no such paper had arrived for me, for, as I sadly knew, my mother was away; yet I was determined not to miss this chance and I was sure that she would have signed the paper had she been at home.

Somehow or other I managed to smuggle myself into the lorry without disclosing that I had no paper. But it was evidently going to be very difficult when we arrived at Old Sarum. On the way over I could not make up my mind whether to claim that the paper was lost or whether to own up that I had not got one. When the time came honesty prevailed, and was unexpectedly rewarded. Someone must have taken a

44

risk in order not to disappoint me, with the result that a couple of hours later my turn came up and I found myself sitting in the observer's seat of a Bristol Fighter.

The first flight of one's life must surely have been a memorable thrill for everyone of my generation. But for me it was miraculously exciting. I can remember every windswept detail of the take-off, the breathtaking 'moment-of-truth' when the bumping of the wheels ended and I realised that I was airborne for the first time ever; the shadow of the plane getting visibly smaller as we climbed; the vertical bank over the earthworks of the Roman Camp; the long glide down with the engine throttled back; and the delightful relief of tension as the landing was successfully completed. I discovered, that day, and have confirmed it many hundreds of times since, that flying is unlike any other sensation in the world and better than most.

5. STALKING

Holidays from Oundle are now in my mind merged together.
But there are special memories which may have some bearing
on my story, and particular events on the Norfolk Broads
which had their influence on me. We took a converted wherry,
the *Golden Hind,* and made our way through the Broads along
the usual route by the wooded Broads of Salhouse and Ran-
worth, up the River Ant to Barton, and in due course up the
Thurne and the Kendal Dyke, through Heigham Sounds to
Hickling, where I met for the first time Jim Vincent, the
Warden of Lord Desborough's then quite new bird sanctuary
at Hickling Broad. Jim showed me his young Bitterns, his
young Montagu's Harriers, and his Bearded Tits, for the first
of many times. He remained a delightful friend until his death
twenty years later.

After Hickling we took the turning into the Meadow Dyke
leading to Horsey Mere, which was later to become our regular
summering place. On this first passage through the Meadow
Dyke, I found for the first time the beautiful striped caterpillars of the rare Swallowtail Butterfly.

The wide landscape of the Broads has a character and
beauty of special and perhaps specialised appeal. From this
earliest visit it has been the setting of two of my lifelong enthusiasms—water birds and sailing.

At Potter Heigham I remember that my stepfather had hired a half-decker. This was a comparatively safe eighteen-foot half-decked sailing boat, carrying a balanced lug, and it was in this that he gave me my first sailing lessons. By the time we went on our next holiday to the Norfolk Broads I was already quite handy in a boat and could sail on my own.

Many of my holidays from Oundle were spent at my stepfather's cottage in Wiltshire. It was called The Lacket, and was on the outskirts of the village of Lockeridge near Marlborough. It was, and still is, one of the most perfect thatched cottages I have ever seen. It nestles amid ancient yews; and across from the cottage there is a gentle slope of fields to the West Woods. These woods were our particular delight, and we had our own names for all the places in them, which we marked on our own special six-inch-to-the-mile map—Archer's Dene, Brock Dene, Pleached Alley, Mole Joke. Often we used to walk far over the Downs and into Savernake Forest.

Always on these walks I used to collect wild flowers and bring them home; and while my stepfather read aloud to us each evening I would draw the flowers meticulously in watercolour. Finally I had quite a complete collection of small drawings of the common wild flowers that grew around The Lacket. I have always found being read to aloud an excellent stimulus to my drawing.

I was about seventeen when, at the end of the summer holidays, my guardian, Lord Knutsford, invited me to stay with him at the shooting lodge which he had taken in Scotland, Tournaig, in the deer forest of Inverewe on the west coast of Ross and Cromarty. This was my first introduction to stalking, a sport which had delighted 'Uncle' Sydney for very many years. And perhaps because my family had been basically opposed to blood sports, my introduction induced something of a reaction. The shooting of my first stag was steeped in the romantic traditions of the sport, and overnight I was an enthusiastic stalker.

I had two great days stalking on Inverewe, one each side of my seventeenth birthday, and on the second day I shot a stag. After that I acquired all the famous books on stalking and read them as fast as I could. Later this led me to begin to draw deer, and for this I went frequently from The Lacket to watch them in Savernake Forest where at that time there was still quite a large Red Deer herd.

That there could ever be any serious conflict between the outlook of the naturalist and the sportsman did not occur to me then, or for many years afterwards. I thought that if one followed the guiding principle of the statutory close seasons, the code of what was done and what was not done in sport, it was quite unnecessary to have other doubts.

My stepfather was at this time a delegate to the League of Nations at Geneva and some of my school holidays were spent there.

I had read in a book that the black Alpine Salamander was to be found in Switzerland only above the 1,000-metre line, and I was determined to find one. From Geneva the simplest way to reach this altitude was to take the train eastwards along the north side of the lake, past Lausanne and Montreux, and up the valley to the south as far as Bex. I decided to do this by myself as a day excursion. Arrived in Bex I simply started up the nearest hillside. There was some kind of path, but the hillside was thickly wooded and I climbed on until I calculated from my map that I had achieved the necessary height. I stopped to get my bearings and my breath, and then moved off the little path into the thick woods and turned over the first loose stone I could see. Underneath it was an Alpine Salamander. It was slimmer in build than the yellow and black species—smooth and shiny and all black. I could hardly believe that my mission had succeeded so easily. It took twenty minutes and at least twenty more stones to find the next one, and most of the day to catch a dozen, which I put into the small brown cardboard suitcase in which I had brought my sandwich lunch.

Up on the hillside I met a chamois hunter returning from an

unsuccessful stalk, who told me of his adventures as we made our way down into the valley. Just before we parted he insisted on looking at my Salamanders, and assured me that he had never seen one before.

'You are the successful hunter,' he said. 'I, the unsuccessful.'

'But tomorrow it will be the other way round; you will surely get your chamois,' I said.

He shrugged his shoulders. 'Who knows?' he said. 'But that's hunting.'

6. THE RED HERRING

In the autumn of 1927 I went up to Trinity College, Cambridge, to read Natural Sciences, Zoology, Botany, Physiology and, later, Geology. At Oundle I had had a fair capacity for work and had finished up quite well placed in the Biology Sixth Form. I won no scholastic prizes and at the very end of my time there had only just scraped into being made a prefect. How would it be at Cambridge?

The Master of the college at that time was J. J. Thompson, the famous physicist. I remember having tea with him at the Lodge early in my first term and being miserable because my shoes were dirty. I had managed not only to get rooms in college but in Great Court, by dint of sharing them with Humphrey Trevelyan (son of the historian who was to be the next Master of the college and who was a close friend of my stepfather's). I have often wondered how Humphrey stuck it out for the whole academic year, because I must have been a tiresome room-mate. For a start there was the aviary which occupied half my bedroom, extended on to the roof and incorporated the sitting-room window. Then there was the Flying Phalanger ... But Humphrey remained good-natured all the time. My second year was spent in Neville's Court, and my third year back again in Great Court with another attic room.

Young years are formative years, and just as many of my contemporaries at Oundle must have gained a taste for Bach and Handel by singing choral works in chapel, so I believe that

I am a better man for having lived for three years surrounded by the glorious architecture of Trinity College, Cambridge. Beautiful surroundings seep into one's system, and make one all the more aware of beauty later.

My career at Cambridge began quite respectably. I had no idea of the red herring I was soon to find myself following. I went to all my lectures and demonstrations, and worked away at my books. For exercise I went out beagling three times a week with the Trinity Foot Beagles. One day after trotting across the upland fields we ran down through a little marsh, and as we ran Snipe jumped up on all sides of us. Running beside me was Francis Wayne, who was up at Magdalene, and between puffs he told me that he knew . . . of a place . . . where we could go . . . Snipe-shooting. This was a new and exciting idea to me and I sent home for my father's old Cogswell and Harrison gun. A week later (it was in November 1927) we found ourselves on the washes at Erith. The Washes are not to be confused with the Wash into which they eventually run. They consist of a wide strip of grassland, lying between two high banks, which can be flooded as a sort of safety valve for the drainage systems of the fens. There are Washes on three of the Fenland rivers—the Welland, the Nene and the Ouse, and those of the Ouse are also known as the Bedford Levels. Because the level of the flood-waters was affected by the tide, these Washes were long held to offer free shooting to the wildfowler.

On that first day as we walked over a rough field of brown grass with water at its roots that squelched underfoot, there was suddenly a 'frrp' and a Snipe jumped up at my feet. With a 'scarp-scarp' he twisted and turned, close to the ground, but just as he started that great upward curve I fired, and the Snipe fell into the grass. It was my first shot with a twelve-bore, and my first shot at a flying bird (and for quite a long time the only successful one). It seemed to me to be an occasion for comment if not for celebration, but the rest of the party walked on as if nothing unusual had happened, and I walked with them. At the end of the field Francis shouted across to me:

'You picked up that Snipe all right, didn't you?'

'What?' I said, casually. 'Oh—the Snipe—oh yes, I "picked" that all right.'

But that Snipe constituted the entire day's bag, and if this monumental fluke had not come off perhaps I should never have become a wildfowler and should now be quite a different sort of person. Or perhaps I should be just the same, because of some other fluke.

Of the party that day was my old friend from Oundle, Michael Dilke, now also up at Trinity. Before long beagling had for me been entirely replaced by regular visits to the Washes. The flood-waters were teeming with birds. Great flocks of Wigeon grazed on the puddly fields, Mallards and Teal sheltered among the flooded thistles and when the water became deeper as the winter advanced there were rafts of Tufted Ducks and Pochards and Coots. Two new friends soon joined our excursions—Dick Hull (later to become Chief of the Imperial General Staff) and Christopher Dalgety. Both had been longer at Cambridge, and both had wider experience of shooting than Michael and I.

I began to keep a wildfowling diary from the first day of my new-found delight.

The diaries say how I went here and someone else went there. Occasionally they are unconsciously funny, very occasionally they are useful for reference, but they give no real impression of the places or the people, and it is sad to think of the number of hours so largely wasted in writing them. They fill six thick volumes covering the next six years—a fascinating souvenir of the wrong use of time. Yet perhaps they have some bearing on the kind of chap I was at the age of eighteen.

On the upper stretch of the Washes at Sutton, Christopher Dalgety had installed a duck-punt which he had bought second-hand at Keyhaven on the Solent. She was a single-handed sea-going punt, long and low and slinky, about twenty feet overall with a two-and-a-half-foot beam and her name was *Penelope*, because that is the Latin name for a Wigeon. On her bows he mounted a punt-gun borrowed from Cornelius

Smith, landlord of The Fish Inn at Sutton Gault: it was a small muzzle-loading gun that fired only about eight ounces of shot and one and a half ounces of powder, and it was one of those guns which might or might not go off and probably would not!

One bright November afternoon Christopher and I stalked hopefully down upon a company of Diving Ducks sitting in the open water. Owing to some reeds and thistles, our quarry were unsuspicious, and already we were drawing into range, and were ready for the shot. 'Popwoomph', it was almost a 'hang-fire', and a cloud of blue smoke filled the air—well, at any rate, she had gone off, and we jumped up to see what we had shot. There on the water lay one single drake Pochard. He was stone-dead and we pushed up and collected him.

Two days later we were out again in *Penelope*. From the flood bank we had spied three Grey Geese far out on a spit of grass among the flood waters. We intended to go after them even though it involved rowing a mile and a half against the stream. By the time we reached the spit it was beginning to get dark. There were a lot of ducks there, but nowhere could we see the geese. We sat up in the punt—and then towards the west, I saw reflected in the water three large black silhouettes. In an instant we had flattened ourselves, and I was poling the punt with all speed in their direction. At about ninety yards the geese decided that we looked dangerous, and spread their great wings; there was a movement in front of me, and a click which was followed by a loud curse—the gun had misfired.

I remember we got one Mallard from the punt with a twelve-bore just before dark, and then we drifted back to the river and rowed down with the current, which was running like a mill-race. We had a bridge to go through, and there were a few breathless moments as we sped down peering into the darkness for the great black shadow which we knew to be there. Suddenly it came, and we were under it in a flash, narrowly missing one of the pillars. We pulled quickly to the shore, made fast the punt and went up to the bank to The Fish just as it began to rain.

To me these adventures were irresistible: the beauty of dawn and dusk, the planning of the campaign, the slight risks to be taken and above all the animals—not only the quarry but also the others who had business on the floods, the Otters, the Peregrines, the Harriers and the Short-eared Owls.

7. THE LURE OF THE GEESE

The flood-waters of the Bedford Levels were exciting enough in those early days, but if we were to be wildfowlers, then wild geese must be the real quarry. According to the books, the place to go for wild geese was Wells-next-the-Sea on the North coast of Norfolk, and there Michael Dilke and I decided to go for a week of the Christmas vacation.

Upon some personal recommendation we had selected as our guide the well-known professional wildfowler, Sam Bone, and went round to see him on the evening of our arrival.

Unfortunately we had chosen the time of the full moon, which, because of the tides, he told us, was not the best time to shoot geese at Wells. But we had seen few geese in those days, and we were content to see them even if we never fired a shot, though we did not say this to Sam. That night as I lay awake, I suddenly heard the magic sound of geese and ran to the window, and from over towards the marsh came the call of the Pinkfeet. There must have been a big lot on the move, for the sound seemed like a single singing roar made dim by the two miles of marsh that lay between.

Next morning we stood on the shore. There was an orange glow in the east, and out of it came skein after skein of geese. Since then I have seen Pink-footed Geese in flight many thousands of times in all their winter haunts in Britain; I have followed them to their breeding grounds in Iceland, I have assisted at the capture and ringing of more than 20,000 of them; and yet the thrill which I felt on that first morning is repeated again every time I see the great skeins stretched across the sky. The spell is as strong as ever.

During the day Sam took us to Stiffkey salt-marsh and there we tramped about, crossing the creeks by the old tumble-down bridges. Here Redshanks abounded and Curlews were sometimes to be found. Sam persuaded us that Redshanks were suitable game, and we returned to lunch after many miles of tramping with, I believe, three of them.

I think it was Christopher Dalgety who first heard about the saltings at Terrington, to the west of King's Lynn. They were comparatively unknown to wildfowlers in those days. We kept the place darkly secret, inventing our own code name for it, 'Sandbanks', for it was only forty-four miles from Cambridge —an hour and a half's drive in Christopher's old Morris Car. Nowadays the marsh is controlled by a Wildfowlers' Club, so the secret need no longer be kept.

'Sandbanks' consisted then of a rough salting half a mile wide, bounded on the seaward side by mudflats, and on the landward side by a sea-wall protecting mile upon mile of flat neatly ditched fields. The salting was finely divided by a net-work of deep muddy creeks which branched and wriggled their way in from the sea. The flatness of the scene was broken and at the same time emphasised by a single stunted willow tree which grew just behind the sea-wall. But the sky and the birds made it for me a place of incomparable beauty and romance.

It was out on the salting here that I shot my first goose. There had been a great flight of Mallards that night. For half an hour they had whispered overhead, high above the saltings, and now the geese were beginning to move, out at the edge of the tide. In little parties they were starting in across the marsh to find good grazing or to pass on over the sea-wall into the black potato fields.

I could follow them by their calling as they circled and passed wide of me. Then, from almost behind, I heard the low intimate talking of another bunch, heading, it seemed, straight for where I sat. Almost at once the black line of them appeared, a dozen geese full low and passing close behind me. I swung round and fired one shot over my left shoulder, and throwing myself on my back I fired the second. As I watched, one of the geese seemed to be separating from the others. At first, being upside-down, I did not realise that it was falling, but as I jumped up I heard a thud on the soft muddy turf. I ran to the spot, and there he was, stone-dead on the salting—my very first goose.

He turned out to be a Bean Goose—a considerable rarity. But at the time he was to me a plain wild goose, and that was all that mattered.

Success was rare in those early days and when it came my enjoyment was great—the primitive enjoyment of the hunter. If anyone asked me, and they frequently did, how I could equate the killing with my evident love of the living birds, my answer was given without hesitation. They were man's traditional quarry and it was part of a man's instinct to hunt; it was part of the birds' instinct to be hunted. My delight and admiration for wild geese was based as much upon their supreme capacity to remain watchful and to look after themselves as it was upon their beauty and grace. There was nothing sentimental about my regard for them. Our relations were simple and straightforward, to be carried to the logical conclusion—to the death; and there, when I was eighteen, the argument ended. Today I find that it goes a good deal farther and its conclusions are rather different.

8. GREY GOOSE

Expeditions to the coast from Cambridge were only occasionally possible, but the flood-waters were easier to get at,
although as the winter advanced boats became more and more
essential. At Sutton there were *Penelope* and the 'black canoe',
but farther down the Washes at Oxlode, a newly discovered
area for wildfowling, there was only the 'black boat', a leaky,
tarred vessel with pointed ends and vertical sides which was
clearly very old. For wildfowling we must have a proper punt,
and a boat-builder in Cambridge was commissioned to start
work on one straight away, to be made from our own designs.

He was very quick and had it completed within ten days.
She was launched in the Cam, in the pool just above Silver
Street Bridge.

We poled her up the little backwater there to the mill pool
and practised stalking with hand-paddles and pole. We
christened her *Grey Goose*, and arranged for her conveyance
to the Fens on the very next day. Meanwhile we had bought an
old muzzle-loading punt-gun, which fired half a pound of
shot—small for a punt-gun, but it seemed large enough for
our purpose.

Next morning *Grey Goose* was hoisted on to a lorry and the
journey to the Fens began. At Erith Bridge at the head of the
flood-waters, she was lifted from the lorry, and launched in the
river. We had then about nine miles to go on the flood-water to
Oxlode. On the way we should pass the reaches we already

knew from our adventures in *Penelope*, and as we expected to find ducks there, we decided to be cleared for action.

The first thing to do was to test the big gun. Laboriously we loaded it, ramming down only a light charge of powder, a tow wad, a charge of shot and some hay to keep it in: then, standing well to one side in the shallows, I pulled the trigger, the roar, the spatter of shot on the water, and the cloud of smoke were all perfect. So with high hopes we reloaded again and set off down the river.

After about a mile we saw some Tufted Ducks, and lay down to stalk. The gun went off with a terrific roar and a burst of flame. Was this usual with punt-guns? We supposed so, and jumped up anxiously to see our luck. Not a bird had been struck, and disappointedly we pushed to a bank opposite the Jolly Bankers Inn to reload. Only then did we find that the gun had blown up; half the nipple-holder in the breach had blown out sideways—a piece of metal about the size of a wine cork, and it had fortunately gone out without making a hole either in us or the punt.

The rest of our journey was carried out under sail, and late in the evening we arrived in our new operating area among the washes of Oxlode.

It was a long time before our new punt brought us any luck, and it was not until the following winter that I scored my first 'right and left' at geese. The tide was just flooding those same saltings at 'Sandbanks' under an orange full moon that had just risen. The place where I knelt was still dry, but behind, between me and the security of the sea-wall, the creeks had filled and the marsh was covered.

The geese were farther out also on a dry part of the marsh, but I knew that the tide must reach them at any minute. Before long I should be plainly visible, surrounded by water; but if they came soon, not only should I be hidden on the black island of salting but the island itself would be a landing-place for them. Then all at once there were geese everywhere. They came with hardly a sound. Many went on inland, but suddenly I saw a little bunch of six quite close and very low. They were going to settle beside me. I crouched down as low as I could, and they came on with set wings. Geese have comparatively poor eyesight at night, and they did not see me at all until it was too late. Indeed, one of them never did see me, and another only for a second. So fell my first right and left of geese.

The feeling of achievement was complete. I do not think at the time I experienced any trace of regret at the destruction of these beautiful creatures, such as I should feel were I to do the same thing today. I was simply the successful hunter, and as I walked home with my two geese I might have been returning to my cave.

Moonlight flighting was without doubt the most exciting kind of wildfowling we did in those days (even though no boats were involved), for geese were the most worthy quarry, to be placed far above any other fowl. Soon after the rising of the full moon they would move in, some perhaps on to the saltings, but others over the sea-wall into the potato fields. When the tide had filled the creeks on the out-marsh we usually waited behind the high bank, or in the fields themselves. While the moon was still low and red, the first geese, often a family party of six or seven, would cross the bank and sweep silently round the chosen fields before settling. Later the bigger flocks would stream in on the same flight-line. Often we ran feverishly to try to get under the line, or to intercept a bunch we could hear approaching; and almost as often they went straight over the place where we had been. Although the main flight was usually over by nine o'clock, there were always a few geese going out to the shore to drink throughout the night. By eleven, though, these movements were so sparse that we gathered for hot curry from a Thermos flask. If we had been out on the salting and had wet knees and bottoms we would start the car and dry our clothes by sitting on the radiator.

By about two in the morning we often thought it was time for some sleep, either in the car or in a straw stack, but it was usually too cold, and after a while we would have to run about to get warm. At four-thirty it was time to start out for the edge of the mud and wait for the geese coming out again, and the ducks, and the sunrise—and perhaps fall asleep in a creek. Then after the high tide, at about eight or nine, we would start back for breakfast. Sometimes the geese would defeat us completely and we would return empty-handed. But however the nights went, there was always the wild call of the geese.

That year Christopher and Michael and I had shot each of the six wild species of geese that come regularly to this country, and we felt the need to bag a Canada. There are several parts of the country where Canada Geese have been established for so long that they are now practically wild and the species has been given a place on the British list, but it was not so at the time of which I write. The Canadas in the marsh we had chosen for our project, though not nominally wild birds, were in fact exceedingly wild.

The night was one of bright moon with snow on the ground and a hard frost which had frozen the ditches so that they would bear our weight. With white pyjamas over our clothes, we should be invisible to man and goose.

By midnight Christopher and I had walked three miles along the beach and were at the edge of the fresh marsh, listening for our quarry. There were Grey Geese feeding in the marsh under the moon, but on that night they meant nothing to us. We could hear the Canadas farther on. We took a ditch apiece and started to stalk in, one of us on each side of the nearest bunch. My way led me along the side of a railway. There was a ditch of open running water which I suddenly came upon. It was full of Ducks and Teal which rose with a terrible clatter and clamour. This marsh was proverbially well keepered and it seemed that if anyone was about that night they must surely hear the noise and wonder at the cause.

I turned off down another ditch of thin ice, which cracked ominously, and crawled along the edge of it. The moon was now hidden by cloud, but the snow made the world surprisingly light. There was a little bank in front and when I looked over this I thought at first that the moles had been very busy since the last snowfall. But a moment later I realised that the dark spots were not mole-hills, but Canada Geese.

I crawled over the bank to get closer, but they saw me and in a flash they were up. It was a long shot, but a goose fell dead, and with that the whole marsh seemed to rise. With a tremendous clamour the great flock curled away, and I heard a surprisingly distant 'pop-pop' as they went over Christopher. I picked up my bird and without any delay, set off towards the shore. A Canada Goose is a bulky bird, and while I knew that in our white clothes we ourselves were nearly invisible, I felt that to an observer a goose careering across the marsh hung up by its neck might arouse suspicion. I had to pass through a belt of trees where I might be ambushed, so I ran fast parallel to it before turning in the wood. I reckoned I would hear anyone running to cut me off. I was worried now. I came to a fast-running main drain that was quite unfrozen and dared not wait to find a bridge. So I plunged across in water nearly to my waist, but there was no time to be cold.

It was a mile to the rendezvous which we had fixed, and Christopher had arrived less than a minute before me. In our white pyjamas we had walked along no more than 100 yards apart and neither had been aware of the other. My goose was our entire bag, but we had achieved our object. The ducks began to flight to sea over our heads on the remaining mile-and-a-half walk, and dawn was breaking as we set off for Cambridge in the car.

My enthusiasm for the wild marshes and the birds and the chase occupied too much of my time. We were, of course, entitled to be away from college on a limited number of nights during the term, but the restriction meant little, for it was not difficult to climb out of college. This, combined with a scheme by which the bedclothes on our beds were ruffled to indicate that we had slept in college, enabled us to spend as many moonlight nights down on the shores of the Wash as our consciences would allow, which was a great many more than our tutors or directors of studies could have approved.

Climbing out of college was only one aspect of climbing.

Roof-climbing was a well-supported activity in the University in those days. I was one of the party which made the first complete circuit of Trinity Great Court, but the climb that frightened me most was the ascent of St John's College Chapel. There was an overhanging cornice about sixty feet from the ground which required the most determined disregard of my indifferent head for heights. I never extended these activities to rocks and mountains, perhaps because the call of the marshes was too insistent.

Wildfowling was a new subject for my drawing and painting and I found a new delight in painting the birds that I spent so much time pursuing. My pleasure was to recreate the tense excitement that I felt when I was out on a marsh, recapture some of it each time that I looked at the picture, and convey some of it to those who had shared the experience.

My paintings of geese and ducks and snipe led to a small exhibition of my works at a Cambridge shop. I do not now remember the number of water-colours in this my first one-man show, but there must have been a dozen or twenty and I remember that at prices up to five guineas they were nearly all sold, which made a welcome addition to the funds available for future wildfowling expeditions.

9. OF PINKFEET, PUNTS AND
BLUE GEESE

During our Christmas 1928 holiday on the Solway we had heard rumours that very large numbers of geese assembled at the head of the great estuary upon their first arrival from the Arctic in late September.

So, on 20th September, 1929, I set out from London alone in the family's Austin Seven and arrived at Sark Bridge Farm, Gretna, eleven hours later. Next morning I found that many thousands of geese had already arrived at Rockliffe. All that day more were coming in. This was the first time I had ever seen geese arriving on migration. There were little bunches coming in high over the Metal Bridge, heading the westerly wind and planing down on to the marsh—some in threes and fours, some in groups of a dozen or twenty. The little parties were scattered about the sky almost wherever you looked. It is a pattern I have seen many times since, but never more impressively than on that day in 1929. I know now that these geese were coming from Greenland and Iceland, but in those days Spitzbergen was thought to be the breeding ground of most of the British Pinkfeet. Wherever they came from, it was far away in Arctic or Sub-Arctic lands, and it added immeasurably to the mysterious appeal of these wonderful birds.

Nowadays no such concentrations of geese are to be found on Rockliffe Marsh, though great numbers of Pinkfeet still come to the Solway; their headquarters is now ten miles farther to the westward around the Lochar mouth and the

67

sanctuary provided for them on the Kinmount Estate near Annan.

Rockliffe Marsh was private shooting, but by crossing the Esk in a boat it was possible to intercept the geese at the marsh edge, or from 'lying-pits' out on the sand, and in the week that I was there I shot twelve geese.

For my last two days in Scotland I moved westward to Wigtown Bay in order to go punting with Major Hulse—the Expert as we called him. I joined him at Creetown, and we spent the two days afloat in pursuit of Wigeon. Our bag was meagre, and the occasion was chiefly memorable for my meeting with Adam Birrell and for a stirring return journey in the punt in a gale of wind. I had met Adam very briefly at the end of a previous day's punting with Major Hulse, but now for the first time I recognised this was no ordinary fisherman-wild-fowler. He was a considerable naturalist, with an astonishingly wide knowledge. He was delightful company whether on a fowling expedition or bird-watching or fishing, and we remained in regular communication thereafter for a quarter of a century.

On the flood water of the Bedford Levels we had *Penelope* and *Grey Goose*, but we still had no sea-going double punt for the Wash, and this must clearly be remedied. Mr Mathie, a boat-builder in Cambridge, was commissioned to build one, based mainly on the design and specifications of the Expert's punt. She was to be twenty-four feet long, four-feet beam, with a twelve-foot cockpit, and she was to be called *Kazarka*—the Russian name for the Red-breasted Goose.

Kazarka was launched just below Magdalene Bridge in Cambridge on 11th December, 1929.

By now punting had become, for me, the most enjoyable of all forms of wildfowling (and therefore the most enjoyable of all activities). The marshes were wild, but the mudflats were wilder still—the wildest remaining part of this country. At sunset on a clear day, drifting homeward on the tide, we would look to the westward across the waste flatness into a brilliance of scarlet and gold. The flat land beyond was a thin black line. Above it, only the serrated edge of a distant spinney, or the outlines of the old lighthouses at the Nene's mouth encroached upon the sky. Below it, a little dimmer and more broken than the sky itself, the wet mudflats stretched to our feet. In our ears was the bubbling of the flowing tide and the call of curlews.

Although my ideas about killing have changed since then, I can still relive the thrill of stalking a great pack of Wigeon or geese, lying flat and hidden in a craft which only showed a few grey inches above water, and drew even fewer below. As the punt swept silently closer the excitement grew, until one felt as if one had just run 100 yards 'all out'. If one was pushing the punt there was good reason for this feeling, for punting with one hand from a prone position was gruelling exercise. The stalk had always to be done as fast as possible, and the 'pusher' usually felt as if he had run a mile rather than 100 yards by the end. But the 'gunner' had no excuse for being out of breath except just plain excitement.

The beauty of the setting and the immediate thrills of the chase were not the only things. A punting expedition was a campaign. It required organisation, generalship and seamanship. It was difficult and arduous—usually disappointing, and sometimes dangerous. I felt that it was one of the few remaining sports which offered adventure. Inescapably I was a devotee.

Nowadays I do not really think that any killing for sport can be justified, but I still look back and wonder just how different my life would have been had I never been a fanatical wildfowler. Was the madly enthusiastic pursuit of ducks and geese an essential ingredient in my painting and in my specialised study of the *Anatidae*? How would it all have been if instead I had continued to run three days a week with the Trinity Foot Beagles and gone more regularly to my university lectures?

Re-reading my shooting diaries in the course of writing this book I came upon the entry for Friday, 13th December, 1929, which is of more interest than I realised at the time. There was a moderate west-south-westerly breeze blowing as we walked out along the old drove at Terrington, and out to the edge of the salting. 'I was in position at 6.40,' says my diary, ' "streak of dawn" having been at 6.10. As it got light geese began honking all round. A lot of Mallards had been sitting at the edge of the mud as I came up and now a lot more came over. At last I saw about eight geese coming straight towards me. I had a shot, but without success. The sound of the shot put up a big lot of about 200 which had been sitting farther to the east. These pitched against about 200–300 yards away. I looked at them and thought that one on the left of the flock looked different. With the glass I could see at once that it was a White Goose. His head, neck and breast were pure white and his back was dark brown, darker than the surrounding Pink-feet. From the fact that he was a head taller than the rest (and longer in the leg) and also that his bill was very large and thick. I felt no doubt that he was an albino Greylag. In general size he was much larger than the Pinkfeet and was much more on the alert. He had his head up the whole time—once when only three other geese in the whole 200 had their heads up. After the flock had walked towards me a little, they sat for a while, and then I think they must have scented me, for away they went.'

Well, there it is! There is the first record of the Blue Goose for Europe. The description is perfect. We even know that he was the rather less common form in which the white of the head extends on to the breast and belly. I may have exaggerated the size a little, and I gave him (and his fellow Pink-feet) a sense of smell which I do not now believe could have accounted for their departure. But the thick bill, the upright stance, the extra-dark back, all seem to me conclusive evidence. That the bird was a Blue Goose I do not have the smallest doubt. He could have escaped from some collection or zoo, but I think it is rather more likely that the bird was a genuinely wild one.

If wildfowling occupied too much of my winters, what of my summers at Cambridge? They might have been the time to work doubly hard to make up for it. But alas for my academic career, there were still plenty of birds to watch!

But the summer was not only for the birds; at week-ends there was also sailing, for I had joined the Cambridge University Cruising Club. Thus I found myself one Saturday afternoon in a fairly primitive and heavy catrigged dinghy, with a balanced-lug, racing on a stretch of the river at Ely which was scarcely more than fifteen yards wide. I was decisively beaten in my race by Stewart Morris, who spent his holidays sailing on the Norfolk Broads. After the racing we went to the inn for tea and then took the train back to Cambridge. This became the pattern of many a week-end in the summer term. I did not, of course, recognise that this first meeting with Stewart Morris, Olympic Gold Medallist, and now probably one of the half-dozen best helmsmen in the world, was of any importance. I could scarcely have guessed at the influence it was to have on the future course of my life. Without doubt his enthusiasm and subsequent skill was responsible for my interest in dinghy sailing and thereafter in the wider world of yachting. In those early days at Ely, George Tozer, Captain of the Cambridge University Sailing Team and at one time a punting companion of the Washes, was selecting a team to represent Cambridge against Oxford, and although Stewart was an obvious choice, it was far from certain until the last minute who would occupy the sixth and last place. After winning a single-handed race at Ely in a strong breeze, I just scraped into the selection and sailed annually against Oxford for the rest of my time at the University.

Stewart was always the principal spur. I was invited by his parents to stay on the Broads in their beautiful converted wherry *Sundog*; she moved from regatta to regatta with a string of racing dinghies and one-designs towing astern. For these holidays I was usually Stewart's crew, but when his new fourteen-foot dinghy *Clover* was built for him in beautifully selected teak, I wondered if I would be considered good enough to crew him in important races. Much later, when I had crewed in less-expertly handled dinghies and finally graduated to my very own fourteen-footer, I wondered if I would be good enough to beat Stewart? Without this friendly rivalry over the years I should never have been selected to represent Great Britain at the Olympic Games (with Stewart as my spare man) in 1936; I should never have won a Bronze Medal there—and likely enough I should never have become (quite accidentally as it transpired) the President of the International Yacht Racing Union.

10. BRENTS WITH THE EXPERT

The expeditions to the Wash continued and some success began to attend them, but although we were rapidly gaining experience and improving as marksmen, successes were still very elusive. And yet were not the failures part of the appeal? The sight of the great gatherings of birds, the mastery of punt-handling, the beauty of marsh and mudflat, sea and sky—were not these the main points of it all?

As the wildfowling season of 1929–30 drew to a close, we planned a three-day excursion to the Wash as a finale. The party was Christopher Dalgety, Dick Hull, Mervyn Ingram and the Expert himself. Major Hulse was held in considerable awe by us all, and we thought it a great compliment that he had elected to join us.

The last day of the season was Saturday, 1st March, 1930. Hulse and I arranged not to get up early, but to go out to the punt after full sea. When we got up at six o'clock we were surprised to find that the rest of the party, in spite of their intentions the night before, were still in bed.

After breakfast Hulse and I went down to the punt. As we reached it a pair of Mallard rose from the creek and flew once all round us before going off to seaward. A moment later I saw seven dark birds landing at the edge of the salting; but almost at once they were up again and making off to the eastward—seven Brent Geese. Brents were by no means common at 'Sandbanks' and I was excited to see them, for they are the traditional quarry of the punt-gunner, and in theory the most difficult of all to approach.

As there were no more than a few duck about the mouth of our creek, we decided to wait hidden in the marsh edge for the tide to fall; then we drifted slowly down on the last of the tide.

Where the mud gives way to sand the Mallards sat to the west of us with every indication that they would move down to the Wisbech Eye rather than into Scotsman's Sled. There must have been nearly 3,000 of them three-quarters of a mile away. To the east were a few scattered bunches of Wigeon, nothing more.

Round the hairpin bend we came upon a party of a dozen Mallards, and Hulse pushed me up to them. I misjudged the range and thought they were too far away until they rose, when it was too late. But it was not a very good chance, though we might perhaps have had five or six. On the left bank of the corner leading round into the Sled lay a seal, away up on the high sand thirty yards from the water. He was a rather small Common seal, grey with a tinge of yellowish or olive brown. We lay down and stalked him, just to see how close we could get, but he had seen us and when we were about 100 yards away he started for the water's edge. After a feverish shuffle he finally made it when we were still thirty yards from him, wriggled in and swam out watching us. He sank down tail first and disappeared. A minute later there was a splash on our beam; evidently he had come up rather closer to us than he expected. Next time he came up a little farther away and took a long look at us. He had a delightfully appealing expression in his eyes. Afterwards, we found this was a favourite low-tide basking place, and we always called it Seal Corner.

We rowed up into the Hairpin Reach, and spied a bunch of eight ducks on the north shore. To these I pushed Hulse at great speed and it looked quite a good chance, for they had not seen us at all at 150 yards. But when they did, at ten yards less, they were up and away on the instant, and we were sadly crestfallen. The whole distance covered by the punt on such a day as this was perhaps no more than ten miles in twelve hours, and with the tide behind her when rowing or pushing, the punt probably made three or four knots. Thus there were, of necessity, long periods of sitting and waiting for the tide to ebb or to flow. There was now a long wait while the tide filled in ahead of us. Up the Hairpin Reach on the tide came a little grey and white bird with a slender neck and a long pointed bill. At first I took it for a Great Crested Grebe, but as it came closer I realised that it was too small. And then by the shape of its bill and the very white cheeks which contrasted with the slightly darker neck and breast I realised that it was a Red-necked Grebe. The light was so good that I could see every detail of the bird—the first Red-necked Grebe I had ever seen. Having come to within about fifty yards, he then swam off down the Sled against the incoming tide, diving perpetually for food. When I last saw him his white cheeks shining in the sun were his most conspicuous character.

Hulse and I sat talking after he had gone. Great numbers of ducks had meanwhile been sweeping in from the sea and from the Wisbech Eye, and settling on the mud high above us to the east. It was a wonderful thing to watch them swirling in and rounding up to settle. But there was nothing we could do to get near them; so we rowed on up the creek where we caught up the first of the tide and found a small bore going up ahead of us, with a wave six or eight inches high breaking on either bank.

As the light began to fade we decided to wait in the creek for the ducks to come drifting up to us with the flood tide, and push out towards them at the last minute. I lay down to the gun and Hulse lay down to push, holding the punt against the bank of the creek. Slowly the black lines of ducks in the water came closer, but we were impatient and went out a little too soon. Again the birds lifted at 150 yards. We retired at once into our creek, but we had cleared its immediate neighbourhood of ducks and that seemed to be the end of our day—and of our season. Hulse suggested we should unload the big gun while there was still enough daylight to see what we were doing, but I was for waiting a little yet. I was about to stand up and spy with the binoculars when Hulse said, 'Quick, lie down.' Seven geese had pitched at the edge of the salting 200 yards away to the east; but unfortunately they had seen me, and they rose again at once and flew a few hundred yards farther. With the glass I could see that they were Brents. It was a bitter moment, for Brents were to me the most exciting quarry of all, and I had never stalked them in a punt. 'Of course,' said Hulse, 'if they'd been over to the west of us, against the sunset, it would have been all right. We could see to stalk that way for another twenty minutes.' I looked round to west of us, and there silhouetted were seven more geese. I could hardly believe my eyes. They were less than 150 yards away and I could see at once that they were Brents.

As quickly as we could we began to turn the punt round by swinging the stern out into the current. I remember I was tremendously excited as I lay behind the gun, because our chances seemed so good. Perhaps our luck would change and our blank day would be redeemed at the eleventh hour. The stalk was going to be difficult because the strong wind kept blowing us sideways on to the shore of the creek, and the punt was continually running aground. We had lost the shortest pole two days before and now we really missed it. We were still broadside on to our geese going down the creek, and they were only a little over 100 yards away. At last there was enough water to turn left and head towards the quarry.

But the geese had seen us, and were swimming rapidly away, all bunched together. We gave chase at high speed. Now thoroughly suspicious they stopped, spread out and prepared to jump. But they seemed to think better of it and turned to swim away again, bunching as they did so. We were gaining on them now, and Hulse was fairly driving the punt along.

When the Brents headed the wind for the second time I decided that this would be the last opportunity. Four of them were fairly well bunched together on the left, the other three being spread out to the right. Hulse in an urgent and breathless voice said, 'Now's your chance!' I steadied the gun on them and pulled the string.

The smoke cloud blew away from us straight towards the birds and from the side of it three of them flew off. When the smoke had cleared four geese lay on the water. I got out and cautiously waded in eight inches of water to pick them up. They were all adults of the Dark-bellied form.

We pulled back into the creek, vastly pleased at the result of my first stalk at Brents, and set off for home.

So ended three days in the magic world of the wildfowl—to me, at that time, the only world of reality. The University of Cambridge might have been upon another planet.

The mechanism by which my presence on the Wash should have remained unknown to those in authority had broken down and serious trouble was only averted by assigning the three days to those normally permitted, and staying up for three extra days at the end of the term. News of my absenteeism, however, reached my stepfather, who wrote more in sorrow than in anger.

This was my reply:

University Pitt Club

'Dear Bill,

'It was true—and I was away for three nights—the last of the shooting season and no doubt the last I shall do for a long time. I suppose it was very bad and I merited all you said and more; but I am not entirely convinced. Somehow or other being out in the wilds seems so much more necessary to me than learning the fossils of the Devonian period than I cannot quite manage to "put it from me".

'It's such a rare thing to be able to enjoy and understand a wild place; that sounds stupid I know but it's what I feel. Anyone can learn the names of fossils and the classifications of animals, but I don't want to do things that anyone can do. Anyone can't paint—and I suppose that's why I like it, and anyone can't "understand" and get the best out of the elements and the wastes—the places where "anyone" wouldn't even want to go.

'I suppose it's scope for imagination that I want and there

77

isn't any that I can find in the inside of a dog-fish. I think I have a rather particularly vivid imagination; but not only do I think that I should use it, I know that I must use it or I shall just fade away and lose it.

'This isn't really an excuse and I don't really expect you to understand it. I can't express it properly either.

'I know it was naughty to go away, but of course I have to put in the three days at the end of the term just the same.

Yours,

PETE'

There are a good many things in this letter which now seem naïve and foolish. Particularly, perhaps, it is strange that I was then unmoved by the romantic side of geology and comparative anatomy. In my mind they did not touch that part of zoology which interested me most, the behaviour of the living animal. In my enthusiasms I lacked all sense of proportion. I did not readily distinguish work from play, and so far as my academic work was concerned I had become totally irresponsible. There were three factors in this, the nature of the work, the appeal of the diversions and my own character. I was in a mood to consider only the first. If the University could not keep me interested in Part 1, Zoology, there was either something wrong with the University, or something wrong with Zoology, or both. There was too much dissection, there were too many specimens in bottles. In those days the science of animal behaviour had scarcely begun. To know about live animals was something less than science. The web of Ecology —the relationship between animals and plants, water, soil and climate—had scarcely been invented. The suggestion that an intimate knowledge of saltings and mudflats and their plants and animals could in themselves add an important element to my University studies would not have impressed those in charge of my education.

And what of my painting and drawing? It was, of course, satisfactory that I could turn out a reasonably neat and realistic drawing of the central nervous system of my dissected dog-fish, or frog, or rabbit or cockroach; but there was no excuse for spending working time on a reconstruction of the Brent Geese against the sunset, as seen from the punt. Art simply did not seem to be getting a look in, and yet I wanted to be painting for most of the time that I had to be indoors. I had begun to make a few portrait drawings of my friends, and was commissioned by the Editor, Lionel Gamlin, to do a series of University personalities for the University magazine *Granta*. What with these and an exhibition of my water-colours, and the illustrations to the new edition of the *Roof-climbers Guide to Trinity*, was I not perhaps becoming more of an artist than a zoologist?

Both at school and at Cambridge I had been specialising in science, and I came to realise that I had no education whatever in the arts. I could draw a little, but I knew practically nothing about art, nor literature nor history.

As my academic career in Natural Science held no great promise I decided to change horses in midstream, and to complete my time at Cambridge by studying History of Art and Architecture. At the same time my primary objective in life changed. Instead of a scientist I would be an artist.

I have never regretted this great and momentous decision, for at one sweep my whole outlook on life was changed and enlarged. I saw it as the missing half which had suddenly come up into balance. Perhaps I was going to be complete after all. In order to take a degree in the new subject I stayed a fourth year at Cambridge, and worked a good deal harder than I had done in my first three.

My first pictures of wildfowl to be published, apart from the little drawings in the schoolboy book, had appeared in the magazine *Country Life* in August 1929. They were rather simple water-colours of wild geese, accompanied by a blood-thirsty little article, describing my wildfowling adventures. The birds were poorly drawn and I had as yet no idea of how to make the air support them; they were simply stuck on to the sky. But the compositions were quite pleasant and already I had begun to understand that the movement of birds through the air could more easily be suggested by the pattern of the flock than by the shapes of the individuals. After that my paintings appeared regularly in *Country Life,* about twice a year, for many years to come.

This outlet for my work may have played a very small part in my decision to become a professional painter, although I never seriously believed that there was likely to be any commercial demand for my work. If I had ever hoped that the painting of birds could provide me with a modest livelihood, I had long since dismissed the thought. 'Portraits,' they had told me, 'ah, now there's money in them—but birds . . .'

My last term at Cambridge was the autumn term of 1930 and it was during this term that I first met William Michael Malpas Bratby, who was up at Sidney Sussex College. I record that 'on Wednesday, 29th October, I went to Childerley Hall with Malpas Bratby. It is a shoot taken by him for £40.' The principal bag on that day, I remember, was pigeons.

William Michael Malpas Bratby was a remarkable character : you had only to listen for him for a few minutes to realise the originality of his mind. It was closely linked with his sense of humour, and he might easily have become a comedian or a funny writer but for his flair for finance, which later led him to such delight in his work as a very successful stockbroker. In Cambridge days he was already a glorious deflater of pomposity, and he also had a line in sheer fantasy, so that he could give a long and detailed account of supposed adventures which bore little relation to the truth—and kept all of us who listened in fits of laughter. This particular capacity at times amounted to inventive genius. Here, I realised, was a splendid new companion for our various adventures. He remained one of my closest friends from then until the day he died in 1959.

He had a large collection of gramophone records of American railroad songs and 'Western' ballads. He could not himself carry a tune but in a curious monotone he hummed these songs perpetually on car journeys and the like. I found myself singing them, too. I was well aware by this time of the extraordinary power of popular tunes to associate themselves with occasions and adventures. During our wonderful expedition to the Solway Firth a year before I had been humming two tunes. One was 'The Year of Jubilo' and the other 'Down in the Cane Break'. I have only to hum these tunes to see again the tightly packed flocks of Barnacles sweeping in over Caerlaverock Merse from the 'Blayshie Bonk' or the Greylags coming out from inland and tumbling down to the shore.

The memorising of lyrics and verse is quite a common way in which we fill the pigeon-holes of our minds. Of serious poetry I have never memorised much—a little Keats and rather inaccurately, some Browning, *The Revenge*—no more. But at a fairly early age I took the trouble to commit the whole of Lewis Carroll's *Hunting of the Snark* to memory, and have retained it down the years. I have found it very useful, not only for whiling away any dull half-hour, but more particularly perhaps for its quotability. There is a verse which is appropriate for nearly all occasions, especially nautical ones.

In the winter of 1930 we had established the punt again on the Wash, though for this last term I went only seldom because of my exams. It was important to get a degree in my new subject, and this I duly achieved. Mervyn Ingram and I took our degrees together on the 17th December and went snipe-shooting on the same afternoon. A couple of days later, with Christopher Dalgety and Michael Bratby, we were off to the Wash. This was a Swan song, and the end of my season, at least, for I was to go abroad almost immediately to study my new trade: I was to attend the State Academy at Munich to learn to be a painter.

11. MUNICH

Painting was now to be my profession. Natural History was deeply embedded in my system. A zoological training was part of my background. Wildfowling was my obsession. Sailing was my summer's delight; fourteen-foot dinghies had entered my world and seemed likely to stay there. I had been Stewart Morris's crew for the season, in *Clover*, built for him by Morgan Giles to answer the challenge of the boats of Uffa Fox, who had established himself sensationally as a designer of fast boats. Skating was primarily a winter interest, and although it did not compete on even terms with wildfowling, it was my principal contact with the juvenile females of my species, which gave it a significant place.

I had become quite proficient on the ice, especially in free-skating, which involves fitting together a sequence of movements to be performed to music. It is in fact a dance, with various steps, jumps, spins and spirals. Above all free-skating was fun, with that added sense of achievement when a difficult jump came off.

There is in skating the magic of the movement over the ice, and the physical satisfaction of speed and power. There is also pair-formation (just as complex and ritualised in humans as in birds), and my comparative skill in waltzing ensured an array of partners. And it was on the ice that I first saw a new princess. She was good, too—good enough to be the champion skater of Sweden. But she knew also, as I discovered later,

83

how to draw, and she was delightfully pretty. It was through her that I discovered real humility for perhaps the first time. Our romance was gentle and tender, but I was simply not good enough for her. Beside her, in skating and everything else, I felt a clumsy clodhopper.

It had been decided that during my year's study at the State Academy School in Munich I should stay in the family of one of the Professors of the School who was himself a distinguished painter of animals, particularly horses. The Herr Geheimrat Professor Angelo Jank's family consisted of his charming and rather stout wife and five children—two boys and three girls. The eldest boy and the eldest girl were already grown up and living elsewhere, but still at home were the three younger ones—Ruli, a very tall, fair-haired, sardonic lad of about my own age, Anna-Louise (also called Mouse), who was seventeen, and Jula (who was thirteen and irrepressible).

For some reason I was not able to go at once to the Academy and spent a term at a private art school. This was perhaps as well because when I arrived in Munich I had no single word of German. It was obviously necessary to learn at least the rudiments of the language before I could expect to get anything from the professional training.

My mother believed any school was good enough provided it gave you a model to draw and unlimited time to draw in. Although this may have been an overstatement, there is some truth in the notion that artists are born and not made, and that individuality can easily be suppressed and overlaid by teaching.

During my first weeks in Munich, however, no one stood much chance of influencing my artistic individuality in any direction for lack of a common language. But in a very few weeks Frau Berman (the twice-weekly successor to Mlle Herbulin) had established the first bridge across the chasm. It was purely by chance that I was living in the house of the Professor of the Animal Painting School, but when the time came to enter the Academy it seemed sensible to go into his class, although the animals involved were horses and cows and pigs, and did not ever seem likely to include such animals as wild geese and ducks. The Herr Professor himself was a kindly man, and I can remember showing him the first oil painting which I had ever made—a picture of geese against the background of a sunrise. The sky was very dark, the birds almost black, silhouetted against a streak of fiery orange. It was an undistinguished picture, but it had a snatch of the atmosphere about it and I was extremely proud of it. The Professor's criticism was in friendly vein, but it was plain to see that he did not think much of it and that he did not understand at all why I had painted it.

Next week in the Tiermahlschule we were painting an old bay mare. The Herr Professor came round to me and stood for a long time in front of my picture. I stood back with him and the longer the silence lasted the greater was my despair. The proportions of course were right; the thing was inescapably a horse ... inescapably *that* horse. As a portrait it was really quite a good likeness, but as a painting it was dull and ordinary. There was nothing rich or interesting about tone or colour or composition. I had been an effective colour camera, but no more; I had made no contribution of my own. Nor did I need the Professor to tell me this: I knew it quite well. After you have looked at a picture for a long time—as you do when you are painting it—it is easy to become blind to the most glaring faults. It is worth cultivating the capacity to turn away from the canvas and clear your mind of its image, and then to turn back and see it with a fresh eye. I had tried to do this as the Professor moved from the last painting to mine, and what I saw appalled me. Perhaps I should go back to biology or become a skating champion after all. At last my teacher spoke. 'I do not think you are moved by this horse,' he began. 'It does not seem to interest you in the same way as the Roe Deer you painted last week out of your head, or the jumping trout. Technically the brushwork's not bad,' and he passed on to the next pupil. He was, as I have said, a kindly man.

Another guest in the Professor's family was a rather earnest young American. I remember he asked whether I liked opera.

85

'Not much,' was my reply. 'You see, I really don't care for the human voice unless it sings in chorus.' 'Well, of course,' said he, 'there are choruses in some operas. Take *Meistersinger*, for example . . .'

I had never been to an opera in my life and my taste for choral music came from the works we had performed at Oundle. All the same I must have realised that I was on thin ice, for I have remembered the exchange to this day. *Die Meistersinger von Nürnberg* was the first opera that I ever saw—in the theatre in which it had first been produced sixty-three years before—and in spite of its great length I was at once a fanatical devotee of opera and of Wagner.

As a student I was entitled to a 'Student Card', which among other things reduced all opera tickets to half-price. It was not long before I had seen all the Wagner operas in the company's repertory, and most of the Mozart operas, which were usually produced in the glorious little Baroque Residenz Theater. The Verdi and Puccini operas were not supposed to be so well rendered in Munich as the works of the German composers, but in truth I enjoyed them almost as much. There were three special favourites in the repertory which I never missed: Smetana's *The Bartered Bride*, Rossini's *Cenerentola* and Weinberger's *Schwanda*.

On my student card I used to go to the opera two or three times a week. When I knew the opera well I sat at the back of the gallery where for a shilling ticket I could listen and walk forward whenever I particularly wanted to look down on to the stage. The music students sat all round me reading their scores, but I usually took some drawing paper. Of all the operas I saw in this way I suppose I was most impressed by the works of Wagner. Apart from the beauty of the music, I was prepared to boggle at the immensity of the undertaking, the gigantic achievement of one man creating a whole opera—story, words and music; and so many of them, and all so long!

I had not been very long in Munich before I decided to attend the World Skating Championships in Berlin. In order to do this without interfering with my work at the Academy I decided to travel by air. Airline travel at that time was still a comparatively adventurous business and this was my second flight ever.

I had never been to Berlin before, but I found my way by tram to the Sportpalast where the Skating Championships were being held, and there among the competitors was my Scandinavian love. For three days I watched the skating. Winner of the Women's Championship was a young Norwegian girl, Sonja Henie, with a programme full of fireworks. My girl was third or fourth, but that did not matter. I was sure myself that she had more artistry than all the others.

Watching the competition was the British teacher and stylist Bernard Adams, a gentle little man with white hair and moustache and black eyebrows. He had never himself been a great performer, but he was acknowledged as one of the greatest of all teachers of the art. In London I had known him well and had some lessons from him. Here in Berlin he made me an interesting offer. 'If you will give me your time uninterrupted for the next two years I will make you World Champion.' It was an interesting thought. Did I really want to give up everything else to become a champion figure skater? Sitting beside the rink in Berlin as the World Championships took place before us, this seemed to be an uncommonly attractive proposition. But when I had returned to Munich and was back at my painting, I thought to myself 'Perhaps not.' Did I really want to give up two years of my life to this particular and rather limited objective? On balance I felt that I did not.

Although the eldest daughter of the Jank family was living and working elsewhere in Munich, we met often enough, so we decided to take dancing lessons together. In due course we emerged reasonably skilled in the German style ballroom dancing of the day. Our dancing suggested the composition of some dance tunes; so many of them seemed to be ruined for dancing by what seemed the unnecessary requirement of singable words. I began to make up dance tunes in my head, but I had no idea of how to write them down. Here I was helped by an English music student who faithfully committed to paper the tunes which I hummed to him. I took the best of them to Herr Kohl-Bossé, the leader of the dance band in the famous Four Seasons Hotel. To my surprise he was interested. He played it on the piano a few times and eventually changed the final phrase, which had been the most original part in my view. Looking back on it now, it is more than ever clear that I was right about this. But ruined as it was I was still thrilled when the band first struck up my tune. For want of a better name we had called it 'The Elephant's Cake-Walk'.

Herr Kohl-Bossé played it at least four times at that first Thé-dansant. It was on the last time, as they struck up, that I overheard a young man say to his partner, 'Good heavens! Don't they know any other tunes, this band?' Dear Herr Kohl-Bossé! He did not overhear it, and every time we came to dance in his hotel I could be sure that my tune would be played at least twice. There were other tunes and other bands later, but this first time was the great event.

For all this ballroom dancing with the eldest Jank daughter as partner, it was Mouse, the second daughter, who interested me most. She was shy, and scarcely looked up from her plate at meals. But when she did, you could not miss her dark eyes and her gentle half-mile. I was sure she had hidden depths. And she liked me well enough. This I knew because she rolled up the sleeves of her jersey against family opposition after I had told her it was becoming. If I was not to have a Swedish wife, perhaps I could have a German one. Mouse came and stayed with my family in Norfolk the following year. She enchanted me, as always, and right up to the time I received an invitation to her wedding, to which, alas, I could not go.

An hour and a half from Munich in the electric train is the village of Oberau, nestling in the foothills of the Alps beside the River Loisach whose milky melt water thunders down from the high snows. It was early spring when I first went there with Stevie Johnson, a young Englishman who was also learning German in Munich. Stevie was a fly-fisherman and the Loisach and its tributaries were full of Trout. The valley was so beautiful on that first week-end that we had to go again for the next, and the next and the one after that. It was spring —lovely and full of living things, of Roe Deer, and water birds, and butterflies, and all the spring flowers of the Alps. Only then did I realise how much I had missed the wild countryside during my city winter in Munich.

The Loisach valley floor at Oberau is about a mile wide. At the sides the wooded mountains rise precipitously. The road and the electric railway occupy the comparatively narrow strip between the river and the western hillside; across the Loisach the water-meadows are wilder and more remote. I knew them well for all that summer and for part of another. To me now they are a collective picture of all the seasons, full of gentians and orchids and columbines and great beds of lily-of-the-valley. I remember the excitement of the week-end when Swallow-tail butterflies were everywhere, I remember the Dippers which lived on the rapids, the Firebellied Toads which came out after rain, the Trout and the Grayling and the Chubb.

Flowing into the Loisach a mile or two below Oberau was a tributary stream, the Lauferbach, and here we fished with a dry fly.

One late summer's day, walking up the river along the edge of a hayfield, I almost stumbled over a small reddish animal curled up in the tall grass. It was a day-old Roe Deer fawn, and of all the animals I have ever seen I think it was the most appealing. He was tiny, with long coltish legs, unafraid eyes, a bulging forehead and huge expressive ears. He was deep russet and handsomely marked with sharp white spots in a row down either side of his back and spreading down his sides and flanks. He was almost too beautiful to be true. He seemed to be entirely without fear and lay confidently in my arms; he sucked my little finger, he stood quietly while we photographed him and was finally happy to be left in his original nest. His was a perfection that suited the perfection of our valley on that sunny morning.

Fierce thunderstorms were common there; they built up, black and brooding, over the mountains to the south, flickering among the high peaks and then burst with an exciting fury in the evening; I found these Alpine thunderstorms stimulating, awe-inspiring, beautiful, but annoying because the rain ruined the fishing. It was on a day when thunder threatened that we encountered the badger, and caught it in an umbrella.

I was walking home from the Lauterbach as the great cumulus clouds gathered at the head of the valley. The fish had not been rising and I had given up fishing and bathed instead. Over one shoulder was a damp towel, my trout rod over the other, and hanging on my arm was an umbrella against the threatening storm. Crossing a recently cut hayfield I came towards one of the little wooden huts in which the hay is stored in most of these Alpine meadows. As I came round the corner of the hut there, sitting right out in the open, was a baby badger. The moment he saw me he started to run for his sett which was actually underneath the hut, and thinking it would be interesting to have a look at him, I jumped to head him off. We both had about ten yards to go, but as I went I had a brainwave: I pushed my umbrella about half-way open and blocked the hole with it. The badger finished a close second and went full tilt into the umbrella. It was a well-grown baby and it looked quite savage down at the bottom of the umbrella, so I wrapped my bathing towel round my hand and gave it to him to bite. He seized hold of it and while he was busy biting it, I picked him up with the other hand and had a good look at him. Then I took him back to show the others.

We decided that he was too old to be tamed, but the thunderstorm was upon us and we decided to keep him overnight in a box in the garage. Next morning we found he had eaten a large plate of bread and milk, and escaped from his box, but he was still in the garage and still as ferocious as ever. I carried him back to the little hut by the hayfield and popped him down his hole. Then I listened. I heard the rumble as he ran down and then a great babel of grunts and squeaks. Greetings, scoldings, recriminations? Who knows what treatment a young badger can expect from his family after a night out?

12. ROYAL ACADEMY SCHOOLS

At the end of the academic year in Munich I returned to England, ready to go to the Royal Academy Schools in London. Meanwhile there were invitations to Scotland for the summer holidays. In Skye, even more beautiful than I had been led to imagine, there were sea trout to be caught, stags to be stalked (unsuccessfully), and grouse to be chased. From there I went to Struy Lodge near Beauly, for more stalking. They were long energetic days on the hill, and to begin with also unsuccessful. But one day after a blank morning we spotted a single stag with a number of hinds laying just beyond him. We started our stalk, trying first a burn, but that did not go close enough so we climbed up again and began a much more difficult approach along the top, straight towards the stag. Finally we had to crawl about fifty yards, stopping at one point and then finding that we could get closer. When at last we got into position we could not at first see the stag, but then we made out his horns with eight points and the ridge of his back. He was lying down with his head flat. The plan was to wait until he should get up to feed. It was already 3.30 in the afternoon, and deer always feed in the evening. We hoped it would not be too long to wait. After about twenty minutes the stag lifted his head. The range was no more than 100 yards, so in high excitement we waited. And then at last, after more than half an hour, the stag stretched his neck. Two of the hinds which had been getting up periodically and sitting down again, had now got up and begun feeding. 'He's thinking about it,' said Rory McCray, the stalker, then, 'He's getting up.' And so he was; first his hind legs, then his front and he was up, facing us, scratching. Then he took a few paces downhill and began feeding broadside on. 'Wait till he stands,' said Rory, and a moment later he stood stock still.

The aperture sight was up and I took careful aim and began to squeeze, but the rifle would not go off and at last in despair I pulled right through, forgetting the first pressure, and when it went off it was nowhere near the stag. 'Over his back,' said Rory, and I reloaded.

At the shot the stag had looked up and stood with hind legs slightly bent ready to jump away at any moment, but he did not know which way to jump. So I took careful aim and squeezed. There was a thud and the stag fell. My first sensation was one of intense relief that I had saved the situation, if only by a hair's breadth: I flopped backwards and sat down with a bump in a pool of water. The stag was a good eight-pointer with a very wide head and he was a fairly heavy beast.

Looking back on it I can remember a dim awareness of remorse at having killed that beautiful creature, but it was overwhelmed by the sense of success after the days of failure in Skye and the blank day we had already had at Struy. For those days I had walked and walked over the hills with one express object in view—to shoot a stag. I had taken good exercise, I had steeped myself in the atmosphere of the Highlands, I had seen all kinds of animals from Red Deer to Fox Moth caterpillars; I had learned something of the art of stalking, and the use of dead ground, how to flatten my body as I crawled, when to move fast and when to move slowly, the importance of the precise direction of the wind and the eddies which might carry my scent—but I had not shot a stag.

Three days later (it was my twenty-second birthday) I shot another from a ledge on a corrie. I had clean missed twice, but the third shot was in the heart, the stag galloping for fifty yards down a bank before falling stone-dead. He could not have known much about it, but it was a clumsy piece of work, and although the two stags I had shot were the heaviest of the season and therefore causes for congratulation, the seeds of doubt had been sown in my mind.

I only ever shot one more stag after that—a year later on the steep slope above Loch na Cray in Skye. The doubt became a certainty. Stalking was wonderful, but killing stags was not for me. So now I do not walk for days over the wild hills; I see the high tops only in memory. There is no doubt that I am the poorer in mind and body for this, and it is questionable whether the Red Deer are the better for it. What I learned of stalking probably saved my life one day in Normandy, but unless I were starving I could not now be persuaded to shoot a stag.

Back in London that autumn of 1931, I became a pupil at the Royal Academy Schools in Burlington House. I was two years at the school, two happy years of drawing and painting.

I won no prizes at the competitions, I had no very advanced ideas about the future of art, yet I believe my training at the Royal Academy Schools was of the greatest value to me.

But for this period of my life, as it had been in Cambridge days, my most serious limitation was an unbridled craving for adventure. I wanted things to *happen*; for me to be happy things had to be happening, and in a curious way they seemed to happen all the time.

Wildfowling provided many of the adventures. Thus the winter week-ends found me back on the old familiar beautiful marsh on the Wash, sometimes with my original companions, sometimes with new. Punting still held its special appeal, now more perhaps for the boat handling, the silent and secret comings and goings in the creeks, the intimate views of the wild creatures, than for the shooting; though it would not yet have been worth the long days if the guns had been left behind.

It was during one of these trips that I met William G. Tinsley, a shy, fifty-year-old bachelor farmer, who lived at the Poplars in Holbeach Marsh.

Will's father had died about a year before I first went to the Poplars and most of the farm business was undertaken by 'Gran', his stepmother, who had in fact brought up Will, his three brothers and his sister. Will's preoccupation was birds. He had little inclination for farming, although he spent his days doing it. His great interest was wildfowl, and particularly the geese which came to feed on his potato fields. He had shot them and had kept the wounded ones alive; he had brought in and hatched the eggs of Shelducks which nested locally under the stacks. Around a small pond at the back of his garden were most of the common species of British ducks, pinioned in an enclosure, and in the orchard were a number of geese. His enthusiasm was impressive and infectious. At once I recognised Will Tinsley as a man after my own heart, and I stayed often at the Poplars.

In those early days his collection of waterfowl was small, though later it was greatly enlarged. His observations during the Second World War were to influence the establishment of the Wildfowl Trust on the Severn Estuary. And it was Will who introduced me to the art of decoying ducks, piloting me twenty-five miles inland to Borough Fen decoy, at Peakirk, near Peterborough.

At the door of the farmhouse—the Decoy Farm—we met Billy Williams, the decoyman—a small man of about fifty, with twinkling bright blue eyes. His family, famous in the history of early duck decoys, had worked Borough Fen since it was built, about 1670, which makes it one of the earliest, though probably not the first, of the two or three hundred duck decoys that were built in Britain.

I had read something about duck decoys, but I had no very clear idea of how they worked until my first visit to Borough Fen. The decoy wood lay 200 yards from the farmhouse— eighteen acres of trees, among them tall poplars, elms and oaks standing out in the vast bare expanse of fenland fields. Inside the wood was a small secret pond of two and a half acres, of a regular but complex shape. It had eight very small bays, from which led eight curved tapering ditches each about sixty yards long and five yards wide at the mouth. The ditches were spanned by hoops made of ash or willow saplings, over which tarred string netting was stretched to make a tapering tunnel, curving to the right as it went farther from the open water of the pond. Along the outside of the curve were ranged a row of screens made of reeds, three or four yards long and six feet high, set up in an overlapping pattern like a Venetian blind, which could be seen through from one direction but not from the other. These eight devices, radiating from the central pool were called the 'pipes' and Borough Fen was therefore an eight-pipe decoy.

To operate a decoy it is necessary to entice some of the ducks which have collected on the pond (often in thousands) to come into a pipe, this may be achieved in three ways. First, the banks of the pond can be made vertical except in the pipes, so that ducks which want to go ashore and preen and sleep can do so only on the 'landings' in the pipe or at its mouth: this is called 'banking'. Alternatively, the birds may be encouraged to come to the pipes with food spread on the 'landings'. But the most surprising and interesting method is the use of a trained dog. In this the decoyman exploits the curious behaviour pattern of ducks in the presence of a predator. If, for example, a fox appears before them when they are sitting on the water, they appear to feel safe enough to swim up within a few feet and mob it. The behaviour of small birds round a hawk or owl, and the behaviour of young cattle round a dog is clearly analogous. The attraction seems to be all the greater if the predatory animal is retreating.

The application of this principle in Holland in the sixteenth century is still today the operating basis of most of the duck decoys which remain in existence. The dog is trained to run round the overlapping screens, appearing, retreating along the screen and disappearing again progressively farther and farther up the pipe as the ducks follow it. At Borough Fen, as in many other decoys, the dog jumps over a two-foot-high screen called a 'dog leap' and appears with startling sudden-ness which seems to be even more stimulating. The 'dog

95

leaps' occupy the space between the ends of the high screens making, in plan view, a zig-zag pattern.

When as many ducks as possible have been lured under the archway of netting, the decoyman appears suddenly at the mouth of the pipe. Because of the overlap of the screens he is still invisible to the ducks out on the pool, but is in the full view of those which are in the pipe. They dare not fly back towards him, for he appears to have cut off their retreat to the open pond. Instead they fly away from him up the pipe, thinking perhaps to escape round the bend, but there they find the pipe growing ever narrower. The decoyman is following close behind them as they run up the final slope from the narrow channel, into the detachable tubular net at the pipe's end. From this 'tunnel net' they are removed, and in the days when I first went to Borough Fen Decoy they were speedily killed and sent to market in London. Nowadays Borough Fen Decoy, and some others (including our four-pipe decoy at Slimbridge, built in 1845) are used exclusively for ringing and measuring ducks, which are then released.

Back in 1932 I was tremendously excited with my first introduction to this fascinating technique. To be operating silently within a few feet of the ducks, and within 100 yards of perhaps thousands of them, was a new thrill.

Many times Billy and I talked of the days when the decoy's economy would allow us to kill no more, but to ring and release the catch instead. This was not finally achieved until 1955, only two years before Billy's death. For several years before that, only Mallards had been killed, all other species being sent away with rings on their legs.

When I had known Billy for three months I proposed that we build an Observation Hut, and he seemed to be in favour.

We selected a site on one of the 'pointings' jutting out between the north and north-east pipes, from which with the prevailing south-westerly wind we should get a good view of the ducks without risk of disturbing them. It involved cutting a path through a thick blackthorn thicket and then building a small reed-thatched hut at the far end.

The hut was successful: it could be reached in secrecy and gave an excellent view of the ducks on the pool, with a chance to count them, to assess the relative abundance of the different species and check sex ratios. Although it remained there for a good many years I was never quite sure that Billy Williams entirely approved of it. But in the first winter after it was built it was a novelty and was much frequented by visitors to the Decoy.

One morning in the following February when the ice on the pool was half an inch thick, my diary records that we went down before dawn to break it and to feed the house pipe: 'The birds came in very early so that we had to leave it before we had finished and go back to the house; after breakfast there were a few ducks and Wigeon in the house pipe. Then we went into the hut where the sight was simply staggering. Filling the pond from edge to edge was a huge mass of birds. There must have been 3,000 ducks sitting on the ice, possibly 4,000. There were quantities of Wigeon and Pintails and about forty pairs of Shovelers.'

My initial idea of an observation hut which could be entered and left without the knowledge of the birds turned out to be the prototype of many huts built since, and perhaps it was fortunate that the first attempt should have proved so satisfactory.

A year later, with the Academy Schools behind me, I had got to start making my way as an artist. I went to live at Borough Fen Decoy. I was likely, I thought, to paint best those things which moved me most. That meant my wildfowl. They had never been painted in the way I saw them. Other artists did not *know* them quite as I knew them. What I wanted to do was extraordinarily simple and easy. I had only to put on to canvas the birds as I had seen them at dawn or dusk or moonlight, or in storm or frost or snow, and I could not fail to be doing something original. It remained to be seen whether those who looked at the pictures would be moved in the same way as I was when I watched the flight of the wild geese, and heard their music.

I painted hard during the winter, picked out what I thought were the three best pictures and sent them in for the summer exhibition at the Royal Academy. To my surprise and delight two of them were accepted.

During the winter at the Decoy I had painted about forty pictures and these, with a few earlier works, were accepted at a one-man show in the summer of 1933. Nearly all the pictures were oils, and the highest price was £25. During the month all but two or three were sold.

The show led to a number of commissions. One was for a large painting to hang above the stairs in the hall of Sir John Beale's country house at Oulton Broad in Suffolk. The dimensions of the canvas were to be eight feet by five feet, and I was considerably alarmed by the prospect. It was more than four times larger in area than any picture I had ever painted before. For a long time I was frightened of starting it, but Sir John Beale was not a man to be fobbed off with excuses or postponements. A deadline was agreed, and Sir John said that he was coming to see the picture on a certain day the following week. 'As it is already half finished,' he said, 'I'd like to see how it looks. Perhaps it won't be too late to make small alterations . . .' The untouched canvas was hastily taken from the wall against which it had been standing for so long. It was plain and white and vaguely terrifying. But I had in my mind the sort of thing that I meant to do; so, with my biggest brushes I started to slosh on the sky. By the end of that day there was also a reed bed, some water and the outlines of the birds. I still had two days in hand and if I worked very hard I might paint up the birds and still get in the tall reeds which were to sweep up the foreground of the picture. Towards the end of the third day, after the initial background had been given time to dry, it was evident that I was not going to get the reeds done. There were a lot of tall stems to go in, reaching almost from top to bottom of the picture; these took time and there were at least twenty reeds to be painted. The only answer was to ask my mother to help. She went to work on the reeds on the left-hand side of the picture while I plodded on with those on the right. When Sir John came the picture was practically finished and he seemed delighted with it. For the rest of his lifetime it hung in his house at Oulton Broad, and was sent later to a Royal Air Force mess. Meanwhile it was to be reproduced as one of the illustrations in a new book, *Morning Flight*, to be published by *Country Life*. The title of the picture in the book was 'Norfolk Spring—Shovelers and a pair of Garganey Teal', but there was a misprint in which the dash had been replaced by a hyphen. They appeared as Norfolk Spring-Shovelers, and all Shovelers have been Norfolk Spring-Shovelers ever since.

This title was too long when the picture was reproduced by the Medici Society, and they called it 'Taking to Wing', under which corny name it has since sold more than 350,000 copies.

My first book—*Morning Flight*—was published in 1935. I had written about 50,000 words of my wildfowling experiences to go with the lavish illustrations, and in spite of its then high cost of three guineas the book was unexpectedly successful. The first edition quickly sold out and a cheaper one appeared in the following year, which was kept in print by new impressions for the next ten years.

It was in this book that I tried to record something of the almost frightening intensity of my feeling for birds in wild places, and the way in which the sounds of the wild geese worked on my emotions like the great *Sanctus* chorus of Bach's B minor mass.

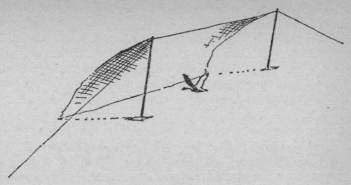

13. NETTING GEESE

Not far from my old school at Oundle was the Lilford Estate
where on the floods we had watched the White-fronted geese
in my school days. Near the Hall was a fine collection of
captive birds presided over by Mr A. F. Moody, who was
Lord Lilford's curator. On visits to the Wash we had saved
many birds caught in flight-nets (now happily illegal) and had
taken them to the aviaries at Lilford—Curlews, Redshanks,
Knots, Dunlins, Grey Plovers and others; we had also brought
wing-tipped geese both for him and for Will Tinsley's collection in the orchard beside his farmhouse in Holbeach Marsh.
The idea of keeping birds alive had suddenly become an important new objective.

To be sure, we still liked to go wildfowling as often as
possible at 'Sandbanks', our beautiful marsh at Terrington.
But gradually the idea of a wider interest in the birds was
catching hold.

I am writing, still, of a time which was long ago, when my
views on many things were different from the views I hold
today, and in order to put those youthful thoughts into perspective I must go back to the subject of killing.

When people used to say, 'I don't understand how you can
draw those beautiful creatures and at the same time want to
kill them,' I used to answer that this was admittedly strange,

but that my particular regard for them was not a sentimental one; it was not a 'dear-little-dicky-bird' attitude, but rather a respect for a wild creature which was supremely able to look after itself, and which did so, by and large, very effectively in spite of all my wiles. It was in fact, I would say, this capacity to look after themselves which primarily attracted me to wild geese. This simple argument no doubt left many in disagreement.

But after many years of wildfowling the first inklings of a changing attitude came to me when I was out with David Haig Thomas. David had rowed bow in the Cambridge boat for four years. I had met him first out shooting on the Wash, one frosty November morning before I went to Munich. He was wading in bare feet because he had overspent his allowance and could not afford rubber boots. Tough, ruthless and irresistibly charming, he became a staunch friend and a fine companion in adventure. One early spring day in 1932 we had shot twenty-three Greylag geese. Among them were two wounded ones, and as soon as we had picked them up we hoped that they might not die. The birds which a few moments before we had been trying to kill, we were now trying to keep alive.

The two geese survived and we kept them for many years. Having got this far it began to seem strange that we should ever have taken delight in killing geese at all. And yet we had, and to a certain extent still did. When a bird was cleanly killed in the air there was a satisfaction of good marksmanship, but was it any greater than the satisfaction at breaking a 'clay pigeon' fired unexpectedly from a spring? And if so how much greater, and why? When a bird crashed with a thud on to the ground, how could I ever have thought the sound satisfying?

Then came the problem of wounding. I was a moderately good shot in the days when I kept myself in practice, which meant, if I was shooting geese and employing the essential self-control only to fire when the birds were in proper range, that I was likely to bring home one bird for every three cartridges I fired. Yet, when you are firing a pattern of pellets, is it likely that the other cartridges are all clean misses?

I once heard a keen wildfowler say that he had 'the satisfaction of hearing his shots slap into the birds' although none of them came down. I have taken a wildfowler round the pens of the Wildfowl Trust and heard him say when a flock of Snow Geese came low over his head—'My word, I could knock a couple of those down.' When the same Snow Geese landed at our feet and walked up to feed from my hand I could sense that he was very much ashamed of the remark. The expression suggests a blunt stick to beat the beautiful birds out of the sky.

Back in the 1930s my own desires were beginning to be superseded by the desire to catch the birds alive. This involved achieving the power of death over the quarry without exercising it. It seemed at once to be a step forward. There was the initial objective of keeping the captured birds until they became tame, and thereby learning more about them; and when enough had been caught for these purposes there was still the technique of bird ringing—then fairly recently developed—which would require an almost unlimited number to be captured.

This advance, if advance it was, was no sudden change in my outlook. I was still much too captivated by wildfowling to give it up altogether. So many things went with the actual shooting—the beauty, the natural history, the exercise, the memories, and particularly the technical skills which in the course of years I had acquired. Especially was this so of punting; the seamanship, the boat handling, the knowledge of weather and tide—all these appealed to me as much as ever.

It was one thing to decide to try to catch geese alive and quite another to find a way of doing it. Not for twenty years did we perfect a means of catching wild geese by the hundreds, but our final success adds some interest to these early beginnings.

The best system seemed to be that developed by the Plover-netters of the Fens—a modification of the double Clap Net in which a single net, attached to two poles, swung over like the page of a book at the release of springy stretched rope.

At the end of August 1932 Will Tinsley and I went over to see an old Plover-netter, Barney Shawl, who gave us a demonstration of how his net worked. I took careful notes of the way in which the rope was pegged down. My diary records the special devices for release, so that both poles go over simultaneously. It goes on:

'In this way I am perfectly convinced we can catch numbers of geese. Netting geese will, I believe, prove much more exciting than shooting them, and with the tremendous advantage that never a wounded bird will be lost, and that the prize will be a bag of fine live geese instead of bloody corpses.'

But by mid-November, after many unsuccessful attempts, I was not so sanguine about the goose nets. My diary reads:

'I have come to the conclusion that it is not going to be so easy to net these geese as we fondly imagined. We have had an easy time so far in concealing the net. Stubble fields and clover make good cover. Setting them on bare plough, where footprints count, is going to be a very different matter. Our net is twenty yards long and three yards wide and covers twice that area in the course of swinging over, but this is still only about one-fortieth of an acre. It looks a pretty small patch in a field of eighty acres.

'I don't think that catching them as they fly over will ever be a success as it is extremely difficult to judge the lead to give them. The only chance of a flying shot would be if they were to pitch downwind of the net; it *might* then be possible to put them up and pull on to them before they got too high. One does not realise how big a goose is. When he looks as though he is only a few feet up he is probably twenty feet in reality. After all, the net's height is just under twice the wing span of a goose. I think if we go at it we might catch some, but it will be very difficult and we shall never catch as many as we can shoot in the long run. But still a live goose in the net is worth ten dead ones.'

The most serious limitation of the Plover-net device was the length of tautly stretched rope leading to the point where the operator was to hide. If we could get away from this there seemed a much better chance of catching geese. Some other way than a stretched rope must be found for the motive power. We turned our thoughts to break-back mousetraps and wondered whether the poles could not be pushed over in the same way.

By the beginning of December I had brought these plans to a practical stage and my diary records:

'During the week I had springs made to throw the poles over: two torsion springs, the coil four inches in diameter with legs about eighteen inches long and the whole made of seven-sixteenth-inch spring steel, to be set through three-quarters of a revolution. My idea is that with a spring we can do away with the all-too-visible 100 yards of springy rope, which will leave nothing but the poles to conceal, a much easier proposition.'

Hopes were very high and I went for the Christmas holiday to stay at the Poplars with Will Tinsley. We set the net in various fields in Holbeach Marsh. The whole of Christmas Day, for example, was spent unavailingly sitting over the net. Boxing Day was a thick fog and then came Tuesday, 27th December, when I went by myself to Trevathoe Farm. While I was setting the net some geese came on to the next field. Very soon a little lot of three geese came. Fortunately they did not see the thirty or forty geese on the field next door, nor four others on the far side of my own field, so in they came to perfection and pitched. I looked up and saw at once that they nicely covered the area of the net. One of them must be under, so I pulled. There was a clang as the new tubular steel 'poles' swung over. In the first instant I saw two geese getting up and sweeping back to the left. The wind was blowing almost along the net and they had got it under their great wings and had shot back on it. But the third . . . what of him? Then suddenly I saw him jumping and straining in the meshes of the net. I should think I covered the intervening sixty yards in something under six seconds and was on the spot to extricate the very first goose ever caught in my net.

The extrication was a great deal more difficult than I had anticipated; he was completely 'taffled up'. I had to reset the net in order to get him the right way up and then I set to work; I should say it took five minutes to get him out. When I eventually did so he was a somewhat bedraggled object but he was nevertheless my first netted goose. I returned to the dyke and popped him into the bag I had brought for the purpose. I had got one, anyway.

Two days later on the same farm I caught another single goose, and then on 2nd January, 1933, after two days of waiting, I netted just one more goose, and my diary records :

'These two days have been two of the most enjoyable I ever spent in the pursuit of geese; and the total bag has been one goose . . . but alive.'

14. THE LIGHTHOUSE AND BOND STREET

The stretch of saltings lying between King's Lynn and the River Nene, which had been known by us as 'Sandbanks', is marked on the map as Terrington Marsh. At the western end it is sharply bounded by the artificial cut which brings the River Nene out into the Wash. The completion of this cut, built at the end of the eighteenth century as a final stage in the draining of the Great Fens, was commemorated by the construction of two small ornamental lighthouses, one on each side of the river at its mouth. They had been a landmark to us ever since we first began to visit these marshes, and I had been thinking of trying to acquire the disused East Lighthouse for some time, but it was not until 1933 that I made an approach to the Nene Catchment Board for a lease, which was immediately granted.

The Nene had a rise and fall of about thirty feet and at low water there was a steep slope of soft mud held together by often-renewed faggots. At the point where the sea-wall, running east and west to protect the reclaimed fields, met the bank of the river running north and south, you arrived at a gate, and seventy yards beyond it stood the East Lighthouse on a short projection of the river bank which jutted out into the saltings. A hundred yards away across the river stood its twin —the West Lighthouse. Nowadays the reclamations of the Wash have pushed far out over those saltings, but in the 1930s the spring tides surrounded my lighthouse on three sides, covering the great expanse of salt-marsh to the foot of the bank.

It was a conical brick building looking rather more like a windmill without sails than a conventional lighthouse. It had four storeys, the bottom one sixteen feet in diameter, and above it three rooms which became progressively smaller, until the top one was little more than six feet across, but it was a room with a wonderful view from each of its two round windows, one looking up the straight river on a scene of parallel lines converging at the vanishing point, the other down over the wash and its sandbanks and mudflats and saltings.

There was also a basement room reached by outside steps in which a rather splendid nomadic character called Charlie had his home when he was not sleeping under a hedge. Charlie was a great big friendly red-headed man who collected cockles and samphire in the summer and did handyman jobs in the winter.

At first I had visualised the lighthouse as a temporary headquarters for wildfowling week-ends, in which some of the gear might be stored in the dry until the following week-end. It was not for several months that I began to see it as a permanent dwelling-place, and then it was my home until the beginning of the Second World War. During those five years there were, of course, many developments. I added, for example, a flat-roofed studio overlooking the marsh, a larger bathroom and a bunk-room connected with the garage and boathouse which I had put up initially. The additions included a new front door leading from the gravel driveway into a small hall. This was altogether more respectable than the original entrance through the kitchen. With a front door it became a proper house.

But the arrangements for keeping live waterfowl on the marsh all round the house were even more important.

For some time we had been sending birds caught in the flight-nets on the saltings at 'Sandbanks' to Mr Moody at Lilford. One dark night more geese than usual flew into these nets, and next day about a dozen were offered to us by the flight-netters. I decided that these must form the nucleus of my own collection, to which would be added the three I had caught with my spring net.

First an enclosure must be made and this had to be done quickly; at the ironmongers in the village of Sutton Bridge I bought a fifty-yard roll of six-foot wire-netting and some metal stakes. This roll was set up round a little pool on the salting within a stone's throw of the lighthouse. It could only be twenty yards long and five yards wide and into this tiny area the fifteen wing-clipped geese were introduced. Soon I realised that something very much larger was necessary, and this required a certain amount of planning and could not immediately be provided.

The fifteen geese had only been there a week when, during a fog, a wild goose flew into the pen, but was very soon chased out again by the ganders in possession. The newcomer was a young bird and he refused to be driven right away, but walked up and down just outside the pen where he was safe from the attacks of the pinioned birds inside. He stayed there for a week or so and became quite tame; for security, when anyone appeared, he would flap up over the fence and into the enclosure. We called him (for no reason that I can remember) Egbert.

One day in the middle of February when there was a strong north-east wind and a big spring tide the waves raced in over the saltings and right up to the sea-wall. They beat on the wire-netting of my little goose pen and the weight of the debris, the dead leaves of the marsh plants and other flotsam, lay against the wire until it collapsed. Out swam the fifteen geese and half an hour later I saw the little flotilla far out among the breakers nearly a mile from the shore. When the tide began to fall the geese had long since disappeared from view. It was very cold with sleet, and searching with glasses out of doors was almost impossible. That night we went to bed feeling very miserable, and wondering how our pinioned geese would fare.

Early the next morning I went up to the round window at the top of the lighthouse to spy the marsh with glasses. To my astonishment sitting in the middle of the mangled remains of the pen was a goose. I thought at once that it must be Egbert who had flown back, but it was not: it was one of the pinioned birds who had walked back into the middle of the pen and was sitting there apparently feeling quite at home, and waiting for his breakfast. That day a local wildfowler brought another back. We made up the pen again and on the following morning I was awakened by a familiar honk; running to the window I was just in time to see Egbert circle round and settle again in his usual place just outside the pen. Of the rest of the geese, as far as I know only one met with tragedy: he was shot. All the rest were caught and all but three were returned to me, the three being sold to someone else before I heard of their capture; but I was assured they had gone to a good home.

Egbert developed a rather dangerous habit of flying down to the river to wash, and as the new pen which I was then building contained perfectly good washing accommodation, I thought that his habit should be discouraged. I was not all sure that some character with a gun might not shoot Egbert from the river bank, even if he knew full well that it was Egbert. So I stretched a net over half the pen and then walked the geese under it. Twice Egbert flew up, refusing to go under the net, but each time trying to settle on top of it. When he found that awkward he flew down to the river. But each time after a few minutes he came back, swinging in over the wire and settling in the open half of the pen. At the third attempt he walked under with the pinioned birds. His escape was quickly blocked and soon afterwards Egbert could no longer endanger his life in that foolhardy way.

In due course the new enclosure of about three acres of salting was completed and the twelve Pinkfeet (including Egbert, now in permanent residence) were released into their new home, there later to be joined by ducks and geese of many other species as my small collection grew.

In earliest days the 'tame' geese at the lighthouse were far from tame. In the larger pen I found that they spent most of their time keeping as far away from the observer as possible. To make my birds tamer they must see more people, not less.

But it also helps if there is a nucleus of hand-reared birds thoroughly accustomed to seeing people near by and unwilling to be disturbed by them. When once these principles were understood the birds round the lighthouse quickly grew tame and soon they came to feed from my hand.

The lighthouse itself was in the middle of my new enclosure. The geese would finally hardly move out of the way of cars or people as they came along the top of the bank.

Birds need regular feeding, so I employed Kenzie Thorpe, a well-known local poacher, to look after them.

Kenzie Thorpe had Romany origins; he was a middleweight boxer, a skilled wildfowler and an inveterate poacher. But he knew something about the local wildfowl, and I could not help liking him, in spite of the circumstances of our first meeting.

One morning at 'Sandbanks' several years before, David Haig Thomas had shot a goose which slanted away across the ditch on the other side of the field. From far to one side a long shot had been fired at the bird which was already half-way to the ground, and Kenzie and a companion had jumped out of the ditch and gone to collect it. When David went over to fetch his goose Kenzie refused to part with it, disclosed that he was poaching and threatened to sock David on the jaw if he came any nearer. I had joined in the argument when we met him on the out-marsh later in the day. From then onwards I had met him only occasionally, but on the principle that poachers make good gamekeepers I decided to engage him to look after my collection. By and large the arrangement worked well, and Kenzie was soon quite expert in the care of live waterfowl.

When my new studio had been built, the lighthouse was as near perfect for all my purposes as I could make it. I began to paint hard.

I selected oil paints rather than water-colours, and large canvases rather than small because I wanted to escape from the preoccupation with tiny detail which had so greatly affected my early work. I painted from memory, which is to

111

say that I did not find it necessary to have what I was painting in front of me as I worked. In the case of flying birds this would in any case have been difficult. I had in my mind the idea of what had stirred me when I had seen it out on the marshes.

My earlier works painted at the decoy had shown a certain hasty and ignorant crudeness. Now at the lighthouse I seemed to have advanced beyond that stage, but there was always the danger of losing the original freshness and vigour.

I quickly discovered that if I worked for too long on a painting I was quite capable of ruining it. Working fast was the secret of quality as well as quantity. And I was also brimming over with new ideas. I could not wait until one picture was finished before starting the next, and soon I found that this was, in fact, a practical method; the first stage of one picture could be drying while the next was started. It also gave me the chance to adjust my work to my mood. If I was feeling creative I could start on a blank canvas, if not, I could go quietly on with the chores—putting on a large area of blue sky, or laboriously painting up flocks of birds whose shapes and pattern I had already determined. I painted in bouts of intense energy, working all day and long into the night with two Aladdin mantle lamps, one at either side of the canvas; often I had no idea how the colour would look when I saw it again in the daylight. I can remember the tremendous excitement of coming down in a dressing-gown in the morning to see how it looked; and the bitter disappointment when my corrections for the artificial light had been faulty and half the picture had to be painted all over again. I can remember often, too, going to bed when a half-finished work was on the easel, and just before I went to sleep seeing the picture finished in my mind's eye—in that moment of truth between waking and sleeping—and then being furious that it had gone from me by the morning. But in those wonderful days there were few frustrations. I was not trying to do anything very complicated. I set out to put my birds and my wild places on my canvas and, by and large, my training allowed me to put them there more or less as I meant

112

to. Sometimes the idea rather than the image took charge, so that the painting finished up quite unlike what I had initially imagined, but occasionally rather better.

I was painting hard for another exhibition after the unexpected success of my first in 1933. I had to produce about forty more pictures. At the speed I worked this was not difficult, and I still had plenty of exciting ideas—far more than I could ever undertake.

My exhibitions at Ackermann's Galleries in New Bond Street followed annually. Forty new oil-paintings and a few drawings a year, mostly of my beloved wildfowl with occasional portraits or pictures of sailing-boats. If one of the requirements of a portrait was to paint a likeness, the same requirements must surely, I thought, apply to a picture of a bird. Gradually as the years went by, the likenesses of the birds in my pictures improved, and my earlier works, when I saw them again, left me dissatisfied. But these improvements in my work went unnoticed by all except the few who really knew the birds.

In the social and financial fields, however, the exhibitions were increasingly successful. In 1934 the opening was performed by John Buchan: in 1935 by Hugh Walpole; in 1936 by Sir James Jeans, the astronomer; in 1937 by G. M. Trevelyan, the historian; in 1938 by James Stephen, the poet; in 1939 by Vincent Massey, the High Commissioner for Canada. Each of them came to New Bond Street on a summer's afternoon, said a few well-chosen, often witty words, and launched me into another London season. It had all become alarmingly, dangerously, but delightfully fashionable. I used to go daily to the gallery, which was a pleasant opportunity of meeting my friends.

The first royal visit to one of my exhibitions began disastrously. I was sitting on one of the print cupboards in the outer room of the gallery, dangling my legs over the edge and talking to Betty Gilbert, who helped to sell the pictures, when two ladies came in. One of the faces was vaguely familiar, so I smiled, nodded and went on talking to Betty. The two ladies

113

passed on into the inner room. Betty said, 'Wasn't that the Princess Royal?' 'Great heavens! Of course it was—how awful!' In confusion I dashed through to apologise, but Her Royal Highness would allow it no further thought, and in a moment we were discussing the Whooper Swans which came to the lake at Harewood.

The Queen (H.M. Queen Elizabeth the Queen Mother) came to a later exhibition and bought a fiery picture of Pink-feet coming out from inland to the mudflats of the Wash at dusk. She told me she had once seen them against such a sunset on the Wolferton marshes below Sandringham. Queen Mary also came to Ackermann's Galleries during the series of pre-war exhibitions, but gave no real indication of what she thought of the pictures. Perhaps she liked them, for she came again some time after the war, in a wheel-chair.

It seemed that success in Bond Street was a handicap in artistic circles. My pictures were less readily accepted by the Royal Academy, though I knew they were better than the earlier ones. From time to time they would take a very large oil-painting of flying birds, chiefly, I think, because they thought it would be comparatively easy to hang. A great sky full of birds could be 'skied'—would indeed look the better for being hung at the very top of a wall of pictures. Recognising this particular niche which it seemed possible I might continue to fill, I sent in each year an elongated, frieze-like picture of wild geese in flight against the sky, with no ground in the picture at all.

Reproductions of my works in print form were now beginning to sell well. *Norfolk Spring-Shovelers* or *Taking to Wing*, published by the Medici Society, had already had some success; proofs in colour collotype printed by the Chiswick Press for Ackermann's in a limited edition, in accordance with the provisions of the Fine Arts Trade Guild, were appearing twice a year and being sold out. Each 'Artist's Proof' in these editions of 550 copies had to be signed in pencil. Signing one's name 550 times in succession is a curious task. To begin with I found it impossible to think of anything else except signing my name. If my mind wandered, I began to write other words than my name. Signing the 550 proofs in those early days seemed an endless business. Perhaps under the influence of the autograph-hunting craze or perhaps only because of longer practice, the ceremony has largely lost its terrors. I find now that I can carry on a lively conversation while signing my name continuously and that, by sloping the pile and with someone to turn back the signed ones and the interleaved tissue paper, 550 prints can be signed in slightly under three-quarters of an hour.

15. *EASTLIGHT*

My family had now been spending its summer holidays in Norfolk for some years, and sailing had become increasingly important for me. There were regattas and 'weeks', and a new circle of friends. My Cambridge contemporary Stewart Morris was regarded as the most promising helmsman, and in 1932 he had won the Prince of Wales's Cup—the Championship of the International fourteen-foot dinghies. I resolved to try and be a champion too, and to gain all the experience I could. I was crew to Alan Coleman in *Telemark* during 1933, and he invited me to join him as crew on a trip to America, where he was taking a team of three boats. Also on the trip was Uffa Fox, equally impressive as a designer and a helmsman, unconventional, gay and delightful. His rugged philosophy has often been of great help to me over the years.

In return for my passage I looked after Alan's boat, and by the end of the trip I reckoned I knew enough about care and maintenance to justify my owning a boat myself. So I commissioned Uffa to build me my first International fourteen-foot dinghy.

In the spring of the next year I went down to his retired ferryboat workshop at East Cowes for the launching, and soon afterwards for her first races. With me was John Winter, whom I had first met sailing at Cambridge. Tall, dark and good-natured, he was obviously destined to be a champion. *Eastlight* was the name I had given my boat, for the dawn of

117

my sailing career and because I lived in the East Lighthouse. Her initial success so greatly encouraged me that I decided to keep a detailed record of every race. Just as I had recorded every bird and beast that was shot during our wildfowling expeditions, I now recorded the exact position of *Eastlight* in every round of every race that I sailed her in. More than twenty years later when I was bitten by a new sport, gliding, I found myself recording every detail in the same way. I am an incurable recorder.

Sailing my very own fourteen-foot dinghy was utterly satisfying. I enjoyed it most in a breeze of wind. Beating to windward I sat on the gunwale, shoulder to shoulder with my crew. With our toes tucked under a special strap we both leant as far out as we could to bring the boat upright, trying to counteract the heeling moment of the wind. If our combined weight was not enough, then by easing the mainsail a little the heel was reduced. In one hand I held the mainsheet leading from a block on the transom, and I played the wind as one might play a fish. In the other hand I held the tiller extension or 'joystick' hinged out at right angles to the tiller so that, leaning as far out as the strength of my tummy muscles would allow, I still had perfect control.

The boat was deliciously sensitive. A tiny movement of the hand holding the tiller was instantly reflected in a movement of the jib luff along the horizon. The heel of the boat could be controlled also with the helm. If I luffed up a little she came upright. To keep her as upright as possible was my aim, and at the same time to work her as close to the wind as she would go.

In 1934 a transatlantic team racing fixture was organised between Canada, the United States and Britain, and the races were to be sponsored by the Royal Canadian Yacht Club at Toronto. As reigning Champion, Stewart Morris was to be Captain of the British team. Four boats with their helmsmen and crews sailed in the *Empress of Britain* for Canada on 7th July, and *Eastlight,* was one of them. Stewart was to be crewed by Roger D'Quincey, John Winter by a namesake of mine though no relation, Tom Scott; David Beale was to be crewed by Oscar Browning and I by Nicholas Cooke, who was to be my crew for the next two years, though we had not sailed more than a dozen times together when we set off for Canada as part of the British team. Uffa Fox came with us as team manager.

When we took the boats out of their covers at Toronto we found that in each had been screwed a small, carefully painted black cat, wishing us luck from the ship's staff of the *Empress of Britain*. These black cats became mascots of great value to us, ultimately being moved to the dinghies we subsequently owned.

The Canadian dinghies which opposed us were quite different from our own. To begin with they were not open boats like ours, but had fairly extensive decks; they were also a good deal lighter in construction, but they were not made for planing along the surface of the water and in the event they were no match for ours. The American boats were less good than the Canadian. As a result we beat Canada in the team race by three races to one, and the United States was beaten in all its races by us and the Canadians.

Eastlight scored one private triumph by winning the Wilton Morse Trophy for a separate individual race, which at that time was regarded as the most important of the year for Canadian dinghies. A Canadian boat was second and Stewart Morris third.

But although Nick and I might style ourselves Canadian champions, the most memorable race of the whole trip was one of the team races. It was the second race of the series, four boats a side, and the course was twice round a triangle, six miles in all, out in the open lake.

Lake Ontario is thirty miles wide at Toronto, and being fresh water it can provide a shorter, steeper, nastier sea than you will find anywhere on salt walter. When we started out from the harbour after lunch it was almost dead calm.

We were towed out in a long string by the Committee boat, and as we came into the open lake whose surface was like glass, we could see, away to the west, a cloud. Our Canadian opponents began hurriedly reefing their sails, and we immediately followed suit, although reluctantly because it was likely to ruin our beautiful light weather canvas. Suddenly the squall hit us. It was a stiff breeze, and we were all at once scudding along at ten knots. From our point of view in *Eastlight* this was a most agreeable turn of events, because in 'planing' weather our chances against the Canadians were greater than ever.

At this time we were still waiting for the preparatory signal which was due at any moment, but before the gun was fired, and almost as suddenly as it started, the weight went out of the wind and we were left with a pleasant light breeze. We had begun to shake out our reefs when, without warning, the wind suddenly hit us again.

When the starting-gun went, thunder began to crash all round and the lightning flashes left our eyes full of purple streaks. The waves were short and very steep, and every other one came in solid and inky black over the bows. My crew did not dare to belay the jib sheet because of the cannon-ball puffs. He held it in one hand and was baling hard with the other, and at the same time trying to 'sit out' in between scoops so as to keep the boat upright.

The first leg of the triangle had been a beat to windward, but as the wind was following the storm round, it became a reach and the waves were now so big that it was hard to see the buoy; the rain which had started to fall in torrents made it harder still. Owing to our weight, however, *Eastlight* was now lying third, and we were well in the front of the rest of the fleet. We rounded the mark and found that the wind had so changed that the next leg, too, was a beat, but we were sailing across the seas instead of into them and so not shipping as much water. This enabled us to sit out a good deal more and that made us go faster so that we were rapidly catching the two leaders. When *Riptide* tacked we were ahead of her, and at the next buoy only twenty yards behind *Judy*. Now was our chance to break through, because off the wind our boats were likely to plane along on top of the water at great speed, which the Canadian boats could not do.

But as we rounded the buoy, all ready for the killing, to our dismay the wind died light as suddenly as it had arisen; there was not nearly enough to make us plane. At the same time a thick mist arose off the water. We hoisted full sail and a spinnaker, both of which my crew did so smartly that, even without the planing, we blew past *Judy* and out of the mist. We were leading by twenty yards as we passed the Committee boat at the beginning of the second round.

But the wind had become light and flukey, and although we kept *Judy* behind us, as team tactics demanded, some of the others who had taken a different course were ahead when next we met. We found ourselves fourth with *Riptide* second and two of our side first and third.

All four of us were close together when suddenly the mist came across again. We could see about twenty-five yards, and beyond that only the tops of the sails. The mist was in a layer over the water about six feet thick. Standing up on the mast-thwart Nick could see over it, and I told him to stay there in the hope that the top of the buoy, which could not now be much more than 100 yards away, might just be visible to him. We were scarcely moving, so light was the wind.

Nick stood up there for a good while, and when I told him to come down he was reluctant because it was 'lovely and warm up there'. Certainly the mist itself was unbelievably cold, and as we had only thin shirts on, which clung clammily to us, I could not blame him for climbing up again. And it was as well that he did, for suddenly he saw the buoy fifty yards away and well to leeward of our course. We called softly to one of our team-mates, without letting our opponents hear, and it was some seconds before they noticed, from the top of our sail over the mist, that we had altered course. By that time they were almost past the buoy although still much closer to it than we were, but they had to turn at right-angles and run, while we were still reaching. So much faster do sailing-boats go when reaching with a light wind abeam than when running, that although we had twice the distance to go, we got there first, with *Riptide* close on our tail. Then we stood up and laid a course over the fog on the Committee boat and the finishing line—a broad reach home. Soon after this we ran out of the mist and, still leading *Riptide*, we crossed the line first by twelve seconds in the most unusual race I have ever sailed.

Back in England *Eastlight*, like the rest of the team, was entered for the Prince of Wales's Cup which was to be held at Falmouth.

There were thirty-nine starters and as usual six replicas of the Cup would be given; it seemed that at least we had a good chance of gaining a replica. But we reckoned without three things; first, the snorting cold which descended on me the day before; next, the glassy windlessness of the day itself; and finally, my own lack of 'big race' experience.

It was a long and gruelling race, in which at one point we were becalmed in the lee of a large anchored merchantship, and dropped from fifth to twentieth. In the end *Eastlight* finished sixteenth. John Winter in *Lightning* won by seven minutes. Stewart Morris was sixth. For me it was a bitter disappointment.

In seventy races in 1934, *Eastlight* scored fifty-one guns, twenty-three first prizes, twelve seconds, fourteen thirds; she finished fourth ten times, and fifth six times. Except for four races in which she retired she was only once below fifth, and that was sixteenth in the Prince of Wales's Cup, the one time when I really wanted her to be in the first six. On reflection it seems that the fault must have been more mine than hers.

But when the race was over, there were consolations at Greatwood, the house my family had taken. With the relaxation of tension the house party could really begin. And Deirdre was due to arrive. I had first seen Deirdre the previous year, one of the crew of a Broads One Design, with a retired Colonel at the helm. The boat was invariably last, and it was not only sympathy with its helmsman that led me to suggest I should join his crew for a day and perhaps discover why! Deirdre loved sailing and dancing, and we were in love.

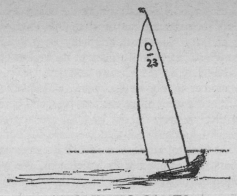

16. OLYMPIC GAMES

In the race for the Prince of Wales's Cup at Falmouth third place was taken by *Whisper* belonging to David Drew. She was probably no faster than *Eastlight*, but she was the prettiest of all the boats in the fleet; her timber had been very carefully selected, and the most glorious grain continued across her sides from plank to plank, so that she appeared to have been carved from the whole trunk of a tree. Her colour was that beautiful purplish-chestnut of some kinds of mahogany, whereas *Eastlight*'s colour was yellower, and seemed less mellow. *Whisper* was so lovely, and incidentally had done so well in the light airs, that I decided to sell *Eastlight* and buy her. The price, as I recall, was £130. *Eastlight*'s number had been 318, *Whisper* was 324; although she was six boats later, the vintage was the same, and her performance was almost identical.

In the race on the day before the Prince of Wales's Cup in the following year Nicky Cooke and I were out in front, doing very well in a fresh breeze, when one of the rigging wires of the mast broke and the mast itself bent alarmingly. I let the sheet go just in time and the mast was saved. The wire which had parted was the bottom diamond wire on one side, part of a stressed structure of single-strand wires on spreaders of aluminium tube which kept the mast straight. Congratulating ourselves that the wire had broken the day *before* the big race and not during the race itself, we got the boat back to Cowes, whipped out the mast and took it up to Uffa Fox's yard where the boat and its spars had originally been built. A new diamond wire was fitted in the place of the broken one, and all seemed to be ready for the race the next day.

It was another day of strong winds, which suited us perfectly. Nick and I went off on the first beat, and before long it was clear that we were in the lead. As we approached the weather mark I suddenly saw that the mast was bending. The wire had not broken, but it seemed to have stretched, or else the wire knot had slipped at its attachment. We went about quickly on to the other tack, and found that the mast stood up quite straight. It only needed one more short starboard tack to get ourselves round the weather mark, still first by nine seconds from Stewart Morris. On the broad reach Nick did his best to tighten up the slackened diamond wire, but it had stretched too much and the rigging screw would not take up enough to get it taut again. On the wind in the second round the mast again bent alarmingly. We gilled along gently not daring to fill the sails, and then, as we sailed only at half power, we found ourselves overtaken by Willie Hicks from North Norfolk, who had been going very well to windward. He crossed us once and we were faced with a major decision. There were three and a half more rounds to the race. If we sailed on at half power we should drop down and down. There was just a chance that if we drove her hard, the mast would bend until the slack diamond wire was tight, without actually breaking. We decided to haul in the sheet, drive her as fast as we could, and hope for the best. As we hauled in, the boat surged forward again, but the mast bent like a bow; it was clear that it would not last long. A moment later we came over the crest of a big wave and with a splintering crack it broke. The rest of the fleet sailed past, and that was that.

Stewart was the winner, John Winter was second and Willie Hicks third. It was small consolation that *Whisper,* with a new mast, won the race the following day in identical conditions

124

over the same course. It was *not* for the Prince of Wales's Cup.

The following year, 1936, I decided to sell *Whisper* to Michael Bratby, and order a new boat, to be called *Daybreak*, from Uffa Fox. I had entered for the Prince of Wales's Cup which this year was to be held at Hunter's Quay on the River Clyde where the winds were light, and *Daybreak* was specially designed for light weather. But when the day came it was blowing a gale. The race was postponed to the next day, and the next, and still it blew; but we raced and in spite of her narrow beam *Daybreak* came third to win my first replica for me.

Then early in the summer of 1936 I decided to enter for the trials for the single-handed sailing in the Olympic Games. The event was to be sailed in the German Olympic monotype, or Olympia-jolle. It was not taken very seriously by British yachtsmen in those days. By some extraordinary chance I won these trials. I still do not quite know how it happened, but I suppose you cannot have bad luck all the time. Stewart was second and became my spare man for the Olympic Regatta at Kiel.

Although we had placed the Olympic Games far below the Prince of Wales's Cup in importance in the season's racing, my failure to win the Big Race was probably an additional spur in the regatta at Kiel.

Apart from the initial trials my only experience of the boat I was to sail had been a week on the Buiten Y, a part of the Zuider Zee near Amsterdam, in Early June. Dutch, German and Norwegian helmsmen were racing, and Stewart Morris and I were both lent boats for the regatta. I managed to win the points cup for the week, with two firsts and two seconds, and Stewart came fourth with one first and three thirds. In Germany, Stewart was much more than my spare man; he was my team manager and my coach, and looked after me and my boat with meticulous care.

The series began on 5th August, and in the first race it blew hard, and I went away to win quite comfortably from the

German Willi Krogmann, and that night we dried the sail in the cruiser *Neptune* which was lying in the harbour at Kiel. But in the next few days the wind fell away and my performance was gradually outshone by the Dutch helmsman Dan Kagelland.

By 11th August—the day of the last race in the series—Dan was so far ahead on points that he had won the Gold Medal. He had no need even to start, though in fact he did so. Willi Krogmann and I had an exactly equal number of points, but again we were so far ahead of the Brazilian who was lying fourth that he could not possibly overtake us. So far as the gold, silver and bronze medals were concerned, the last race had only to decide whether Willi or I should have the silver one.

At the start we manoeuvred with eyes only for each other and Willi got the better of it and went away ahead of me. Then followed a spirited race in which we ignored the other twenty-five competitors entirely. By the second round when we lay respectively thirteenth and fourteenth, I was coming up on Willi fast. The wind had freshened, which favoured me because I was heavier, and it was quite clear that in a short while I should overtake him. He tacked to cover me and we sailed along side by side going to windward on a starboard tack. At the outset of this tack his boat lay about fifty yards to weather of mine, and he was therefore in effect still about fifty yards ahead. In the fresher breeze we both lay out to the very limit of our strength. I was gaining on him by sailing just a little bit closer to the wind. The two boats remained level, almost stem to stem, but their courses were gradually converging; I was shortening that fifty-yard lead. As I sat out on the starboard gunwale Willi was directly behind my back. I did not need to look round at him; I could hear his bow wave, and by its direction I could tell that we were both sailing at the same speed, but by sailing closer to the wind I was still closing the gap.

Of a sudden the wind changed its direction very slightly and both of us were able to point a little higher than we had been

126

pointing. This minor change in our positions relative to the wind's eye, meant that the wind shadow from Willi's sail now fell across my sail. There was nothing for it but to tack immediately. I scarcely looked behind and flung the boat round. To my consternation I felt a little tap as she went round and realised that I had nicked the stern of Willi's boat. This, of course, I had no right to do; it was a collision and the fault was most certainly mine. Although I knew I had been gaining on the German boat, I could not believe I had reduced the fifty-yard lead to a boat's length in so short a time. But there was a second reason. In the quick glance behind me I seemed to have room to tack astern of him, but I was thinking in terms of a fourteen-foot rather than a sixteen-foot boat. My familiar fourteen-footer would have cleared him, but the Olympic Monotype did not.

The damage was done; there was, as I saw it, no alternative but to retire immediately. I dropped the mainsheet, bore off down the wind and sailed out of the race. It was a very bitter moment and small solace that it was regarded as the correct thing to do.

One way and another 1936 had been a full year: apart from winning a replica of the Prince of Wales's Cup and an Olympic Bronze Medal (in spite of the disappointments, I was very proud of both) my book *Morning Flight* had been published in its first 'Ordinary Edition', I had had an exhibition of pictures at Ackermann's and had illustrated my stepfather's book *A Bird in the Bush* which was published in the autumn. It was very well received and reviewed, but I was not at all satisfied with my drawings. I knew that they were not in the same class of excellence as the text. A few of the designs were fine and bold, but with too many of the small birds I was groping for a likeness. For so exquisite a book the illustrations should have been perfect and I was sad that they were not. It was a poetical book and by chance Bill was President of the Poetry Society, as well as Minister of Health, when he wrote it.

Birds and sailing had met on the common ground of East Anglia for so many summers now that my family decided we should have a permanent country home in that part of the world. So we came to live in holiday times at Fritton Hithe, a Victorian house thatched with Norfolk reed, which overlooked Fritton Lake, near Great Yarmouth. In front of the house, which rambled about, mostly at ground-floor level, was a wide lawn leading down to the reed-fringed lake side and a small jetty from which we could bathe and fish and sail, though the lake was so sheltered by the surrounding woods that there was seldom a steady breeze.

Fritton was a part of my life for about twelve years, and the house was full of young people, contemporaries of my brother and me, especially during the regattas in the summer.

'Sea Week' at Lowestoft in 1937 was more than usually important because the Prince of Wales's Cup was to be held there again. For this, my fourth attempt, I had commissioned Uffa to build me a new dinghy, for best performance in a strong breeze. It was to be called *Thunder*. (As owner of *Lightning* John Winter claimed that his must always come before the thunder, but I was not to be deterred.) Charles Currey was my crew.

Thunder was the most beautifully finished sailing boat I had ever seen. Not only were the fourteen-footers thoroughbreds but they looked like thoroughbreds. They were built with the precision and artistry of a violin; Uffa had set new standards of workmanship in boat-building, and to own one of his fourteen-footers in the 1930s was to own the most perfect little boat in the world.

The day of the race had dawned absolutely calm and there was little hope of more than a zephyr all day. I still owned the narrow-beamed *Daybreak*, but had chartered her to David Pollock, and now it was *Daybreak*'s weather. There was nothing I could do about it but watch David take the lead almost from the start.

We were away close behind him and stayed hard upon his tail. I felt confident that we should find an opportunity to pounce on him at a later stage in the race, but to begin with he was offering us no chances. We were a good deal more concerned that John Winter in *Lightning* and Stewart Morris in *Alarm* were not very far behind us. Early in the third round *Thunder* went into the lead, but we couldn't cover both John and Stewart, and while we were looking after Stewart, John got through. In the last heat we were a minute behind John in a freshening breeze, and our additional weight began to tell.

We crossed the finishing line sixteen seconds ahead of John after a race of three and a half hours. Twenty-two seconds after *Lightning* came Stewart Morris. It was a moment of immense elation. During the last minutes of the race there had been no time to savour the golden instant when we took the lead. Now the gun had gone; the unbelievable had happened; at the fourth attempt we had won the Big Race. The years of failure had perhaps built it up to a disproportionate significance. But even now I look back on those few minutes after the finishing gun as among the most triumphant and utterly satisfying moments of my life.

17. WILD GOOSE CHASE

In the early spring of 1936 I had been invited by the magazine *The Field* to go as their special correspondent to the great plains of Hungary during the northward migration of the wild geese. My companion was my cousin Eric Bruce who was on leave from his job as District Commissioner in Sarawak.

We went to the Hortobagy (pronounced Hortobarge) by train from Budapest and at once began looking for geese in the sky, but it was not until shortly before our arrival at Nagyhortobagy that we really saw any. At first there were small groups in the distance, but all of a sudden we were among them on both sides of the railway, at first scattered and then gradually thickening till the climax by a little copse where there were not less than 10,000. Nearly all were White-fronted Geese.

Nagyhortobagy is a tiny village in the middle of a vast grass plain that has small pools all over it. The inn or Csarda was the principal building in the village, and from here we went out each morning in a cart to lie in wait for the geese in specially dug holes, or pits, in the clay soil. The principal guide was Farkhas Istvan, who knew exactly where the holes should be dug and could dig them with expert speed, rectangular and five feet deep, with a seat on one side.

It was the first time that I had seen geese in really big numbers. On the second morning there were geese murmuring upwind in a semicircle. It was a cloudless dawn and cold—thin ice on the splashes. Suddenly there was a noise like a train; and a grey mist appeared just above the horizon in front of me: it seemed that all the geese in creation were in the air. They flew round and settled, and a few minutes later as many again were up over on the right. Then a grey mist lifted above the horizon on the left, and another behind me. There were not less than 5,000 geese in each of these flocks, and not less than five flocks within a couple of miles of my pit. All this was at least eight miles from where we had seen great numbers on the previous morning. If there were not more than 100,000 geese on the Hortobagy at that time, there were certainly not less.

The shooting was too easy: a bag of 100 geese to one gun is altogether excessive and nothing to be proud of. But those morning flights were memorable for the wide variety of birds we saw—the Great Bustards, the Cranes, the Eagles—and particularly for the Lesser White-fronted and Red-breasted Geese. Those geese which were only slightly wounded I kept alive for bringing back to the collection at the lighthouse. Already in the first days I had assembled a group of Common Whitefronts which I planned to take back; I hoped that I might perhaps manage to add Lesser Whitefronts and Red-breasts before the end of our week.

One morning the cart arrived to pick me up at my pit with Eric already on board. He called me to look under the front seat where we always kept live birds, and there was our first Lesser Whitefront.

I had not expected to find Red-breasted Geese in Hungary, but there were two skins in the small museum at the Csarda which had been set up by the enterprising proprietor. I had been told that Red-breasts were *very* rare, but I decided particularly to keep my eyes open for them. And on the following morning I saw a flock of them. A big wave of geese came over and high above, and behind them I heard a new noise, short but very squeaky, not unlike a Whitefront, but fairly easily distinguishable. I grabbed the glasses. Were they? Weren't they? *They were*—thirteen of them. I did not see much of the colour, but the shape was more compact and perfect than in any other goose.

A little later I heard the noise again in the distance. It was another little bunch—sixteen Red-breasts and one Lesser Whitefront planing down with set wings from a great height.

At the end of the week the Lesser Whitefront came safely back with me to the lighthouse in company with a number of Common Whitefronts and a Bean Goose. But among 100,000 wild geese on the Hortobagy there seemed to have been no more than thirty or forty Red-breasts; the chances of getting any of them alive seemed negligible.

In the following autumn I went again to the plains of Hungary. This time there were only four Red-breasts among the migrating hordes. Farther east, I thought, there would surely be more, and I pushed on through Roumania and to the Black Sea and the Danube Delta.

I arrived at the same time as a blizzard, and on the second day at a place called Gropeni I drove in a sleigh past a flock of 500 or 600 geese on some meadows by the side of the Danube. They were mostly the familiar White-fronted Geese and they were feeding sitting down so as to keep out of the wind and to keep their toes warm. I looked at them with the glass and saw there were fourteen little Red-breasts with them.

From Roumania I went back again to the Csarda at Nagy-horobagy to collect a group of sixteen live geese which had been saved for me from the bags of the autumn wildfowlers, and put into a temporary pen; among them were a Bean Goose and four Lesser Whitefronts. The Csarda was officially closed to visitors, but Nemeth Ur, the proprietor, came out from Debrecen to see that I was comfortable.

I had to wait there for a few days to get permits for the live geese. When the permits arrived I set off for England with the geese in three large crates. At Budapest they were loaded into an aeroplane and we flew to Vienna. At Vienna there were reports of bad weather and fog ahead. I and the geese were the only passengers and the pilot told me that if the fog were bad we would not stop at Prague but go straight on to Leipzig.

But the fog was bad at Leipzig too, and we had not enough petrol to go on. Three times we tried unsuccessfully to get down (once with an unnerving glimpse of a tall building), and then flew a few miles to a military airport at Erfurt where we found a thin patch in the mist and landed safely. We refuelled there with 400 gallons poured from tins, and then flew to Cologne.

At Cologne the service was suspended. England was shrouded in fog, and the geese and I could go no farther by air, there was a chance, they said, that I might catch the boat train to the Hook and be in London the next morning; and I was anxious to do this because the crates were small and the geese unfed; I had been counting on a short journey.

I just managed to catch the train, but with no money at all. However, a fellow traveller lent me some. A confidence trickster would hardly travel with crate-loads of wild geese. From then onwards the journey went very smoothly and by the next evening we had all arrived safely at the lighthouse—eleven Whitefronts, four Lesser Whitefronts, one Bean Goose and I.

The following year I decided to extend my search for Red-breasted Geese to the Caspian Sea—their true wintering ground.

I set off alone on my wild-goose chase in November 1937. My destination was the Persian shore of the Caspian.

I knew that the Red-breasted Geese wintered in large quantities on the Mughan steppe in Russia, and I hoped that when, in the middle of winter, this steppe had become snow-covered, the geese would migrate southward to a lagoon near Pahlevi, in the bottom left-hand corner of the Caspian.

This was a great gathering place for wildfowl, including literally millions of ducks which fed at night in the rice-fields. I had never dreamed that my favourite group of birds could exist together in such concentrations. Most of the ducks were Mallards, Teal and Pintails, but there were, in varying quantities, most of the ducks of Europe and many of the Asiatic ones, too.

Here I first saw the White-headed Duck—a Stifftail and the

Eurasian counterpart of North America's Ruddy Duck; and unexpectedly I saw large flocks of Smews.

Of geese there were also large numbers, but only Eastern Greylags and Whitefronts—no Red-breasted.

On several days I watched flocks of Pelicans, perhaps nine feet across the wings, rising into the sky and circling upwards in a great spiral. They gained height without moving their wings at all—merely by soaring in an upward current. I did not then understand the mechanism of a thermal which later became so important when I took up gliding. As a background to all these magnificent Caspian birds was the frieze of snow mountains—the noble peaks of the Elburz range.

I learned that the wildfowlers had an extraordinary way of catching wild ducks at night. To discover how to do this myself I went to stay for ten days in the charming village of Siah Derveshan.

At night great numbers of ducks come to feed in specially preserved Broads surrounded by trees and well grown with low vegetation through which waterways have been cut. The wildfowlers go afloat in two boats. In the bows of the first, burning on a tiny earth-covered foredeck, is a flare consisting of bulrush fluff soaked in paraffin. Immediately behind this is a hood of rush matting and behind this again stands the duck-catcher with a great elongated hand-net. He and the rest of the boat are in darkness, shaded from the light of the flare by the intervening hood. The boat is propelled with a punt pole from the stern. The second boat is propelled also with a punt pole, but from the bows. In the stern sits a man incessantly beating a gong. It seems that the object of the gong-ringing is to drown all other noises of the approaching boat and to bewilder the ducks so that they do not fly until it is too late. Often it is difficult to persuade them to fly at all. They swim along with their heads low on the water hoping not to be seen. The wildfowler makes a high-pitched squeak which seems to be heard above the ringing of the gong. Immediately the bird jumps into the air, the wildfowler makes a swipe with the net and the duck is caught. It is even sometimes possible to pick the ducks

135

up by hand as they swim against the boat. Many species of ducks are caught with flare and gong and hand-net in these marshes, or murd-abs, as they are called, and sent to market. One year, rather earlier in the season, over 600 had been caught in a night on this one murd-ab.

After a little practice I became fairly proficient with the net, and one evening I caught a dozen myself under the watchful eye and with the helpful tuition of my host.

At Babol I collected an interpreter—a Persian lad named Ismail Khodjeste who spoke a few words of German. We hired a large sailing-boat to explore the lagoon at Bandar-i-Gaz, and were accompanied by a guide who had looked carefully at my reasonably realistic water-colour of a Red-breasted Goose. Yes, he said, he knew them well. They were locally called 'Ghazal Goz' and he could show us thousands. Two days later when we had sailed far up the lagoon he pointed proudly to his flock of Ghazal Goz. They were flamingoes. My drawing, though perhaps not perfect as a likeness, deserved better than that!

From Bandar-i-Gaz we drove across the steppe to Gumbad-i-Kabus, a magnificent tenth-century tower built by one of Genghis Khan's lieutenants and still in astonishingly good repair. It is a round brick tower of great height, with a conical roof and beautiful angular flutings in its walls.

The south-east corner of the Caspian makes a sharp corner and we headed northward in our tumbledown car across a corner of the great plain which stretches away and away north and east to Bokhara, Samarkand and Tashkent. The unending expanse of the steppe was vastly impressive. At last we reached the Russian frontier, only to find the great marshes of the River Atrek virtually devoid of geese of any kind. We saw Red-crested Pochards, but a small party of Greylags were all the geese that we saw.

During the night we heard Lesser Whitefronts passing southward on migration, and next day on a lake called Atagel we saw a small bunch of them resting. But there was not a sign of Red-breasts.

We followed the Lesser Whitefronts back towards the mountains, and our quest led us back to the lagoon where we had seen the flamingoes. It transpired that on the voyage in the sailing-boat we had gone to within two or three miles of a magnificent marsh where huge flocks of these little geese were wintering, but we had turned back just before discovering it. Now we decided to explore it fully—it was our last chance of finding the elusive Red-breasts.

Although the people of the village knew the Red-breast as a straggler in small numbers, I satisfied myself that there were none there now among an estimated 30,000 Lesser White-fronts which might have been twice as many.

So finally and reluctantly I abandoned the search and headed for home.

The birds I had come so far to see had completely eluded me. I had not seen a single one; and yet I had seen a thousand other new and exciting sights. The thread on which I had hung my journey mattered scarcely at all by comparison with the journey. I had become a traveller.

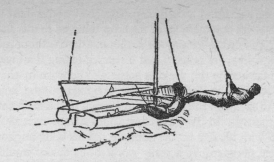

18. THE TRAPEZE

As the summer of 1938 approached I began to think of a new sailing plan. John Winter and I had long had a theory which we had now decided to put to the test.

We believed that the crew rather than the helmsmen should be responsible for the tactics of a dinghy race. The helmsmen's attention should be exclusively occupied with watching the luff of the jib and sailing the boat, especially to windward. The crew was in a very much better position to look all round at the other competitors, assess the tactical situation and decide when to tack.

There was the additional advantage in the new idea that, in sitting out, the helmsman uses rather different muscles from the crew; if we sailed one round each of a long and gruelling race, by changing over we should be much fresher, and therefore much less likely to make mistakes or to be clumsy in our exhaustion. Some years before we had planned to become joint owners of a boat in which we could put our theory to the test, and we had commissioned Uffa Fox to build us a new boat. In order to make it quite plain what the new boat was and how the system would work she was called *Thunder and Lightning*. John planned to retain *Lightning* and I retained *Thunder*. If the idea did not work we had our escape routes ready.

We had also had another idea—the device which is now universally known as the trapeze. Some years before I had crewed Beecher Moore in his Thames Rater at Surbiton to which he had fitted a 'Bell Rope' attached to the mast at the 'hounds', and one member of the crew hung on to this and was thereby enabled to lean much farther out than without it. Uffa, Charles Curry, John and I had discussed taking the invention a stage farther by the use of a harness to be worn by the crew which could be hooked on to a wire hanging from the 'hounds', that is to say from the point of attachment of the main shrouds to the mast. In this way the crew would lean or even sit in the harness with his feet on the gunwale and his body horizontally stretched outboard. If it really worked this device would give enormously greater and more sustained righting moment, and therefore driving power, to the boat than had ever been possible with toe-straps in the middle of the boat and the crew leaning out just as far and as long as his belly muscles would sustain him. The Canadian dinghies had also used a method of belaying the jib sheet to a cleat on a sort of breast-plate strapped to the crew. Our harness would combine the two.

Thunder and Lightning was completed only very shortly before the Prince of Wales's Cup Week, which that year was back at Falmouth again. As a result there was no chance to try out the trapeze in realistic conditions. First, it had to be kept secret, or moderately so, and secondly, during the early races of the week the winds were quite light.

On the evening before the big race John and I sailed out from Falmouth Harbour, round the corner into Carrick Roads and there, safely out of sight of all our competitors we tried out our new device in a very light wind. If I sat out to leeward and pulled the sheet in tight, it was just possible for John to go out to windward on the wire. The device seemed practical. How would it affect our performance? Of this we still had no clue.

There was in our minds no doubt that the trapeze was legal. However, so that there should be no question of the legality if we used it, we leaked the information in the bar on the night before the race, when it was too late for anyone else to apply the system to their own masts. There were jeers. We even showed them the harness and breastplate, which had been made for us. It brought loud ironical laughter, and the cry, 'No big race has ever yet been won by a gadget.' There was risk too in our device for we planned to use a light wooden centreboard instead of the normal lead ballasted one. Our trapeze was a strong wind gadget and if it did not work we should be at a disadvantage without the lead.

The day of the race dawned utterly calm, but by the time we reached the Committee boat a light breeze was blowing and just before the start it had become a planing breeze.

There was a big fleet—more than fifty boats. We were carrying *Lightning*'s old mainsail—a sail which had won two Prince of Wales's Cups already, and been second in two more. It was getting old now, and perhaps more suitable for heavy weather; through stretching it was flatter than it had been, but it seemed just right for a good whole-sail planing breeze.

I was to sail the first half of the race and I did not make a very good start. Immediately to windward of us and slightly ahead was Robert Hichens in his latest home-made dinghy *Venture II*. We were both on the starboard tack and in a matter of moments John had belayed the jib on a cleat and was out on the trapeze. Standing horizontally out from the boat with his feet on the gunwale, he was a startling sight even to me. Robert Hichens was now almost directly ahead; his crew looked at John with amazement, drew Robert's attention to him and for a critical ten seconds Robert sailed his boat 'off the wind', which allowed us to luff across his wake and get our wind clear. At one stroke we had escaped the consequences of my bad start, and we rounded the weather mark first by thirty seconds. Stewart lay second for a while, until he was overtaken by Colin Ratsey, sailing brilliantly in a very broad-beamed ugly-looking dinghy called *Hawk*.

We finally finished nearly four minutes ahead of him, with Stewart third. Although it was satisfactory to win and as a race it was exciting in the extreme, it could not quite compare with the thrill of my first success in *Thunder*, the year before. The holder of a Championship has more to lose than to gain. If he wins, so he should; if he does not, he's slipping.

But as soon as the race was over the trouble began. Was the trapeze legal or was it not? When it was pointed out that the rest of the fleet had had an opportunity to say whether or not they thought it illegal before the race and had not done so, nobody was ready to enter a protest against it after we had won. All that was left was to say that in future it must be banned and I was asked by the Yacht Racing Association's Dinghy Committee (of which as a Cup-Winner I had now become a member) to draft the wording of a rule which would ban our exciting new invention.

I am still sorry about the decision. It may be that it would have radically changed the fourteen-footers; here was a system of keeping a small dinghy upright in strong winds which was eminently enjoyable, required no very great skill, but looked spectacular, appeared to have no danger, and reduced the compression strain on the mast. Most important of all it made the body weight of the crew a little less critical, because it enabled a light crew, for example, a girl, on a trapeze to compete on even terms with a heavy man in wind strengths up to fifteen knots, whereas previously the light ones had been at a disadvantage in any wind above ten knots. All these advantages were there, but because of a prejudice it was outlawed and did not return until the design of the Flying Dutchman seventeen years later. Now it is carried in many other classes as well, and greatly enhances the enjoyment of sailing on a hard day. It is tremendously exhilarating to stand out, comfortably supported by the trapeze, almost horizontal and skimming low over the waves. It is sad to think of the man hours (woman and child hours, too) of enjoyment lost during those seventeen years because of the noses that were put out of joint that day at Falmouth.

19. THE HECTIC TRIP

All this time my collection of tame wildfowl round the lighthouse had been growing. But even more satisfying than the exotic species I had obtained were the wild birds that came of their own free will. Such a one was a Pinkfoot called Anabel. Three and a half months old, she had obviously lost her family on the way from Iceland or Greenland when she came sweeping out of the sky to land beside the lighthouse. She met a cool reception from the others of her kind gathered there, but she soon came to accept me, and she spent the winter in my enclosure.

Next summer she slipped away to catch up the great flocks already migrated. Five months later, in October, I was standing outside my front door when I heard her shout. She came straight down without circling round, and came up to me when I called her. Again she stayed all winter and departed once more in May. All that October I waited for her. But she never came back. Perhaps she went elsewhere. More likely she shared the fate of the majority of her kind and was shot by a wildfowler.

My expedition to the Caspian led to an invitation to stay with the eighty-year-old Duke of Bedford and his wife, the 'flying duchess', a distinguished ornithologist who also piloted her own light aeroplane. They had read of my unsuccessful attempts to catch Red-breasted Geese, and I knew that they had managed to breed these birds at Woburn. The Duke had

143

not only one of the finest collections of waterfowl in the country but also a herd of about 200 Père David's Deer, already extinct in its wild state. The last herd had been destroyed in 1900, but a few individuals had been obtained by various zoos throughout the world. The Duke had managed to get some of these, and had built up a herd from them. I was terribly impressed by this vision of one man on the opposite side of the world who had saved a Chinese species from extinction; and it was not some obscure animal barely distinguishable from its relations, but a magnificent beast with antlers quite different in shape from those of any other stag in the world. This, I remember thinking at the time, was in itself an achievement to justify the work of a lifetime. Such was (and still is) my reverence for the evolution of species, and my horror of the extinction of any single one of them.

Even in the 1930s, life at Woburn Abbey was dauntingly formal, but I left with the promise of a pair of Red-breasts for my collection, which turned out both to be females. Later, however I was able to buy fifty wild caught birds from a dealer, and with these and my original two I had an impressive flock on the greensward by the lighthouse.

In September 1938 I was in New York. I had crossed the Atlantic because I had been appointed Captain of an International fourteen-foot dinghy team taking three boats to race at Toronto. Michael Bratby came as team manager and the helmsmen of the other two boats were Charles Curry and Colin Chichester Smith. But the Canadians had learned much about dinghy design from our previous encounter and this time they beat us. I planned to have an exhibition of pictures in New York in November and also to see some American wildfowl. I wanted to paint some pictures of them to add to the ones sent over from England. My book *Wild Chorus*—the successor to *Morning Flight*—was also due in the autumn and there was still some of the text to be finished and sent back to the publisher. Finally I had brought some slides made from photographs I had taken in Persia with which I proposed to lecture. Altogether it was going to be rather a hectic trip.

In mid-October I made a two-day excursion to Canada to see the Greater Snow Geese. We motored in the early morning from Quebec out to the village of St Joachin and from the car as we drove along the edge of the marsh I suddenly saw my first Greater Snow; and a moment later several more circling in ones and twos before settling with some on the ground, but still out of sight.

After driving through two farmyards we arrived at the hunting club—a nice little green shack on the very edge of the salting. From here we could see a great many white geese out on the marsh, but the main lot could be heard as the distant hum of a big city, a mile up the shore under the sun. Our host was a French-Canadian banker, Henri Des Rivieres, and with him was a nice old ornithologist from Vancouver, Ted White, who spends a week there every year.

The club was a shooting club, but its membership was limited, and each hunter was allowed five geese per day and only fifty geese per season. In effect, this meant that about 400 geese were shot out of about 16,000 which assembled there.

I was keen to get some wing-tipped birds for sending home to my lighthouse, and collected two young birds which were only slightly wounded and which were subsequently shipped back to England in the *Empress of Britain,* and I took some remarkable photographs with my little Leica which were afterwards reproduced in *Life* magazine.

It was on the following day that the Snow Geese provided their greatest thrill. What I saw that afternoon had a special influence on the distant future, for it showed me the potentialities of a window looking out on wildfowl. We had been out in the morning in pursuit of the American Woodcock in the Dogwood thickets, and as we returned we could see that the geese were feeding near the club, 120 yards away, about 900 of them. We went round and in by the back door so as not to disturb them. Gradually they got nearer and nearer, and more and more geese came in to join them.

Farther down the marsh was another big lot, and these came

pouring up to settle with those in front. There were fourteen Blue Geese in our immediate vicinity, but the rest were apparently all Greater Snows. We kept fairly still, and I managed to get a window open and took innumerable photos. The geese came closer and closer and to finish with we had them within nine yards of the open window. During all this time geese were circling about within twenty or thirty yards. By now there were between 4,000 and 5,000 within a quarter of a mile on three sides of us, and plumb in front was a thick mass of 600 or 700 birds, all between ten and fifty yards away. They were making such a babel that we could hardly hear ourselves speak.

They had been like this for about an hour and a half, with two or three young blues in the forefront when the climax came. A good many geese were sitting down with their wings dropped in the warm afternoon sunshine. Suddenly all the heads were up. A dog from the farmyard had appeared. In a moment or two they were up.

So ended an hour and a half of thrills piled upon thrills and a never-to-be-forgotten day. Within a hundred or two which perhaps had not yet arrived from the north, we had seen all the Greater Snow Geese in the world.

On 1st November, 1938, my exhibition opened according to plan at Ackermann's Gallery on New York's 57th Street. That evening I cabled my mother:

'GREAT CROWD ONE SOLD BADLY MISSED YOUR
ORGANISATION.'

After a fortnight, during which sales at the exhibition were sluggish, I escaped rather guiltily to travel across the continent.

I went out to Connecticut to stay with Dillon Ripley, then a young man of about twenty-five who had been round the world as an ornithologist, now Secretary of the Smithsonian Institution. He invited me down to his family house at Litchfield to try to catch some ducks on a neighbouring lake with a flare and a gong, as I had learned to do in Persia.

On the lake I saw my first Hooded Mergansers and my first Buffleheads. There were Scaup, Canvasbacks, Goldeneyes, Black Ducks, Mallard, Greenwinged Teal and Coots. But there were not more than 150 ducks on the three-mile-long lake which was quite open, with no reeds.

We had brought a cymbal and as a flare we had a round lamp, which Hugh Birkhead, a friend of Dillon's, had picked up from some roadworks intending to put it back next day. We had a beautiful net which had been made to my design, and we made a hood out of a petrol can. In a large canoe we set off up a river towards a pool where many ducks were said to feed. Dillon was paddling, Hugh in the middle beating the cymbal which made a noise almost exactly like the Persian gong and I balancing perilously in the bows with the net.

We had not gone far up the river when we saw two drake Mallards. The flare was not really quite bright enough, but the Mallards swam skulking into the reeds, where they immediately went ashore. I clapped the net across the reeds and one of them splashed out towards us, hit the boat and, once behind us in the dark, got up and flew off. The other came out too, and I switched the big torch on to him. This was an immediate signal for him to rise, whereupon I missed him. That night we did not catch any ducks.

We set off again the next night and this time the water was rough and the wind kept catching the net and rolling the canoe. We were spinning along quite fast with the wind on our port quarter when suddenly we saw eight or ten Buffleheads— the principal objects of our search. Some took wing but some dived. They were only six or seven yards away. One female came within six feet of the boat, but dived again at once before I could plunge with the net. We saw it, or another, about fifteen yards away, and then nothing more. Again a blank night, but it had been, we felt, a good try.

Van Campen Heilner, sportsman and writer on fishing and wildfowling, took me to see the Atlantic Brant and the Black Ducks on Barnegat Bay. Next I was to join him at Cape Hatteras which juts out from the coast of North Carolina. But

147

before that I made my own plans for seeing the great concentrations of wildfowl in California, where the birds exceeded all expectations.

Los Banos State Refuge was a large one—about 3,000 acres, consisting of a vast reed bed with pools and open patches in it. The reed is green and luscious, and the white geese eat it. Flying over it I saw my first Lesser Snows.

There were said to be no geese at all at Los Banos, but in fact there were something over 4,000. Quite a lot of them were Whitefronts, although the majority were Lesser Snows.

The largest lake of open water had a nice bunch of geese on it—about 2,500—which included a lot of Cackling Geese and some Lesser Canadas. There was also one very small bunch of Big Canadas which are rare in these parts and twenty-five Whistling Swans.

We left Los Banos Refuge and motored along twenty miles of perfectly straight track northward through the marsh, passing a line of duck clubs, their little shacks spaced out every mile or so. Here there were still plenty of ducks but few geese. I saw my first Ruddy Ducks—all in winter plumage.

About ten in the evening we arrived at Grey Lodge Refuge, Gridley, which was another State Refuge of about 2,500 acres, and most of it thick bulrushes with pools and a few open places. On the way in we had heard the Snow Geese calling and chattering in the bulrushes, and all night I could hear them and the ducks calling. I was told that the geese fed out in the fields at night and returned at dawn. I was woken at six and it was just getting light. Almost immediately afterwards the geese began to come in, together with the ducks—mostly Pintails—from the rick fields—a most impressive flight. For the next half-hour the geese—nearly all Snow Geese and Whitefronts—passed over at the rate of about 1,000 a minute. They were coming high downwind and completely filling the sky. Ducks and geese circled and weaved in clouds over the bulrushes and eventually settled among them. The combined roar of the oncoming masses in the west and the hordes which had already settled, was deafening. I think I certainly saw 50,000 geese go down at one end of the Refuge.

The Pintails went on coming out of the sky, hurtling down from all directions, long after the geese were only straggling in.

To join me in the Sacramento Valley that evening came Jim Moffitt, who almost certainly knew more about wild geese in North America than any other person. He was a keen hunter, too, and had made a collection of skins, especially of the Canada Goose and its various sub-species. Jim was a delightful companion for several wonderful days among the geese round Willows and Colusa. We talked eagerly about geese from morning to night, and I wanted nothing better.

On the second morning we watched the great skeins go out at flight in their thousands, and then about eleven in the morning we saw them returning, and tumbling down to the water where they had roosted. This I remembered was the habit of geese in many dry countries where no water is available to them on their feeding grounds.

By now here in California I was definitely more interested in photography than in shooting, and I arranged to go again to the Grey Lodge Refuge where the photographic opportunities were so remarkable.

Then to Cape Hatteras where my main occupation was to be the pursuit of Black Ducks and Canada Geese. The Canadas were especially interesting to me because they belong almost certainly to the Labrador form, *Branta canadensis canadensis*, in which the base of the neck below the black 'stocking' is almost white, front and back. On the second morning we shot some of these geese, and I knew that Jim Moffitt wanted the skin of an old gander, so I selected one fine bird which weighed 11 lb. 5 oz. and skinned it out. I had not skinned a bird since Oundle days and never a goose in my life, but I managed to complete the job in about two hours and made only one small hole by the tail.

From Hatteras I went to see the Blue Geese on the Gulf of Mexico, and then went on to spend a couple of days with Ned

McIllhenny of Avery Island, New Iberia. From his small flock of tame Snow Geese and from his duck banding traps, Ned gave me a number of birds for the collection at the lighthouse and I left with ten geese, thirty-two ducks and four baby alligators. To meet me in New York came thirty geese which had been assembled in California, and with a baggage list which would have done credit to Noah, I boarded the German liner *Bremen* for Europe at the end of my hectic trip.

20. OUTBREAK OF WAR

I arrived back in England just before Christmas 1938. War with Germany was threatening, but the slogan on everybody's lips was 'Peace in our time'. Even so I felt it would be wise to get my name on a Reserve list, and I was accepted into the Royal Naval Volunteer Supplementary Reserve.

My book *Wild Chorus* had appeared and had been well received by the critics. It was a picture book, with many colour plates. My lighthouse home was becoming known, and people were coming from far and wide to see the birds. Prince Bernhard of the Netherlands was one visitor; another was Archie Jamieson, Chairman of Vickers, who had bought some of my pictures to hang in the wardrooms of his new aircraft carriers. I enjoyed living on my own in the lighthouse, and I used to have guests to stay for week-ends. I hoped that I might one day soon marry Deirdre and that we would both live there.

I had an aerial visit, too, from a great friend, Brian D'Arcy Irvine, who had come to paint at the lighthouse in school holidays. He was now a Cambridge University Air Squadron Pilot and flew over to Sutton Bridge. The bombing range on the Wash mudflats was being used now on Saturdays and Sundays as well as weekdays. 'Peace in our time' was beginning to look even less likely. To me the prospect of war meant change more than anything, and this was unsettling though at the same time exciting. I had always been adventurous and

151

there was no particular merit in the comfortable security of my present existence, but I bitterly resented the prospect of its being interrupted.

There was sailing on summer week-ends, and during the summer of 1939 I went to Venice with my mother. There was so much beauty around me to be appreciated, but all the time there was the growing inevitability of war. Finally I had to make plans for the lighthouse and the birds when war should come: my beautiful (and valuable) Red-breasted Geese would go to Walcot Hall in Shropshire; others to Will Tinsley, and the rest to Horsey Island on the Essex Coast, which David Haig Thomas had bought.

I had no idea how long there would be to do all this, but until war actually broke out there was nothing to be done but carry on with one's present existence. So I went on sailing *Thunder and Lightning* in the local regattas.

The last races of Lowestoft 'Sea Week' in 1939 had an air of unreality. It no longer seemed important to win a fourteen-foot dinghy race. In the season before, and in the season before that, the winning of a yacht race had seemed all-important during the time that one was doing it. But now, as the war clouds gathered, all the significance and excitement of it seemed to drain away as we sailed round in a kind of trance.

I remember leading the fleet home in one race and looking back into the afternoon sun and the silver brightness of the sea. A dozen dinghies were following us with spinnakers set on the run up the coast from Pakefield past the Claremont Pier. The nearest was more than fifty yards astern. As we approached the finishing line it should have been a moment of triumph, but instead I felt a sudden fierce sadness. Not only was this the end of a sailing season but it was also the end of an era, for nothing could now stop the war. Perhaps we should never sail dinghies again.

I was staying at Stafford with my old friend John Winter on the morning in September when Neville Chamberlain, the Prime Minister, came to the wireless to give his famous and sombre message that meant we were once again at war with Germany.

The Royal Naval Volunteer Supplementary Reserve was a special band composed largely of yachtsmen who believed themselves to have an assured place in the wartime navy from the very beginning of hostilities. I was soon to discover that my impatience to start a new life in the Navy was most unpopular with the authorities. When I wrote to the Admiralty I had no reply for three weeks, and when an answer did come it was to inform me that I should on no account write to them again about being called up and that I was not wanted now, and quite possibly never would be wanted at all. About a week later I was called up. I went first as a Temporary-Acting-Sub-Lieutenant to H.M.S. *King Alfred*, the famous 'stone frigate' at Hove. Here in a large underground garage hundreds of men, many of whom had spent some part of their holidays messing about in boats, were made into fully fledged naval officers after a ten-day course.

My stay at the *King Alfred* lasted longer than the usual ten days, for in some way I had persuaded someone that of all the types of vessels at sea, the one which would clearly be best suited to my particular talents would be a destroyer. It would be another three weeks before a series of destroyer courses became available to the Temporary-Acting-Sub-Lieutenants of *King Alfred*, so in the meantime I became liaison officer between the regular staff of the training establishment and the officers who were training.

At last the Destroyer Courses were ready for us and with about twenty colleagues I was sent to do an anti-submarine course at H.M.S. *Osprey*—another 'stone frigate' at Portland. Then I went, with all the other officers on another course to H.M.S. *Defiance*, which was a group of old wooden ships which lay at moorings in the River Hamoaze at Plymouth. This was the Torpedo Control School.

We were to be sent to destroyers as Asdic Control and Torpedo Control Officers, with watch-keeping duties. I rather enjoyed learning about torpedoes, perhaps especially because my father had been a torpedo-man. We were living on board *Defiance*. One morning our appointments came through and each of us learned with great excitement to which destroyer we would be sent. Mine was *Acasta*, an 'A'-class destroyer which was considered quite modern by comparison with the old 'V' and 'W' destroyers, to which many of the course were to be sent. The luckiest of our band seemed to be those who were being appointed to 'H'-class destroyers, then among the more modern in the Navy. Soon after they had joined their ships the flotilla of the 'H'-class destroyers was involved in the Battle of Narvik, and we envied them the more.

I discovered that *Acasta* was working out of Plymouth and that she happened to be in harbour at the moment; furthermore I knew that her First Lieutenant was an old sailing friend, Charles Robinson, from Norfolk. That very afternoon I decided to go down to the Dockyard at Devonport and pay a social call, in order to make my number with the officers of my new ship. I had tea in the wardroom and was taken to see the Captain, Commander Glasfurd. I was shown the cabin I would occupy and made friends with the other officers with whom I should serve. On the following morning I woke up with a slight sore throat and by the same evening I had a high temperature. The Torpedo Control Course lasted a week and I was laid low after only four days of it. The officer in charge of the course came to see me and said, 'You know, I don't think you will have done enough of this course to be able to take up your appointment at the end of the week: I am afraid we shall have to put somebody else in *Acasta* and keep you for another week.' This was a bitter disappointment, but there was nothing I could do about it. I had to spend another week learning about Torpedo Control. When the time came I was appointed to H.M.S. *Broke*. Not many weeks later, at the conclusion of the disastrous Norwegian campaign, the aircraft carrier *Glorious* was returning from Norway, escorted by the destroyers *Ardent* and *Acasta*, when she was waylaid by two German heavy cruisers. In an action of incredible gallantry *Ardent* and *Acasta* tried to protect the carrier with smoke-screens and to attack with torpedoes. They were both blown out of the water at close range by the German heavy ships which went on to sink *Glorious*. From the whole force there were only a handful of survivors. Commander Glasfurd and all his officers went down with their ship.

21. H.M.S. *BROKE*

H.M.S. *Broke* was already an old ship at the outbreak of the
Second World War. She was built in 1926 as a Flotilla Leader
of the 'V' and 'W' class, but she was to be my home, my pride
and joy for two long years. When I joined her she was commanded by Bryan Scurfield, a fine, open-hearted man of immense courage and noble character.

I had created so firm and so false a picture in my mind of
what the destroyer would be like that it could not possibly
have lived up to my hopes, so it was not surprising that I was
disappointed when I was installed in her. There was, for
example, seasickness for which I had not bargained, and a
curious loneliness. My mother had always been seasick, and as
a small child I had been sick in sympathy. It did not affect me
in small boats, but in larger ships I had continued to feel
poorly in even slight motion. How much of all this was
imagined by me I shall never know, but in *Broke* when the
weather was rough the Captain ordered a bucket to be brought
up on to the bridge and lashed behind the Director Tower.
And somehow because the bucket was there I found it difficult
not to use it. Eventually there came a rough trip when I felt so
ill and was so sick that I could no longer carry out my duties. I
was forced to stay in my bunk, and the R.N.V.R. Medical
Officer—my good friend Gerald Gibbens—had me transferred
to the sick bay, a small cabin below the bridge. Here I remained for the whole ten-day trip, drinking orange juice and

157

vomiting. I remember the Captain coming to see me and saying as he left, 'Well, Scott, I hope we shan't have to put you ashore for good with chronic seasickness.' But there was nothing I could do about it by then. I was very weak, and next day I was yellow with jaundice. I had a month's sick leave to get over the depressing disease.

I spent this sick leave at Fritton with the family. My mother had invited the two children of an old friend of hers, Kit Howard. The children were to be Easter holiday company for my brother Wayland. Jane Howard was sixteen and Robin fourteen. I was jaundiced and depressed, and I should not have believed anyone who had told me that in two years time Jane would be my wife.

During this sick leave the *Broke* was sent with all despatch to Scapa Flow in order to take part in the Norwegian campaign. I joined her there, making the last part of the journey by air in an Anson, and had no sooner gone on board than she was as suddenly ordered to return to Plymouth.

The passage back took place in flat calm weather in fog, and off East Anglia we ran aground due to the wrong position of a Channel buoy. The ship had to be docked for examination. So far there had been nothing to test my resistance to seasickness now that I no longer had jaundice. When next we sailed it was late at night and in the morning we were at anchor among the Scilly Isles. When I went up to the quarter-deck there was a barely detectable swell underlying the glass-calm sea; but it was the first swell since my sick leave. Surely *this* was not going to make me sick. Or was it? There were a number of ratings working on the quarter-deck. I was sure they could see how green I looked, and the more I thought about it the greener I felt. At last I was overcome and had to rush to the rail. Without doubt this time my sickness must be purely psychological and as such it could surely be mastered.

I remained at sea for most of the next five years and I do not think I was actually ever sick again; but I always felt poorly for the first thirty-six hours out of harbour.

When the British Expeditionary Force was retreating to

Dunkirk, H.M.S. *Broke* was in Devonport Dockyard under-going a refit. I remember the awful impatience of those hot days of early summer because *Broke* remained in the dockyard till after the fall of Dunkirk, and I had to remain with her. I tried to get leave to go up to Dover and help with the boats, but I was firmly told to get on with the job I had been specially given in my own ship. Nevertheless it was not long before we moved from the edge of the war into the middle of it. Our first adventure ended in frustration and bitterness, but it did not lack excitement.

Although Dunkirk was over, there were still British troops fighting in France, and falling back into Normandy. The enemy had crossed the Somme and was driving on to the west. On the afternoon of Sunday, 9th June, 1940, H.M.S. *Broke* was engaged in anti-submarine exercises with the submarine *Otway* a few miles west of the Eddystone Lighthouse when she received a signal from the Commander-in-Chief Plymouth to proceed with all despatch towards Portsmouth. Before we got there we were re-routed to Le Havre in company with two Canadian Destroyers—*Restigouche* and *St Laurant*.

We learned from the newspapers that the Germans had reached Le Treport, but that Dieppe was still in our hands. Surely Le Havre could not yet be in danger. But an hour later it became evident that it was, for we passed an unfinished submarine being towed away and at half past nine we sighted two large oil fires ahead, which were causing some of the smoke-cloud under which we had been steaming for two and a half hours.

When we arrived outside Le Havre we looked for the Senior Naval Officer Afloat, who was supposed to be in the destroyer *Saladin*. But *Saladin* was nowhere to be found, so we anchored off until we were called to Action Stations at half past three. Very cautiously we entered Le Havre harbour still peacefully asleep, so it seemed, under its high protection of balloons, but with the great cloud of smoke, blue in the morning haze, rising like a steep cliff and sweeping away to block out the whole of the northern sky. We steamed right up the harbour, turned and, as there seemed nothing to be done, came away again, having gained useful knowledge of the harbour should we be required to return. It was five-thirty a.m. on the morning of 10th June when we left; ten minutes later we passed *Saladin* going in. Outside again we were instructed by radio to go off with the two Canadian destroyers and the *Harvester* to turn back any ships heading for Le Havre, because the evacuation had been postponed, and a concentration of ships near the French coast would be a good target for air attack. We spread out—four destroyers in an extended line and headed north. Almost at once we steamed under the smoke pall and it was dark and cold and inhospitable. We did not immediately appreciate how much safer it made us from attack by German bombers.

Two hours later we ran out of the gloom of smoke. We were zig-zagging along when he heard a loud explosion ahead. The Alarm Bell sounded for Action Stations. The starboard look-out said, 'Here they are, sir,' and almost at the same moment I heard bullets whizzing by, all round the bridge, as it seemed. We all ducked down and grabbed our tin hats. As I was putting mine on I glanced up and saw a twin-engined machine just flattening out. There were two or three of them, no one was ever quite sure which: the mist and the suddenness of the machine-gun fire were so bewildering. Then even as I looked up I saw the bombs coming, so straight that it appeared they could not possibly miss us. There were four of them, not very big, and they glinted silver.

An instant later there was a series of heavy explosions and the whole ship shuddered. The stern seemed to lift out of the water, and we had to hold on to keep our feet. I was looking along the starboard side aft and saw one bomb burst on the surface of the sea about eight feet from the ship's side in a puff of dark-brown smoke. Two others, on the port side, had come even closer. But somehow miraculously we had not been hit, though the ship was heavily shaken and the gyro alarm bell (indicating the gyro compass was out of action) was ringing insistently to add to the confusion. Almost at once the ship leaped forward at twenty-five knots. The whole attack was over in fifteen seconds, and we had not been able to fire a single shot. It was my first experience of battle. I had been intensely frightened, but somehow at the same time exhilarated.

There followed a dark period on the bridge. By signal we learned that Italy had declared war, that the German advance through France was even more rapid than anyone had expected, and that three destroyers had been hit during our own operation. Into this gloom came a new signal, which at the time did not seem to be very important. It was from the C.-in-C. Portsmouth. It said, 'Following received from Naval Liaison Officer 51st Division: Request a ship may close Fécamp at 2359 today Monday to embark forty stretcher and forty walking cases.' The fog had cleared when we approached the coast on our way back to Le Havre. There was a big fire at Fécamp, and a considerable battle was being fought to the westward of the town. Star-shells were going up from time to time, and curved red streaks of tracer buzzed about. We intercepted a new signal from the Naval Liaison Officer which said, 'Isolated enemy armoured force is now operating westward of St Valery-en-Caux. Request ship may close St Valery at Midnight to embark wounded. Boats should only be sent if two green Verey's Lights are fired from pier.'

As we were the nearest ship to St Valery, the captain decided that we should undertake this job and we turned eastward again, back past Fécamp which was now blazing more fiercely. We had nearly reached St Valery, which being east of Fécamp was therefore many miles behind the German line of advance, when the Captain told me that I was to be the one to go ashore. I was to take a boat and to make contact with the army, embark the wounded and any others who needed evacuation and come off again before daylight. I was to return on board to report with the first trip made from the shore.

It was two-thirty a.m. when we crept into the harbour in a motor-boat. The green Very's Lights had been fired, but now there was no sign of life. I heard what I thought was a whistle.

I whistled back. Silence. Was it a trap? There was nothing for it but to go ashore and find out. Telling the coxswain of the boat that I would be back in five minutes I climbed ashore, drew my revolver and ran to some houses. I saw the legs of a sitting sentry showing round a corner. Brandishing my pistol without much conviction I popped round the corner and said, 'Hands up.' He jumped up and said, 'Yes, sir, certainly, sir.'

He took me across the village square to where there were men standing about. Nobody seemed to know anything about any wounded, and as my five minutes were up I went back to tell my crew that the village was held by the British. I found that they had already made contact with my sentry and his mate, one of whom said he thought he knew the house where the wounded were hiding. We walked about half a mile down the quay, and there was a man walking up and down who turned out to be the officer in charge of the wounded. He showed us the house and shouted through the door, 'They've come, boys. They've come to rescue us,' which was followed by a heartening cheer.

There were forty-seven stretcher cases and about sixty walking cases. Dawn was not far off and I reckoned we had only three-quarters of an hour to embark them. I got my signalman to signal to *Broke* for more boats. There followed a period of frantic exertion as we helped to carry the stretchers out to the end of the pier. Two drifters had arrived and we filled them with stretcher cases, putting walking wounded in two motor-boats. In spite of my orders I did not feel I could possibly go with this trip, as there were far too many wounded still to be embarked and too many other things to organise. Just then a Motor-Landing-Craft arrived towing four cutters, which meant that I could embark the remaining wounded in these.

By this time it was light, and I was terribly anxious for the ships clustered outside the harbour. A number had joined *Broke*, and at any moment I expected to see dive-bombers attack them. From a Major I learned that while his troops were going to hold the village, there might be 8,000 to evacuate that night. He then brought over the Chief of Staff of the

Highland Division (the 51st), to whom I explained that there were ships prepared for the evacuation, but that as three destroyers had been hit the day before, it would be dangerous to evacuate the troops by day. However, if he could not hold out till evening, I would signal my Captain to begin at once. In a tired voice he said, 'No, I think we can hold on till tonight—but no longer.' I asked him if he was sure, and he replied, 'Well, if we don't, there won't be anyone to evacuate. We're the last remnant of the B.E.F.' I confirmed that I thought as many as 12,000 could be got away in the night, provided enough boats were available and the troops well organised.

With the approval of the Chief of Staff I signalled to *Broke* to suggest that the ships should disperse. Almost all the wounded were now embarked. The Chief of Staff went away in his car, and I promised him we would be back at dusk.

It was ten past five when I returned on board and went straight up to the bridge to report to the captain that all wounded had been evacuated. I had left the ship just four hours before. One hundred and twenty people had been evacuated, ninety-five of them wounded. As we steamed away from St Valery we heard gunfire to the westward.

Half an hour after we arrived in Portsmouth harbour, the Captain and I went up to the Commander-in-Chief's office. The three destroyers who had been outside St Valery harbour were to return at once to Plymouth. Destroyers were not to be risked any more on the French coast. Our job, so we thought, was to keep our promise and be back for the evacuation. While we were in the room a signal came to the effect that 60,000 troops would have to be evacuated. Surely now every available ship would go. But, no. Even though we explained that I knew the harbour and beach and that we had been in in daylight, our sailing orders had to stand. It was a terrible blow not to be allowed to keep our promise to the Highland division and we felt it sharply as we sailed from Portsmouth and turned west to Plymouth instead of south-west for St Valery.

The next day, 12th June, was spent in doing nothing at Plymouth, and on the following morning *The Times* reported a German claim that 20,000 prisoners were taken at St Valery-en-Caux. The B.B.C. news said that 6,000 British troops had capitulated there. It was explained that fog had delayed the evacuation and that there were no extensive beaches as at Dunkirk. Though many had been embarked, many more had not. We felt very bitter about it, our little operation had succeeded in its small-scale object, but failed miserably on the major issue.

But we were to return to France later on a number of occasions, notably to help in the evacuation of Brest.

During the summer of 1940, the summer of waiting for the invasion that never came, I found myself thinking more and more of Jane, the gay girl who had been staying at Fritton when I was recovering from jaundice. She was adventurous and full of original ideas. At Fritton we had sailed boats, played running games on the lawn and acting games in the house (at which she was especially good), talked about music and painting and acting and writing—and begun to fall in love.

Late summer saw *Broke* still on nightly patrols against the impending invasion; we were still operating from Plymouth, and I gained good experience as a watch-keeping officer. However much our world swayed on the brink of a terrible abyss, the land we protected was real and precious to us, and the sunrises were the same as I had seen out on the marshes so often. And sometimes I thought particularly of one sunrise, and a boy beside me, watching entranced the morning flight of the wild geese for the first time. The Battle of Britain had begun, and Brian D'Arcy Irvine was missing in his Hurricane after an attack by Stukas on a convoy in the Channel.

22. FIRE AT SEA

As the autumn days slipped by the prospect of immediate invasion faded, until all at once it became obviously too late in the year, and with sudden relief we realised that we had a winter's wait. At the same time the naval war switched from the Channel to the Atlantic.

Broke was sailed for Londonderry, which was to be her new base. She was, I think, only the second destroyer to steam up the narrow and winding River Foyle and secure alongside the quay in this pleasant market town, which was to be our home port for about a year.

Our First Lieutenant had moved on to command his own destroyer, and Bryan Scurfield, greatly daring, had put me up to replace him, which surprisingly the Admiralty had accepted. This was the first R.N.V.R. appointment to such a job in a destroyer. To begin with I was terrified by the complexity of the work, but my Captain nursed me along until I began to feel first adequate and later even efficient.

The winter of 1940-1 found us escorting Atlantic convoys in grim conditions. But one bright spot was the Goodliffes. Guy and Grace Goodliffe lived in a delightful house just a few miles from Londonderry, though it was over the border in Eire. So it was necessary for us to wear civilian clothes if we went there. Guy was tremendously keen on snipe-shooting and knew all the best snipe bogs within twenty miles of his home. On every possible spare afternoon when *Broke* was in harbour I used to go out with him after snipe, or ducks, or even, occasionally geese. But it is the snipe I remember most vividly. Guy taught me how their whereabouts depended on the phases of the moon, how when they were in the red bogs it was useless to look for them in the rushy fields, but if the moon was full there would be none in the red bogs. Then we would come back to tea by a log fire. It was all in glorious unforgettable contrast to the life at sea. I took my Captain and other friends over to Birdstown. I doubt if the Goodliffes realised how much they helped us, but somehow as we returned in the darkness it had made the whole thing just bearable again, and we could face another gruelling ten days at sea.

On Sunday, 6th April, 1941, I came on watch at four p.m. for the first dog watch and found a wild grey day of heavy seas, driving squalls and a moderate south-easterly gale.

We were on our way to meet a homeward-bound Gibraltar convoy, having parted company with the outward-bound convoy in the early morning, and we were plugging into a head sea at seven knots which was as much as we could do with comfort.

We were in company with *Douglas* (an old Destroyer Leader like ourselves, and Senior Officer on this occasion) and *Salisbury* (an ex-American destroyer) and our position was on the port wing of a sweeping formation.

When I came on to the bridge three other ships were in sight, which was unusual because chance meetings were not common in 21° West—600 miles out in the Atlantic—more especially on days of poor visibility like this one.

These three ships were already some way astern and steering west, and I learned that we had 'spoken them' half an hour before, when they had first come into sight. They were H.M.S. *Comorin*, ex-P. & O. liner of 15,000 tons, now an Armed Merchant Cruiser, the *Glenartney*, a smaller merchant-ship and *Lincoln*, another ex-American destroyer, who was their escort.

They soon disappeared into the smoky haze and my watch passed uneventfully as I kept station on *Douglas*.

About twenty minutes after I had been relieved I was informed in the wardroom that the starboard fore-topmast-backstay had parted, and I went at once to the bridge to organise the repair. While I was there a signal was received from *Lincoln* at six-twenty p.m. It said:

'H.M.S. *Comorin* seriously on fire in position 54° 39′ N., 21° 13′ W. joins us if possible.'

We passed this to *Douglas* for permission to go and were detached at six-forty.

Having told *Lincoln* by radio that we were coming, we made a further signal: 'Expect to sight you at 2015. Is a U-boat involved?' to which came: 'Reply No.'

On arrival we asked *Lincoln* who was lying just to windward of the burning ship, what the situation was, and she told us that *Comorin* was being abandoned, that no boats were left, that the *Glenartney* was picking up some rafts and that she, *Lincoln*, was hauling over rafts on a grass line.

When we drew near the scene was awe-inspiring. The great liner lay beam on to the seas drifting very rapidly. A red glow showed in the smoke which belched from her funnel and below that amidships the fire had a strong hold. Clouds of smoke streamed away from her lee side. The crew were assembled aft and we were in communication by lamp and later by semaphore. From the weather quarter the *Lincoln*'s Carley rafts were being loaded up—a dozen men at a time—and hauled across to the destroyer lying about two cables away. It was a desperately slow affair and we went in close to see if we could not go alongside.

We were close to the stern now and we fired our Coston line-throwing gun. We fired it well to windward, but a little too high and the wind blew it horizontally clear of the ship like straw. But we were close enough to get a heaving line across—after many had missed—and we connected the Coston line to the departing heaving line as we drew astern and finally pulled an end of the grass rope to it and passed it over to the other ship. Then we put another Carley raft in the water so that they could haul it in to windward, but for some time they made no effort to do this and finally their Captain made a signal that he thought the only chance was for *Broke* to go alongside and let the men jump.

I had various discussions with my Captain as to which side it should be. I must confess that I did not believe we could survive such a venture. By this time it was almost dark and the *Lincoln*'s raft ferry had failed owing to the parting of their grass line. I do not know how many people they had rescued by this ferry, but it cannot have been very many as it was desperately slow. Not that it wasn't worth doing, for at the time it seemed to be the only way at all.

We decided on the starboard side of *Comorin*, and the men waiting on the after promenade deck jumped first—fortunately their chance was easy and about nine of them jumped and landed safely and uninjured. The second jump was much more difficult than the first and only about six men came, three of whom were injured. Our policy was not to remain alongside for any length of time as this might well have damaged us to the point of foundering in the monstrous seas. Instead we quickly withdrew after each brief contact in order to assess the damage and decide on the seaworthiness of the ship before closing in again for another attempt.

The jumping continued, and as soon as the jumping men began to injure themselves I sent aft for the doctor who was in bed with a temperature. He came for'ard at once and set to work. We also padded the fo'c'sle with seat cushions and hammocks, though we may have got more turned ankles as a result.

Once on the first approach there seemed to be a chance for a jump. Two men jumped, but it was too far and they missed. I was at the break of the fo'c'sle at the time, and looked down into the steaming, boiling abyss. With the two ships grinding together as they were there did not seem the slightest chance of rescuing them. More men were jumping now and theirs was the prior claim. The ship came ahead, men jumped on to the flagdeck, and the pom-pom deck amidships was demolished:

then as we went astern, I ran again to the side to see if there was any sign of the two in the water, but there was none that I could see.

Having got the injured off the fo'c'sle I went aft to examine the damage to the pom-pom deck and see if the upper deck had been pierced. I heard a very faint cry of 'Help', and looking over the side saw that a man was holding on to the scrambling nets which I had ordered to be lowered as soon as we arrived on the scene. We were going astern, but he was holding on. I called to some hands by the torpedo tubes and began to haul him up. Eventually he came over the guard-rail unconscious but still holding on by his hands; his feet had never found the net at all. He was very full of water, but we got him for'ard at once and he seemed likely to recover.

When I was reporting damage to the Captain on one occasion we were just coming alongside so I stayed on the bridge to watch from there, as there was hardly time to get down to the fo'c'sle. The Captain was completely calm. He brought the ship alongside in the same masterly manner as he had already done so often. He was calling the telegraph orders to the Navigating Officer who was passing them to the Coxswain in the wheelhouse. As we ground alongside several jumped. One officer was too late, and grabbed the bottom guard-rail and hung outside the flare, his head and arms only visible to us. There was a great shout from the crowd on *Comorin*'s stern. But we had seen it and already two of our men (Cooke and George) had run forward and were trying to haul the officer on board. The ships rolled and swung together. They would hit exactly where the man dangled over the flare; still the two struggling at the guard-rail could not haul the hanging man to safety. Then as if by magic and with a foot to spare the ships began to roll apart again. But still the man could not be hauled on board; still he hung like a living fender. Again the ships rolled together and again stopped a few inches before he was crushed. As they rolled towards each other for the third time, Cooke and George managed to get a proper hold of the man and he was heaved to safety and this time the ships crashed

169

together with a rending of metal. The two seamen had never withdrawn even when the impact seemed certain and they had thus saved the officer's life. It was a magnificently brave thing to see.

Another man was not so lucky. In some way at the time of jumping he was crushed between the two ships, and fell at once into the sea as they separated. On the other hand, I saw a steward with a cigarette in his mouth and a raincoat over one arm step from one ship to the other, swinging his leg over the guard-rails in a most unhurried manner, just as if he had been stepping across in harbour. It was one of those rare occasions when the rise and fall of the two ships coincided.

The later jumps were less successful because the remaining ratings were the less adventurous ones whom it was difficult to persuade to jump at all.

Once I sent up to the Captain and suggested that we might perhaps consider rescuing the last few by raft if the damage to *Broke* got any worse; with well over 100 survivors on board it would be out of proportion to risk losing the ship and all of them to get the last few if there were a good chance of getting those last few in another way. We agreed that we would try this as soon as the damage gave real cause for alarm but not before.

Quite suddenly the number on *Comorin*'s stern seemed to have dwindled. At last we seemed to be in sight of the end. There were about ten, mostly officers. The Captain and Commander were directing from one deck above, with a torch.

At the next jump they all arrived, unhurt, except the Captain and the Commander, who remained to make sure that the ship was clear.

Five minutes later the Commander jumped and landed safely. The Captain paused to make sure that he had gone, then jumped, too. He caught in a rope which dangled from the deck above, and which turned him round so that he faced his own ship again. At the same moment the *Broke* dropped away and began to roll outwards. The Captain's feet fell outside the guard-rail and it seemed that he must be deflected overboard.

But he sat across the wire guard-rail and balanced for a moment before rolling backwards and turning a back somersault on the padding of hammocks. He was quite unhurt, smoking his cigarette, and he had managed to return his monocle so quickly to his eye that I thought he had jumped wearing it.

He turned out to be Captain Hallett—a destroyer Captain of the First World War who had served under my father some thirty-five years earlier.

I took him up to the bridge to see my Captain, and at forty minutes past midnight we made the signal to *Lincoln*, 'Ship is now clear of all officers and men.'

During the past three hours no less than 685 telegraph orders had been passed from the bridge to the engine room and executed without a mistake. Captain Hallett told my Captain that there were still some confidential books in the strong room of the *Comorin* and that he would not feel safe in leaving her until she had sunk. He asked us to torpedo her. Having discussed the possibilities of salvage and decided that they were not practical, we fired a torpedo, which missed. But as she was sinking, anyway, we decided not to fire a second one.

By about five-thirty in the morning the whole of the after promenade deck of *Comorin* from which the survivors had jumped was ablaze. It was satisfactory to know that we had been justified in attempting the night rescue and that time had been an important factor. At dawn we left *Lincoln* to stand by *Comorin* until she sank and set off home with *Glenartney*.

In spite of the apparently heavy casualties during the rescue, so many of these recovered quickly that there were finally only about twenty-five hospital cases out of the whole 180.

We arrived at Greenock at about ten-thirty in the morning and were alongside for rather less than one hour before slipping and proceeding to Londonderry.

23. COLOGNE BY MOONLIGHT

On Private View Day of the Royal Academy's summer exhibition in 1941 I met Air Commodore Sir Victor Goddard, who was looking at a war picture of mine, and I told him how much I wanted to fly with the R.A.F. It was a good thing, I argued, for all of us to discover at first hand how the other half of the world lived. It could do nothing but good for me to see the R.A.F.'s night bombing efforts at first hand. No better way could be found of fostering inter-services relations.

'Well,' he said, 'I dare say it can be arranged.' And so in due course, 15 Squadron, who flew the great new Stirling bombers, became my friends. My first visit to their base at Wyton in Huntingdonshire was disappointing because their projected operation was cancelled. But not long afterwards *Broke* was boiler cleaning on the Tyne and I set the wheels in motion for a second attempt, and this time secured a lift in a Stirling in a bombing raid on the German naval base at Kiel. At supper, before taking off, I must confess that I did not have much of an appetite. I had that 'before the big race' feeling so familiar in sailing, and though we talked excitedly, I would have been extremely grateful for any excuse not to go. As it turned out we flew above the clouds for most of the night— bombed by dead reckoning through the cloud and returned rather uneventfully. We made a perfect landing home, and it was a great relief to be on the ground once more. But I had learnt a good deal about the men who were flying the heavy bombers.

Jane used to come often to Fritton. She fitted in perfectly—which was one of the nicest things about her—and she and my brother Wayland got on wonderfully well. She and I sailed on the lake and watched the little Terns fishing. She was very excited about being in love for the first time.

One leave I painted a few pictures of ships and aeroplanes and went to London to see the Admiralty about my chances of commanding my own destroyer, and eight months to a year was given as the time I would have to wait. This seemed a long time, but probably worth waiting for.

On the last day of August 1941, I had arranged for an aircraft to fetch me from Lympne aerodrome at eleven a.m. to take me to Wyton for another bombing raid that night.

Briefing was at six-forty-five p.m. because of an early take-off. A morning mist was expected and it was important for us to be back as soon as possible. The target was Cologne and we were given our route—out over Clacton and thence to Namur, where we were to turn north of east towards Aachen and thence to hit the Rhine south of the target. There were 200 aircraft going. The target centre was the Post Office on the west side of the river. We were to bomb from as high as possible. Our bomb load was five 1,000 and nine 500s—9,500lb—and one package of 'Nickel', the leaflets called 'Luft Post'.

After the briefing I borrowed a parachute and was driven out to Alconbury where we had left our aircraft U for Uncle, after the afternoon test flight. There were crowds on the road watching the take-offs.

It was still broad daylight, but the Wimpeys of 40 Squadron were already getting away. As before the twenty minutes before take-off were charged with excitement. Look last, perhaps, on the countryside of England. Wouldn't it be nice if some defect prevented us from going. Or would it? I wondered if my thoughts were the same as those of the other members of the crew, and doubted it. The diversity of man!

Yet each of us was apprehensive. No so much the fear of death—no doubt we should share that later in the night, but this was the acute consciousness of mortality. Its setting was a gloriously peaceful evening in the English countryside, so much beauty to make life so impossibly unquittable. Our turn to start was last of the five Stirlings, as we were farthest in the row on the crosswind runway. O for Orange (flown by Conran —my pilot of the Kiel trip) went off first, but the others did not follow. The C.O. called all Kiltie aircraft to hurry us up. But we were temporarily held up by a flare which had fallen out on to the ground. It had to be replaced, fell out again and was finally put in a different rack. As a result of all this it was eight-forty-five p.m. when we taxied out and I went to sit on the 'bed'. We swung a little in the take-off, but she got quickly into the air and I returned to the front compartment. There were nine of us in the aircraft. The navigator was a red-headed Cockney sergeant, very pleasant and helpful and determined to see I got my money's worth.

I had a look at the map and memorised the shapes of the estuaries over which we should pass in twenty minutes' time. Then I stood at the starboard window and considered the grandeur of the scene. To the south on our starboard beam was a little more than half the moon, shining brilliantly out of a clear sky. Behind were the remains of a calm orange sunset. Outside the window were the two vast Hercules engines, their nacelles glowing cherry red. We were climbing steeply, as steeply as we could. With all its hazards, it was a gloriously exhilarating feeling to be on the way to Germany.

Below, through the haze, sudden brilliant glints of the moon's reflection followed the winding rivers and dykes of Essex. Then dimly the pale shape of a branching estuary showed to starboard and we were over the coast.

Approaching the Belgian coast half an hour later we could see the first flak and searchlights. By now the cloud was ten-tenths below, fleecy and white and very pretty, but also a very good background against which the fighters might see us. Just before we were due to cross the coast, we described a circle in order to gain a little more height, as we were still only about 10,000 feet up. We had the oxygen on. Every now and then Singh—the Indian Second Pilot—was being asked for the readings by the flight engineer.

There was moderate flak in patches after we had crossed the coast; it was not often at us, but some of it was bursting a long way above us, which was disconcerting because it exploded the idea that Stirlings flew high enough to keep out of trouble. Just before reaching Namur the cloud cleared below us and we caught a glimpse of the river junction there. We followed the main stream east-north-east and suddenly searchlights began to light up ahead and to starboard. There were some very fine cones of about eight or ten beams, looking like wigwams of light. Every now and again more would be switched on and others dowsed.

By now we were at 15,500 and the beams which were looking for us could not see us, though they weaved around often illuminating us. We had been snaking the course a little all the way but now we took drastic avoiding action, banking steeply to port with the nose a little down. The searchlights were left behind and when we returned to our course they were on a parallel course to starboard of us. Clearly they were still working on the sound of our previous course. But we had lost some height, and when a little later some more began to weave on us we lost some more height.

By now we were 1,500 feet lower and suddenly a search-light caught us full in its beam. Evidently we were visible from below, for at once half a dozen more swept on to us and held us firmly. The whole inside of the aircraft was brilliantly lit and we could see nothing whatever outside except the dazzling lights that shone up at us. It is difficult to describe the overwhelmingly naked feeling which assailed us. One felt like saying, 'All right. It's a fair cop. I'll come quiet!' The game seemed to be up, and one could not immediately see how it could end unless in tragedy. I had seen an incredibly accurate cluster of bursts at the point of intersection of one of the other cones we had been watching—and yet the seconds dragged on and no flak came at us at all. But this was small consolation, for it only made us more than ever sure that fighters were in the vicinity, and were about to pounce. Meanwhile the pilot was making frantic efforts to escape. He put us into a tight turn, then dived out of it and jinked the other way. It was astonishing to me that the heavily laden Stirling could cope with such aerobatics. But still the fierce beams held us. At first I had been very frightened, but then I became quite fatalistic about it as I waited for the burst of fire which must inevitably come. In the brilliant glare I could see the pilot's violent twisting of the wheel on top of the control column as clearly as by day. The Stirling pulled into a steep turn to port and suddenly, miraculously, we were out in the blessed darkness again. Someone aft had just said, 'Here come the fighters!' but they didn't. Someone else said, 'Well done, Skipper!' Thirty seconds later four red lights in a row were reported passing overhead by no more than a few hundred feet, from starboard to port. We were all so unnerved at this stage that these lights were taken for enemy fighters, but it seems more likely that they were the glowing nacelles of another Stirling above us.

Some of the crew said afterwards that they thought we were held for five minutes, but I think two minutes would be nearer the mark.

All this evasion had cost us a good deal of height and we were now definitely within the range of the flak. A river appeared below us and we got a reasonable fix of the position. But afterwards the cloud thickened up ahead and was again ten-tenths. This did not prevent the enemy from firing at us. Occasionally I heard a strange knocking sound, which I discovered was the explosion of the closest shells. The burst of sparks was followed by a black puff which flashed past my window. Once we felt a bump as we passed through one of the little black mushrooms. This, then, was flak.

'About ten fighters in formation,' came a report from aft, but it turned out to be the smoke from flak bursts.

At our estimated time of arrival a small hole in the cloud

showed a big bend in the Rhine—apparently the one due south of Cologne. There was a great deal of accurate heavy flak coming up; flares were dropping all about, and bombs too, bursting with a deep red flash. This was much hotter than anything I had seen on the Kiel raid. I found myself speculating on the laws of chance. How long could the shells go on bursting so close without scoring a direct hit? Surely it was only a matter of time—and not a very long time at that. Under the clouds were various glows, some from flares that had gone through, some from incendiaries (very white), some redder ones maybe from fires or maybe from dummies. The Captain ordered, 'Open bomb doors.' We were down to 14,000 feet owing to the earlier searchlights, but the cloud protected us from them. I doubt if there were many there, anyway, as the main lot were in the belt we had passed through. The flak, however, was still heavy and accurate and often bursting all round. We flew north still weaving slightly and saw a fire on our starboard bow. This was clearly a building on fire. It shone dimly through the thin clouds, but one could see the square perspective outline of a house on fire.

The navigator was down in the lower compartment and kept asking if we could not go in and bomb each fire we passed, but the Captain kept saying, 'This is no bloody good. We'll have to look around for something better.' When we saw the building on fire, however, he agreed that it was a reasonable target, and since it was very near our dead reckoning position, being a little east of the centre of the city according to our calculations, he turned to run in. Only half our load was to go in the first stick. 'Right right,' said the navigator—then 'Left left— left left—steady—left left—steady—right right.' There was a sudden heavy bump—the bombs had gone. We were slightly turning when they went and this may have been the reason for the jolt, for at Kiel I had not been able to feel the bombs go. There followed a lot of counting on the intercom, to find the time to let the photographic flash go. Then a rich prolonged red glow was reflected on the clouds for about a second. The bombs had exploded. This was followed by a white flash as the photograph was taken. Below there was thin cloud and the dim glow of the fire. We turned to port in a large circle to make another run over the target. Again, there was heavy flak round us. In pained tones the Captain said, 'Well, blow me!' or something like that. Indeed, this seemed to be his only reaction to the enemy's shooting, and was repeated every time the flak burst close to us.

We turned until the glow of our fire was ahead and then a silly blighter went and dropped a flare over it. This lit the cloud so brightly from above that the glow below was invisible. 'We'll have to wait until the bloody flare goes through the clouds.' So we circled again, and again the fireworks burst all round us, showers of golden sparks in the shape of a single flower of gladiolus. Then, while the pilot exclaimed, we would dash past the black lump of the smoke—a reminder that we were going 200 miles an hour. Again I could hear some of the bursts as dull knocks.

The flare went down to the north-east of the burning building and the glow of the fire itself was plainly visible again. We ran in from the north. 'Left left—right right— steady—right right—right right—steady,' and so on—from the navigator. This time I hardly felt the stick go. Then there was the counting and the red glow of the bursts and the flash for the photograph.

Two more sticks fell on the fire just after ours—but we could not see who was dropping them.

'The course is about 265, Skipper—or shall we hang around and watch what happens?'

We circled once more to get on to the course. The flickering flashes of bombs and gunfire and shell-bursts and flares was nearly continuous and through it shone the red flush of the fire.

'Shall I take you home a new way—to avoid those ruddy searchlights?' asked the navigator.

'Yes, if you like,' said the Captain.

'All right, about 290—that ought to take us north of Aachen where they were so bad—mind you it's experimental.'

'All right, we'll try it out.'

After getting badly lost we finally got safely back to Huntingdonshire. Seven aircraft failed to return.

In my two adventurous nights over Germany I had learned a good deal about 'how the other half of the world lives'. I returned to the Navy with a new and deep respect for the R.A.F.'s Bomber Command.

By the middle of September 1941 *Broke* was ready for sea again after her refit and in front of us was another miserable North Atlantic winter.

In the previous year I had put forward a camouflage scheme which would make *Broke* invisible at night and which would I thought be valuable in the U-boat war. The idea was to make her as pale as possible at night because ships nearly always appear as dark blobs on the horizon against the sky.

This camouflage had soon spread to other ships, and in 1941 the C.-in-C. Western Approaches—Admiral Nasmith—had commissioned me to design a camouflage scheme for the fifty obsolete American destroyers, which we had acquired in 1940, long before the United States entered the war. Soon, however, all the destroyers in the Western Approaches Command had turned near-white. It must have been a little before this that a question had been asked in Parliament: 'Was the First Lord of the Admiralty aware that ships painted white had been allowed to sail in convoy thereby endangering all the other ships in the convoy?' But the idea was now becoming generally accepted. At night unless bright moonlight fell upon it, no paint could ever make a ship *whiter* than the sky behind it. A white ship would match it most nearly, and be less easily seen than a dark one. Very pale blue or grey did not seriously upset the principle and made the ship a trifle less conspicuous by day (and also slightly easier to keep clean than pure white).

By early 1941 C.-in-C. Western Approaches was making the following signal to Captains (D) Londonderry, Greenock and Liverpool, repeated Admiralty, Flag Officer Commanding North Atlantic, C.-in-C. South Atlantic:

'Four corvettes having been torpedoed up to date every endeavour is to be made to hasten the camouflaging of corvettes in accordance with Peter Scott Scheme.'

There was another factor to be taken into account. If the U-boats could not see the escorts there was a better chance of surprising them. But if the escorts could not see each other there was a greater danger of collision. Good camouflage was believed to have been part cause of a good many collisions that had actually occurred, including one between *Broke* and another destroyer while I was officer of the watch. But in spite of this the Admiralty finally came down on the side of camouflage.

After being in her for two years and a day I left *Broke*, during a long refit to prepare her for the North African landings, where she was badly damaged in action at Oran, and sank while under tow to Gibraltar. I had accepted command of a Steam Gunboat which was being built at Cowes.

24. S.G.B.9

For a while now Jane Howard and I had been engaged. She was sharing a flat in St John's Wood with a friend, Dosia Cropper. Early in my leave a dinner party was planned. Dosia had invited a friend, Kit Dodd, who was working in the Admiralty, and his girl-friend Philippa Talbot-Ponsonby.

I remember Phil as a quiet, rather shy girl, with some sort of hidden character which I did not discover; but that night I had eyes only for Jane.

With the new boat *S.G.B.9*, being built at Cowes, Isle of Wight, this familiar place of so many happy sailing memories was obviously going to be my headquarters for many weeks. The Admiralty had explained that as no destroyer command was currently available, the Steam Gunboat job would be a useful stop-gap which would in no way spoil my chances of my own destroyer in due course.

As soon as I was appointed, it was suggested that I should visit some of the operating bases of Coastal Forces to gain experience. I lost little time in following up the suggestion, for the same evening I took a train to Dover and before dawn I found myself at sea, fighting a fire in a sinking Motor Torpedo Boat.

But apart from this adventure, the paying-off of *Broke*—the pause in my war—was the opportunity I had been waiting for. At last Jane and I could get married. The wedding was at St Mary's Church in Lancaster Gate only a few hundred yards from the family house at Leinster Corner. Jane was just nineteen. For our honeymoon we went to the Lacket—my stepfather's little cottage at Lockeridge in Wiltshire. It was early spring, a spell of fine warm weather, primroses and catkins, and a chance to show my wife the countryside in which I had spent so much of my boyhood—our own beautiful dene, the West Woods, the downs, the 'Valley of dry bones', where the sarsen stones are in greatest profusion, the Kennet running clear after a spring drought, the great stone circles of Avebury.

After our honeymoon Jane and I went to Cowes and stayed in the Gloucester Hotel, so as to be on the spot as the ship was completed. My mother had come down to launch *S.G.B.9* and in the final layout there were a multitude of minor decisions to be made.

When she came to do her speed trials over the measured miles in Stokes Bay *S.G.B.9* returned a mean speed of thirty-six knots which compared quite favourably with the speeds of her smaller counterparts powered with the less reliable and more inflammable petrol engines. While these trials were in progress some operation was obviously being prepared in the Solent. Two other Steam Gunboats, completed earlier than No. 9, were to take part but it was not until much later that we learned it was the first projected raid on Dieppe. Because of a suspected leak to the enemy the whole scheme was abandoned for the time being.

By midsummer *S.G.B.9* was ready to be commissioned and we took her down to the shore-based training establishment called H.M.S. *Beehive* at Weymouth. My new ship's company included three ratings from *Broke*—Frank Brown, a Leading Telegraphist of great efficiency, Jimmy Jones, my servant who had nearly been blown to bits by a hand grenade in Belfast, and Tom George, a Maltese lad who had earned a Mention in Despatches in the *Comorin* rescue. For five weeks we 'worked-up' until we were a fairly efficient team. Many of the exercises took place in Weymouth Bay at night.

By the beginning of August *S.G.B.9* and her crew formed a reasonably well-knit fighting machine. We were sailed for

Portsmouth quite evidently for something special, though, of course, we had no clue what it might be. Four Steam Gunboats were to be ready by 16th August, and as we were already on the top line there was a week's leave for the ship's company.

I received the orders for the Dieppe raid five days before it took place—sixty or seventy pages of them with a portfolio of relevant photographs and charts, and I sat far into the night trying to form a picture of our particular jobs in the Combined Plan for this one-day frontal assault on a part of Hitler's Atlantic Wall. Two days later we were 'briefed' by Commander R.E.D. Ryder, V.C., who had led the fabulous raid on St Nazaire. *S.G.B.9* was to support the landings at two beaches on the extreme right flank—Orange I and II—and I met Lieut-Commander Mulleneux who was in command of these landings. Our force was to be the Fourth Commando, led by Major Lord Lovat.

The ship's company knew that time was short, but only the Officers, the Coxswain and the Chief Engine Room Artificer actually knew that we were off that night.

We slipped at half past eight in a clear golden evening, and followed the great Infantry Assault Ships down Portsmouth harbour while the siren sounded 'All Clear'. The German evening reconnaissance had been a few minutes too early to see the movement of the assembling ships.

There was a great feeling of relief and elation to be started at last. In the last light of that calm summer evening the force looked very impressive forming up to pass through the East Solent Gate, a gate of netting in the barrage stretching, by way of the old forts, from the Isle of Wight to the mainland shore. There were Infantry Assault Ships (L.S.I., or Landing Ships Infantry), Destroyers, M.L.s, Gunboats and the French Chasseurs of the 'cutting-out party' (to bring back any ships found in Dieppe). They lay stopped all around Spithead awaiting their moment to dive through the gate in their correct order.

After passing through the gate speed was increased to nineteen knots and *S.G.B.9* took station on *Prince Albert* and *M.G.B.312* Lieutenant Nye, R.N.V.R., and so to the channel through an enemy minefield which had been swept a few hours earlier by a special force of minesweepers.

Once past the mid-channel minefield, through which the lane had been swept and buoyed, the various groups fanned out so as to arrive simultaneously off their respective beaches. We split up at 0144 and *S.G.B.9* went up on to the port beam of *Prince Albert* in accordance with the screening diagram.

At 0258 the *Prince Albert* finally stopped in an estimated position seven miles due north magnetic of Pte d'Ailly lighthouse. While we were stopped we suddenly saw a light ahead. It flashed three times and then twenty seconds later it flashed three times again. The Germans had left their lighthouse burning to guide us. Then we *were* achieving surprise! There it winked at us—group flashing three every twenty—just as shown on the chart. We wondered for a moment if it was a trap to mislead us. Perhaps it was not the d'Ailly but a fake light five miles to one side of it to take us to the wrong beaches. Just as the Landing Craft were forming up the light stopped. Had the alarm been given? A quarter of an hour later the light popped up again and winked for three or four minutes.

The L.C.A.s formed into two columns of four and kept close to port of *M.G.B.312* who was leading the Orange force towards its beaches. We followed astern.

Suddenly starshell went away to port. It must be German starshell because no one on our side would risk giving away the quantities of small craft that were approaching the coast. It was 0350, exactly an hour before the touch-down, so it could not be the first of the landing. By the light of the starshell I could see a large ship, perhaps a German merchant-ship (we suspected a German convoy must be passing because of the Pte d'Ailly light being on), perhaps the *Glengyle*—the largest of the L.S.I.s—late at the lowering position (which in fact it was). Near it was a smaller ship, perhaps a destroyer. The starshell died and a tracer battle broke out, fierce white tinsel-like tracer being fired from the south and purposeful red tracer, much of it aimed far too high, from the north. This battle went on for twelve minutes and then subsided, and still the lighthouse winked periodically. Red and green lights on the port bow showed from the breakwater ends of Dieppe harbour. These and the lighthouse were in fact no attempt to mislead us and proved one of two things: either the enemy was completely surprised at least in the timing of the raid, or if he *had* been forewarned, the liaison between his intelligence and the authority which operated his lighthouses was not very good. Historically it now appears certain that the force of about ten large transports, eight destroyers and numerous coastal craft approached to within seven or eight miles of the enemy coast totally unseen and that had it not been for the chance meeting of *S.G.B.5* and the boats for Yellow beach with the enemy convoy, the tactical surprise would have been complete. As it was the battle was enough to send all the Germans ashore to Action Stations.

25. 'LET BATTLE COMMENCE'

The precise moment for landing was to be four-fifty a.m.
when the first grey light would come into the clear eastern sky.
Twenty minutes before this, we stopped a mile and a half
offshore while Mulleneux transferred from 312 to the Support
Landing Craft (L.C.S.) from which he was to direct the actual
landing. Then our eight landing craft divided—three going off
to the left to Vasterival with 312 in support and the other five
going towards the Quiberville beach with us in support. This
included Lord Lovat himself and the L.C.S. with Mulleneux.
At four-forty-two the first aircraft appeared—Bostons and
Hurricanes—and streams of the same white tinselly tracer
went up from the battery round the lighthouse which seemed
to consist of about five guns. To the eastward along the coast
was more tracer, but all going upwards—still the landing craft
were undetected.

About a minute before the touch-down a single White
Verey's Light or fire-ball lobbed up into the sky above the
lighthouse, and the party was on. All along the coastline battle
was joined.

The Senior Officer of the S.G.B.s, who was embarked with
us, directed me to turn stern on so as to present a small target
and be able to fire our three-inch gun. The L.C.A.s of the .
Orange landing party, having landed their troops, withdrew
towards us while the shelling continued. By now it was broad
daylight and at five-fifty a new battery to the east of the light-

house opened up on us; as our first job was successfully completed we drew yet farther offshore.

All this time there were explosions ashore from mortars, guns and bombs. At times there were great sheets of flame, at others very heavy detonations. All the while Bostons and Hurribombers kept coming in to attack the defences. At about six o'clock we sighted *S.G.B.8* coming towards us through the smoke to the east, and we told her to take station two miles on our starboard beam and set off on a course of N. 60° W. at ten knots to carry out 'Task I', a prearranged sweep fifteen miles to the westward in order to give warning of the approach of surface craft. We had been given this job because five German T-class torpedo boats were known to be in Cherbourg harbour, and there was also a possibility of E-boats.

We steamed slowly along the enemy coast as bold as brass, then altered course fifteen degrees offshore. We were not in a healthy place and we suddenly realised it. A few minutes later at seven-twenty there were 'Aircraft right astern'. Two fighters were weaving about and working their way round into the sun. In a few moments it was evident that they had designs upon us and as they turned their noses down I could see the bomb hanging under the first one. 'Hard-a-starboard', and I rang up the revs. To twenty-eight knots. Off came the bomb just as the guns opened up. Not many fired; the pom-pom jammed and one of the point-fives had a misfire. The bomb fell in our wake close astern.

The second Hun was circling towards No. 8. Whether he misjudged the attack or saw that his mate had missed will never be known, but he transferred his attention to us, coming in on the port bow while we were still turning to starboard. As he steadied up towards us in the shallow dive I saw splashes in the water short of us and then our own guns opened up. The F-W 190 was only firing machine-gun—not cannon—and he was himself enveloped in a haze of our tracer. I saw his bomb take the water twenty yards short on our port beam. There was a pause and then a heavy shock and a huge waterspout—but the ship was still afloat and still steaming. I remember thinking it must have been a very small bomb not to have damaged us more. Then I looked at the Focke-Wolf. A trail of wispy black smoke was coming out of it and it was losing height. But when it was nearly down to the water it picked up again and began to climb. I stopped watching it and became concerned with the fact that the ship would not steer, that the alarm bells were ringing continuously, that, in fact, we had been badly shaken. Those in No. 8, however, watched the damaged Focke-Wolf falter again and crash head-on into the bottom of the cliffs.

Our position was now very sticky; we were still in full view of the coast and one Focke-Wolf had returned to base to report that we were disabled. It obviously could not be long before further aircraft were sent to complete the job and despatch us for good. No. 8 took us in tow, but before long we were going again under our own steam. Things were looking up.

A signal had just been received that E-boats had been sighted southward-bound from Boulogne. After a short stop a few minutes later for the engine room to make an adjustment, we proceeded at twenty-five knots and less than an hour later were closing the assorted destroyers and small craft to the north-west of Dieppe while hordes of Spitfires milled comfortingly overhead. Soon no doubt we should be sent out to the eastward to meet the E-boats.

Away in that direction smoke drifted idly north-east from Dieppe and the battle spluttered and rumbled. Heavy fighting was going on by the sound of it. Cloud upon cloud of Spitfires circled above us between 3,000 and 10,000 feet. There were no enemy aircraft in sight at all. The German flak was still lively whenever our fighters or fighter-bombers went low over Dieppe—especially to the eastward.

We closed *Calpe*, the Hunt class destroyer which was H.Q. ship, to ask for instructions but our loud-hailing equipment remained resolutely silent. *Calpe* was lying stopped and surrounded by small craft. Some were alongside, others lay round the other destroyers—*Brocklesby*, *Bleasdale*, *Fernie* and *Albrighton*.

A smoke-screen began inshore of the assembled pool of craft and drifted sluggishly north-east. The smoke itself was white and friendly—the protecting aircraft circled unmolested and the fifty or sixty craft in the boat pool were equally unmolested. We leaned lazily on the bridge screen waiting for orders from the *Calpe*, while even the din of the battle to the eastward seemed to be muffled by the smoke. The boat pool had drifted to the westward so that it lay between Pourville and the d'Ailly lighthouse. 'Maintain a smoke-screen half a mile inshore and to the westward,' came over the loud hailer from *Calpe*. We led off with No. 8 following on our starboard quarter to drop the smoke floats.

Half an hour later we were back beside *Calpe* with hardly any smoke left. She told us to take *M.L.*s *309* and *190* under our orders and continue to maintain the screen. Through our loud hailer we directed the M.L.s when to drop their smoke floats. As we went off a formation of three Dornier 217s unloaded their bombs in the middle of the boat pool from about 4,000 feet without, as far as we could see, doing any damage. The Spitfires were on their tails before even the bombs were released, and almost at once one was set on fire. The crew baled out and the aircraft crashed in the sea a few hundred yards offshore and two miles to the westward. The first two to bale out fell in the sea, the others drifted in over the cliffs before coming down. We went to pick up one of them as a prisoner and got shot at rather accurately by a shore battery for our pains. So we had to leave him to his fate.

Twenty minutes later, when we were back among the boats and the smoke, a heavy air attack began. One bomber blew up in mid-air and the bits fell slowly like autumn leaves. Later a fighter was disintegrated by a shell in the same sort of way. None of the bombs from these Dorniers seemed to have troubled the ships at all.

We had just received a signal that the withdrawal was commencing, and the battle on the beaches seemed to increase in intensity as the Landing Craft went in to take off the troops. At this time we were manoeuvring in thin smoke. Parachutes were coming down all round. We went ahead and began to pick them up. While we were doing it a fierce air battle was going on overhead and whenever possible we engaged enemy aircraft that were in range.

While we picked up the first parachutist—a German—the second one was shouting 'Help—speed.' We took rather a long time getting the first on board, but he was finally hauled in over the transom. Picking up survivors with the air full of enemy aircraft and all our guns firing required a high degree of concentration, and I did not usually make a very good job of it. However, we finally got the second Hun on board (also over the transom) and he was almost drowned. We decided to transfer him, on the advice of the Sick Berth Attendant, to a ship with a Medical Officer. *L.C.F.* (*L*) 5, a beach protection craft flying a medical guard flag, was near by; we went alongside and the man was transferred. By this time the air attack was less fierce but fairly regular. The Dornier 217s—Germany's latest bombers—were coming in in formations of three. One of the three was always shot down, often two and once or twice all three.

All this time it was very hard to know what was going on either ashore or afloat. From time to time signals came through calling for closer support. But how to do it, that was the question. How to know where our own troops were. The blanket of smoke between us and the shore was almost complete. At eleven-forty-five we had made a signal to *Calpe* (H.Q. ship) that 'We have plenty of three-inch ammo but no smoke, can we help?' to which we had received reply, 'Closer support is required, offer of help appreciated.' A few minutes later we signalled *Calpe* again, 'Can you give us a bearing on which to lob shells?', but got no reply to this.

It was an hour after it had been sent that I first saw a signal to *Locust* timed 1112 which said, 'Give support at rising ground at end of Green beach.' It was a bad signal; Green beach had rising ground at either end, and without more precise instructions anything other than moral support was impossible. We called up *Locust* by lamp and made, 'Can we

193

help you support Green beach?' to which came reply, 'Yes—go in.' A general signal had just come through: 'All ships. Make smoke. Executive signal.'

The destroyers were making clouds of brilliant white C.S.A. smoke. Then we plunged into the fog of it and at last emerged with alarming suddenness on the other side. There was Green beach and the village of Pourville about 600 or 700 yards away. We turned to port and opened fire with our three-inch gun at some tracer coming from the top of the cliff at the left-hand end of the beach. There was no sign of activity at all on the beach, but heavy fighting was still going on at Red and White beaches. As we turned away from our bombardment bullets whistled around and Oerlikon shells plopped in the water beside us, but none hit us.

All this time shells were coming from the cliffs to the east-ward of Dieppe—they were not accurate but they were fairly constant, so that hanging about even in the thick smoke was not very restful.

We were receiving such signals as 'Situation critical behind Red and White beaches, can you hasten close support as requested—1114' and later 'Enemy holds all beaches.'

As we came through the smoke-screen for our second bombardment, the coastline loomed up far closer than we expected. We turned again to port, opening fire with three-inch and pom-pom at the eastern outskirts of Pourville which constituted the 'high ground at the end of Green beach'. We passed between the Hunt-class destroyer *Albrighton,* (temporarily aground and no longer firing), and the shore at slow speed and turned back into the smoke. A good many shells and bullets were plopping in the water all about us, but miraculously we were not hit.

Back on the offshore side of the smoke we engaged a Dornier—then another, and at 1308 a formation of three dived down. One of them pressed home his attack on the group of ships all bunched together, which consisted of the destroyers *Calpe, Fernie, Berkeley, Albrighton* and *Bleasdale,* and S.G.B.s 8 and 9. The bombs came out and I saw one slanting down into the water close to the port side of *Berkeley*. Its slant took it right under the ship and when it exploded she reared like a bucking horse. The bridge went up and the fo'c'sle went down, then for a few moments as the ship subsided again into the water the half-detached fo'c'sle waggled up and down. The stricken destroyer was turning at speed, steeply reeled outwards. All the time that she had been steaming in a circle men had been falling off her steep decks and the wake was dotted with the heads of swimming survivors. We followed the circular string of bobbing heads and threw over two lifebelts and a rubber dinghy (to hold five). Then we went on to a Carley raft and collected half a dozen men from that. By this time the other swimmers had collected at the rubber boat and we were able to go straight to that and pick them up. This seems a good idea when there are many people to rescue.

Berkeley was now stopped and down by the bow listing to starboard. *S.G.B.8* pulled away from her side with the last of her survivors and a signal came to us from her Captain who was in No. 8: 'Sink with torpedo.' Meanwhile *Albrighton* commanded by Hanson, who had been Captain of the *Lincoln* during the *Comorin* rescue placed her stern opposite *Berkeley*'s stern and took off the Torpedo Gunners Mate who had been below and left behind.

Then *Albrighton* lay off to the north of *Berkeley* and fired a torpedo. It hit under the bridge and blew off the bows which sank immediately. The rest of the ship, however, relieved of the weight floated more level. A second torpedo was fired and hit the after magazine which blew up. A huge reddish-purple burst of smoke and flame belched out of the wreck and went up into the calm sky in a tall column with a mushroom of dense blackness at its top. For a few seconds part of the ship floated so that we imagined she was resting on the bottom, then she disappeared altogether.

By half past one in the afternoon the ships were forming up into a convoy for the return journey, and soon after the Naval Force Commander made the signal 'Negative Smoke'. What remained of it did not take long to clear, although there seemed a lot of work to be done. *Albrighton* was getting a

Chasseur in tow. The withdrawal from the shore was complete—no more boats were coming off. All who were left behind must now be taken prisoner. But the *Calpe* turned back towards the beaches firing her forward guns in a duel with a shore battery whose shells landed on her starboard side close between her and *Albrighton*. Under *Calpe*'s starboard bow came an L.C.A. heading shorewards. This was evidently a last attempt to get a boat ashore to take off further troops. But it was quite obviously a forlorn hope. They could never make it. They turned away and we turned away with them. Twenty-millimetre shells plopped in the water round us.

All the destroyers were making black smoke. By 1341 the gallant attempt to get the L.C.A. ashore had been abandoned and all ships were withdrawing. The raid was over.

A second L.C.A. had appeared from somewhere and the two of them brought up the rear. We went to look after them and rounded up astern of them. A new battery was firing and the shells fell near the last destroyers just ahead.

Calpe and *Albrighton* increased speed to outrange the new battery. The two L.C.A.s chugged on slowly while we brought up the rear. We watched *Calpe* go off to the south-east in response to a Spitfire which was circling low and tipping its wings to indicate a pilot in the water. She made smoke as she went. A Dornier spotted her away from the Spitfires and did a shallow dive attack. We couldn't see *Calpe* at the time, only the pinnacles of the bomb splashes. Surely the *Calpe* must be hit —and if she was hit there was only us to go to the rescue. And we knew she had many hundreds of wounded soldiers on board as well as the Headquarters Staff.

We increased speed and headed towards the smoke. There was no sign of the destroyer, but a breaking bow wave came out of the smoke across the glassy sea. That bow wave might have been started before the last bombing attack, the *Calpe* might still be sinking in the middle of the 'fog bank' in front of us.

I turned to port to keep north of it and there at last she appeared steaming out at twenty-five knots. We all heaved a deep sigh of relief and signalled: 'Are you O.K.?' to which came back, 'Yes, thanks—please search two miles astern of me for six men in the water.' Two miles! And we were no more than four miles offshore—with hardly any smoke left between us and Dieppe. We turned on to an opposite course and set off at twenty-five knots. Two miles back we still saw no sign of the missing men. The last of the smoke had gone and the sea was so completely smooth that I thought we could not possibly miss them. We turned to starboard in a wide sweep and suddenly I saw five heads in the water. As we approached the swimmers waved and cheered from the water. We stopped among them and they were all on board in a surprisingly short time. It appears that the first attack on *Calpe* in the smoke had caused a cordite fire on No. 2 gun deck (the upper after mounting). Some of the men had been blown overboard, others had jumped to extinguish their burning clothing. The five were no more than slightly injured and it is not clear if there had ever been six as *Calpe* signalled.

The shore looked peaceful except for some columns of smoke rising lazily above the town. As we increased speed to rejoin, I swept the port side with the glasses and saw an L.C.A. away inshore of us. At first I took it for one of two derelicts, one of which had been blazing half an hour before: but this one was under way. I did not want to go right in there, but there was really no choice. We turned once more towards Dieppe at twenty-five knots.

As we closed the boat I aimed a little to one side so that I could sweep round and take it swiftly in tow till we were clear of the shore and the guns, which must, we all thought, open fire as soon as we stopped. The L.C.A. turned towards us. I aimed the other side and the wretched thing turned and came for us again. Eventually I had to go straight to it and turn beyond it. As we approached we saw that it contained three soldiers, two of whom were completely naked except for their Mae West life-saving jackets. One of them was busy semaphoring 'SOS'. After turning we passed them a rope and they managed to secure the eye. Then, miraculously still unshot at, although we were no more than a mile offshore, we set off again to rejoin the now-distant convoy and its cloud of protecting fighters. On the way one of the periodical air fights developed overhead and a pilot was seen floating down to the north-east of us. I decided that trying to get the L.C.A. home was a secondary commitment compared with parachuters, so I took off the soldiers and abandoned it.

We found the airman sitting in his rubber boat; a large red flag with a white spot flying bravely over it. He was grinning and seemed perfectly well and happy. It was a striking contrast between our system and that of the Germans. Their airmen had all been half drowned before we got them on board. This lad, a Norwegian officer, was on board in a few moments and we turned at once back towards Dieppe to collect another pilot whom we had seen descending.

We found the pilot, an American, without difficulty. He, too, was sitting quite comfortably in his rubber dinghy in spite of a badly broken leg and an injured arm. With his good arm he caught and secured a heaving line to the dinghy. Being in a dinghy instead of in the water halved the time that it took to get him on board and in a very few minutes we were off again on a course to rejoin the convoy.

Just then a Dornier appeared out of the clouds. By now we were very familiar both with the appearance and tactics of these bombers. They were immediately recognised. This one came from right astern and dived down as we increased speed. We and the M.L. were the only unprotected targets—money for jam. All guns opened fire and I watched the bombs come out. At once I saw that they were travelling in the same direction as us and at about the same forward speed, perhaps a little more. They would fall just ahead so above the uproar of the guns I yelled to the Coxwain, 'Full astern both.' He didn't hear me the first time, but when he did the result was most striking. Unlike the *Broke* after a similar order, the S.G.B. pulled up dead in her tracks and the bombs went on to fall about sixty yards ahead with four great spouting splashes. Meanwhile the guns had been doing well. The Dornier, which was about

2,000 feet up, was hit by a burst from the three-inch gun under its starboard engine. This caught fire and a thin stream of smoke came from it as the aircraft plunged almost vertically downward. There was great excitement on the bridge. 'We've got him! We've got him!' But when he was a couple of hundred feet up he flattened out and, still burning, disappeared into the haze of smoke over Dieppe.

At five p.m. we came up with the convoy at last, just as it entered the southern end of the swept channel. Since the sinking of the *Berkeley*, enemy air attacks had been totally unsuccessful. An M.L. was stationed to mark the entrance to the lane of flagged dan buoys, the same M.L. that had so nearly rammed us in the darkness sixteen hours ago. When we came up to *Albrighton* I signalled by light to Hanson:

'I think I'd rather have the Atlantic, even with the *Comorin* thrown in.'

'I quite agree,' was his answer.

'Did you have many casualties?' I asked.

'Only six killed, but many wounded.'

We decided that close between *Albrighton* and *Bleasdale* was a dangerous place to be should a determined Dornier turn up, so we crept past and up into the rearguard of the convoy itself.

As soon as we were through the minefield we gradually overtook the convoy so as to tell *Calpe* that we had his five chaps.

I went down to talk to the survivors and one of the Canadians from the L.C.A. told me that he had had conversations with French villagers indicating that the raid had been expected for some time.

We turned up the Portsmouth swept channel half an hour later, and as we passed the Nab Tower clouds of black smoke came from the funnel and we began to slow down.

For more than twelve hours the engine-room staff had been fully extended, nursing badly shaken machinery. Now a combination of 'stuck-up valves' and extreme fatigue was beating them. For the next hour and a half we proceeded in fits and starts in the inky darkness, having lost touch with the destroyers altogether.

Finally, however, we found the gate at about midnight, crept up the Channel, groped our way into the harbour, turned with some difficulty and berthed alongside *S.G.B.4* at forty-five minutes past midnight—just twenty-eight hours after we had left.

In a short while our eleven casualties, five survivors and two prisoners had been disembarked, an operation which was made more difficult by a failure of the shore lighting, so that the wounded had to be moved by torchlight.

It was about three o'clock before we finally turned in to sleep late into the following morning.

In the small hours of 19th November, 1942, we fought a short battle which was to have interesting repercussions two years later. It was on that morning that I first encountered Kapitän-Leutnant 'Charlie' Müller, famous E-boat Commander.

We were in station astern of a west-bound convoy near Start Point and I was asleep in the charthouse when the alarm bells rang. In a second I was on the bridge, and could see a starshell floating down to seaward of us. 'What's up?' I asked. 'Just a starshell, I think the trawler on the port bow of the convoy must have fired it,' said Jock Henderson. Then suddenly 'Clang!' as a torpedo hit the merchant-ship just ahead of us. As I hauled out to port and increased speed there were three more explosions and then we saw the tracks of two more torpedoes approaching. One passed ahead, the other right under the ship, or so it seemed, though most probably the torpedo itself was just ahead of us, for the wake of bubbles is some way behind the 'fish' itself. We and the other escort ships all fired starshell now, and by its light we could see five E-boats about a mile and a half away. As we made after them they disappeared into a cloud of their own smoke. A few moments later we saw tracer bullets buzzing across in front of us. One E-boat was firing at another. It was cheering to find, after an unfortunate incident a few weeks before, that we were not the

200

only ones to make this kind of mistake. Meanwhile we ourselves were sighted by the destroyer *Brocklesby* who was Senior Officer of the Escort, and a moment later her starshell burst over us. By its light, however, we spotted another E-boat and briefly engaged it as it sped away to the south. We followed for a bit, but suddenly we heard another underwater explosion. So there were still E-boats harassing the convoy—we must go back at once.

We had not long turned back to the northward when we saw an E-boat silhouetted against the light of starshell. It was heading exactly towards us. I felt like a fielder in the deep field—could I prevent a boundary? Clearly the E-boat was unaware of us. We reduced speed so that he would not see our bow wave and turned on to a parallel course, not 200 yards away from him. Our own very meagre supply of starshell was exhausted, but so long as the illumination was provided by *Brocklesby* and the trawlers of the screen, we could hardly miss when the moment came to open fire. Still the E-boat had not seen us, and gradually he drew level with us. Now was our chance. 'All right, Number One, open fire,' I said, and exactly at the moment that he gave the order the last starshell petered out and there was utter darkness. With the light behind it for another fifteen seconds we could have blown that E-boat out of the water. As it was we fired towards it and the tracer sprayed around it, but there was no sharp black bull's-eye for the gunners to aim at. The critical half minute which it took the enemy to make his white smoke, and turn away into it, passed without the decisive blow being struck. After all, one direct hit on the waterline with the three-inch gun would probably have done it—would have slowed him down enough for us to try conclusions. But it was not to be.

26. THE FLOTILLA

Jane and I needed a home and the only sensible thing seemed to be to make it in London. It so chanced that 101 Clifton Hill, St John's Wood, which had been the home of Jane's grandfather, Arthur Somervell, the composer, was to let, so towards the end of 1942, we moved in and on 2nd February, 1943, our daughter, Nicola, was born.

I had become the Senior Officer of the Steam Gunboat Flotilla, which meant that I had six boats under my command. This seemed an even better prospect than driving my own destroyer. But there was a snag. The S.G.B.s had only one boiler and this made them vulnerable in action. The Admiralty had ruled that they should not be used on offensive operations until the boiler room and engine room had been protected by thick armour plate.

Early in 1943 the Captain of *S.G.B.6*, Howard Bradford, had broken his arm at the conclusion of his 'work-up' period at Weymouth, and I was temporarily appointed to command his boat. It was the first of the Steamers to complete the new modifications, including the armour. The others would be ready later in the month and my own in early May.

On 16th April I took *S.G.B.6* and two D-class M.G.B.s to patrol in the Baie de la Seine. One of these M.G.B.s was commanded by John Hodder, in whose previous boat at Dover I had had my first introduction to the Coastal Forces. The other was commanded by Dickie Ball.

In bright moonlight we fought a lively battle against a defensive patrol of armed trawlers. The bare bones of the story are told in the covering letter from C.-in-C. Portsmouth when forwarding my report to the Admiralty.

SECRET

Coastal Force Action of Night 15th/16th April 1943
FROM: Commander in Chief, Portsmouth.

To: Secretary of the Admiralty

25th April 1943

1. Be pleased to lay before Their Lordships the following report of an action between S.G.B.6 (Lt.-Cdr. P.M. Scott, M.B.E., R.N.V.R. Senior Officer of Force), *M.G.B.608* (Lt. J. Hodder, R.N.V.R.) and *M.G.B.615* (Lt. R. Ball, R.N.V.R.) and three large armed enemy trawlers.

2. The force had been ordered to proceed through passage II in QZX 771 (which was a minefield) and carry out a search in the Baie de la Seine with the object of destroying enemy shipping

3. At 0014, 16th April, an enemy plot was detected by the H.P.T. R.D.F. Station (radar), Ventnor, at a range of seventy miles, and the position was passed to the force, which proceeded to close. The relative positions of the two forces were passed until *S.G.B.6*'s sighting report was intercepted.

4. During the first stage of the action, which lasted eight minutes, *S.G.B.6*'s steering gear was shot away and *M.G.B.615* expended all her six-pounder ammunition and her pom-pom became irremediably jammed by a round stuck in the barrel.

5. The Senior Officer ordered *M.G.B.615* to stand clear, and forty-five minutes later, having rigged hand steering, proceeded with *M.G.B.608* in pursuit of the enemy, whom he correctly assumed to be retiring towards Le Havre.

6. During the second stage of the action, which was mostly fought at ranges of under 500 yards, the leading

trawler was silenced, stopped and set on fire, while her consorts kept a distance of 1,500 yards, firing inaccurately.

7. *S.G.B.6* endeavoured to sink the trawler with a torpedo which missed, and then owing to the lack of ready-use ammunition and the late hour, and being only ten miles from the enemy coast, the Senior Officer correctly decided to return to harbour.

8. Lt.-Commander Scott reports that the first stage of the action was opened at too great a range, owing to his turning to an opposite course too soon, and the ammunition was wasted at long range.

9. It is disappointing that the expenditure of some sixty rounds of three-inch ammunition failed to sink the enemy, but this would not be probable without a lucky shot in a magazine or certain hits on the waterline at very close range. In pressing home such an attack considerable damage and casualties would have been expected as the estimated armament of each trawler was one four-inch (estimated from splashes), one forty-millimetre, four twenty-millimetre and several light machine-guns.

10. A technical enquiry on the gunnery of the action was carried out by a representative from H.M.S. *Excellent,* and a copy of the report is attached. This discloses an unsatisfactory state of affairs in the gunnery training, and action is being taken on this.

11. The remarks of the Commanding Officer, *S.G.B.6*, on the necessity for fitting extra ready-use lockers are concurred in: and the remarks on the material forwarded by the Commanding Officer, *M.G.B.608*, are also commended to Their Lordships' consideration.

12. I consider that Lt.-Commander Scott showed skill in the handling of his force, and great determination in his engagement, pursuit and re-engagement of the enemy.

13. Recommendations for awards will be forwarded in a separate submission.

(Signed) Charles Little, Admiral.

Copies of this memo were sent to various Commanding Officers and to the Naval Officer in charge of Newhaven.

Paragraphs 12 and 13 were sweet music, of course, but it all seemed rather bogus. Our object had been to destroy enemy shipping and we had failed to do so. Really, we had not been all that clever or brave. John Hodder seemed genuinely to think that I had not led the force too badly, and I took some comfort from that, and the battle brought me, in due course, a D.S.C.

In July 1943 *S.G.B.9*, now officially known as *Grey Goose* (a friendly gesture from the Admiralty bearing in mind that I had once had a duck-punt so named), was at Newhaven with four other Steam Gunboats. For the first time a unit could be mustered for offensive operations which consisted exclusively of S.G.B.s. The patrols began again two or three nights a week, but there were only minor adventures, until on the early morning of 27th July we were involved in a fairly desperate battle. At this time we were trying to co-ordinate the night-bombing efforts of the old Albacore bi-planes with our own attacks, and the shore-based radar on the clifftops of the Isle of Wight were able, on nights when conditions were good, to give us some details of the movements of enemy shipping. The Cherbourg Peninsula was just within their range, but the Seine Bay was outside it. When they detected shipping the details were passed on to us by C.-in-C. Portsmouth and were called 'Enemy plots'.

On this particular night we had left Newhaven five strong. As we steamed south across the Channel, I was leading in *Grey Goose*. Immediately astern was *Grey Shark* (*S.G.B.6*) with Howard Bradford now back again in command. Astern of *Shark* came Grif (Lt I. R. Griffiths) in *S.G.B.8*, now *Grey Wolf*, then came *Grey Owl* (*S.G.B.5*) with Richard Hall, and finally *Grey Seal* (*S.G.B.3*) with Jimmy Southcott.

This was the proud force that set out to intercept an important merchant ship which was expected to cross from Cherbourg to Le Havre during the night. It was soon to be reduced by one when *Grey Owl* developed a defective feed pump and I had to send her home. We drew blank in the Seine Bay, but went after a patrol—which turned out to be rather a strong one—just outside Cherbourg as dawn was breaking.

The moon was well up and giving a little dim light, but not much. We didn't know exactly how close to the shore we were. I thought the shore batteries were already firing and I did not fancy being hemmed in by a strong force and so when I saw the Huns ahead I turned slightly to starboard so as to engage them on the port side firing to southward; a turn to port to go inside them would almost certainly have been better as it turned out. We came to the trawlers first and I let them go past so that the other boats would have something to shoot at when we opened up. When it is very calm it is hard to judge range, but we were certainly not more than 200 yards and possibly a good bit less when I said 'Open fire'. Then a tragedy took place. The port point-five gunner lost his head and fired his guns without aiming, about twenty degrees into the air. This was blinding to the other guns and from that moment all hell was let loose. At least fifteen ships had opened fire simultaneously and the air was thick with the red and green and white streaks. They ripped away from our guns towards the enemy line, fanned out of the enemy ships and come lobbing towards us almost as though you could reach out and catch them, until they whipped past just over our heads. Considering how close we all were to each other it is odd that more damage was not done on both sides.

The Germans must have got under way fairly quickly because by the light of sudden flashes which I took to be hits I could see the R-boats creaming along on a parallel course about 300 yards away. At this stage, it would have been nice to have had some starshell. Our three-inch had been doing very well and I saw three hits with it, which caused big showers of sparks. I looked back and could not see any S.G.B.s following. In truth, I could see very little at all as the tracer was completely blinding. I remember seeing the leading R-boat on our beam and shooting at us and thinking, 'Thank God there aren't any more to pass.' We had passed at least six overtaking at about five knots, and they had done us a bit of no good. We were burning a bit aft—with a lot of smoke; and a scare report came to the bridge. 'All the three-inch guns crew killed, and we are heavily on fire.' We kept on a steady course still because three guns were still firing quite well, it seemed. The fire aft died down, but then suddenly flared up very bright again, and all the Huns started shooting at us so I decided to disengage. A long way astern and on the starboard quarter I could see two S.G.B.s flashing on their recognition display signals (two green). As I turned away more and more ships seemed to be shooting at us, some from the starboard quarter, and fancying that this must be the S.G.B.s I switched on my display, too. It lasted about ten seconds and then—pink—and out it went, shot out by Grif or Jimmy or both. However, they only got two pom-pom hits on us. We found the fuses afterwards and neither of those did any damage to speak of. I found afterwards that my starboard side guns had fired about 200 rounds back. My first Lieutenant, (who was wounded), an Able Seaman and a Stoker put the fire out very quickly with a hail of bullets whistling round their ears. It was a three-inch ready-use locker full of starshell which had gone up. I reduced to ten knots as soon as the worst of it was over in order to let the others catch up. From time to time some hopeful German would direct a burst at us and they would come lobbing towards us. I planned to go to the standard rendezvous two miles north of the action so that we could reform and see if we could go in again.

As I looked back I saw a line of all three S.G.B.s in the light of some starshell which the Hun had just put up.

I watched them go in to attack and suddenly saw one ship get the most terrible pounding. I hoped it was one of them, but I feared it was one of the Steamers because it was very near where I had seen them in the starshell. For about twenty seconds shells were bursting and sparkling all over it. The battle roared on very fiercely and then rather suddenly ceased. There was a pause of a couple of minutes and then the distress signal—a short burst of tracer going vertically upwards directly astern of us. I said to the Coxswain, 'Starboard thirty—steady on south,' and my heart sank into my boots!

The action had begun at 0357 and apparently soon after *Grey Shark*'s steering went which was why she lost contact with me. As soon as it was fixed she plunged into the battle between me and the R-boats intending to ram. She missed, and passed about twenty-five yards from four of them, getting a horrible pasting. She managed, however, to give a pretty fair return and saw a lot of hits on the enemy. But seven of the enemy's armour-piercing shells entered the boiler and with a hiss poor *Grey Shark* came to a standstill. The boiler-room crew escaped unhurt either by the shells or the escaping steam, which is quite remarkable.

Grif was too blinded by the tracer and starshell even to observe that *Grey Shark* had been stopped. All he knew was that he couldn't see the next ahead and that he was being shot at. Then he saw me burning on his starboard side and decided to follow round to starboard. His bridge had been hit, his First Lieutenant, Navigator and Coxswain all slightly wounded and he was at the wheel coming round to north. Another hit on the bridge knocked him down. He picked himself up from the deck and took the wheel again and went a little past the course, altering back to port.

Meanwhile Jimmy had seen Howard buy it, and turned back hard-a starboard. Half-way round his turn he suddenly saw Grif on his starboard bow. They both went full astern but they hit pretty hard. Grif's forward mess deck was holed very badly and although he thought at first he was going to sink, he was in fact quite well able to keep the damage under control.

All those things had happened pretty quickly while we had been putting out our four fires and before *Grey Shark* had pointed her bridge Vickers guns into the air and fired a burst to summon assistance. We turned at once and steered south towards the distress signal and then in the binoculars I saw *four* ships lying more or less stopped. Were they all Huns? Were three of them Huns mustered round the damaged S.G.B.?

Certainly one of the four was an R-boat—he came more or less straight towards us. The others were directly behind him—and which were they? The next one looked all wrong. Surely another German. Actually it was Grif down by the head after the collision, about which of course I knew nothing.

Now came a regrettable moment. The first boat had been identified as an R-boat. It altered course to starboard and passed close down our port side. It should have been blown out of the water. But it wasn't. Ever since I have been wondering just *why* it wasn't. The answer is a combination of reasons I suppose. I was still not sure that two more R-boats were not trying to board the damaged S.G.B. I did not know exactly where the remainder of the enemy were, but I did know from the distress signal that one S.G.B. was fairly certainly going to have to be towed. It was getting light pretty fast and any interruption of the towing would probably spell disaster.

By the time I had identified the other three boats as S.G.B.s the R-boat was too far past us to make it worth starting anything. Grif got under way. I made 'Follow' to him by light, but he didn't receive the signal and in any case he was best out of it. I, of course, did not know how badly damaged he was, until a little later when he made a W/T signal saying he was disengaging.

It appears that the R-boat had closed Jimmy while he was trying to get Howard in tow and started flashing, and Jimmy replied with E.B. ('Wait' in German signal procedure) and the R-boat had waited. Actually, of course, the R-boat must have had a nasty shock finding himself so close to the enemy and must have been very glad of the opportunity to creep away. During this time *Shark* saw and heard a German shouting in the water about fifty yards away. As soon as Grif had gone off I circled round the other two. I watched the R-boat circling to the north of us, and following round to the west with binoculars came suddenly upon a whole bunch of them, seven at least, clustered in the darkest part of the horizon while we were completely silhouetted against quite a bright dawn, and they were closing in at slow speed. And still the two S.G.B.s lay stopped, fixing the tow-line. I could distinguish now, which was 'tower' and which was being towed, and suddenly I saw the towed boat start to pivot round: the strain was on the tow, they were under way.

By this time the enemy ships were less than 1,000 yards away and the obvious course was to lay smoke to cover the tow. I increased speed and started to make smoke and immediately the Hun saw what was happening and opened fire, but the fire was very poor and our B gun was in particularly good form. We saw quite a number of hits on the second R-boat. *Seal* and *Shark* saw the glow of it through the smoke. The first R-boat turned towards us and I expected him to come through the smoke after us, but the second one turned away and the other seemed to follow. Some starshells were fired and several big splashes appeared about fifty yards away, either from the trawlers or from the shore batteries, probably the trawlers.

Meanwhile the tow had whacked it up to about ten knots and Jimmy with most excellent judgement, refused to attempt anything faster, realising that if the tow parted all would be up. We dropped astern of them again so as to be able to repeat the smoke run, and we did in fact make another puff of it for good measure.

I had been looking astern for signs of a pursuing enemy, and when I looked round both *Seal* and *Shark* had disappeared. The sea was so calm that the smoke was completely invisible, and as we were still in the clear I could not for a moment imagine what had happened to the two ships which had been about half a cable away only a few seconds before. I asked the starboard gunners if they had sunk, but they seemed to think they hadn't and suggested fog, and then we ran into it too. In the middle of it we passed only five yards under *Grey Shark*'s stern, which was very hair-raising! After that we ran through several patches of real mist.

By now it was broad daylight—I did not think the enemy ships would dare to follow long because of our air support

211

which they could expect. We had a message by light from *Grey Shark*'s First Lieutenant saying he was the only unwounded officer in *Shark*. Portsmouth made us signals about some destroyers which were coming to meet us and eventually we met the *Stevenstone* and soon after the *Bleasdale* with Grif in company.

We all stopped and, while *Seal* remained attached to *Shark*, I went alongside *Shark* and shunted her backwards alongside *Stevenstone*, so that her casualties could be transferred—and ours also. This took about half an hour or more. There were seven killed and over thirty wounded and many of those thirty kept going, some of them for nine hours or so—till their ships were back in harbour.

The whole do lasted only thirty-six minutes, but quite a variety of things took place in that time. There were a lot of opportunities for exceptional initiative and courage, and there were a lot of chaps who were not slow in taking them.

The results? A lot learnt—some good experiences, a few Germans killed, a few holes in some R-boats—and four S.G.B.s out of action for periods varying between seven days and six weeks, with seven of their gallant men gone for good.

It appears that two R-boats had to go into dry dock and two more were not used after they had returned under their own power to Ouistreham. There is no indication about the trawlers. So far as is known nothing was sunk. One interesting thing is that according to the radar plot after disengaging at about 0436 the R-boats went back to Cherbourg, but just before entering one apparently turned back to the scene of the battle—possibly to look for the man seen by *Shark* in the water.

After that action I had two special worries. The first, which I could never quite escape in any battles where there were casualties, was the degree of my own responsibility for the deaths and injuries of my chaps. Had I made the right decisions?

And then, at the other end of the scale, was the wretched R-boat that got away. Down the years I have lain awake at nights and thought about it. Was it really just plain cowardice that prevented me from saying those two words 'Open fire'?

Paragraph 10 of the C.-in-C. Portsmouth's covering letter says:

'The Senior Officer, when he turned back to the distress signals of *Grey Shark* was faced with a difficult decision when he found himself passing close to an enemy vessel. He could have done no wrong in engaging, and such would have traditionally been the correct course of action, but he was summoned by a consort in distress, and this might have made the difference between her loss or safety. As the battle eventuated, had *Grey Goose* been delayed, diverted or damaged by this potential encounter, she would not have been able to screen the damaged vessels at the critical moment.

'11. The taking in tow of *Grey Shark* by *Grey Seal* in four minutes under fire shows a high degree of seamanship and training.

'12. The action of the Senior Officer in laying a smoke-screen between the concentrating enemy and the tow, and drawing the fire on himself, was a well-judged and gallant action which met with the success that it deserved.'

Soon after this battle I was awarded a bar to my D.S.C. But I still lie awake at night sometimes and wonder.

27. A MOST SATISFYING BRIEF

We fought a good many of these battles in the Channel, mostly less bloody, and some substantially more successful. Then, as I still hoped for my destroyer command after a short spell at the Coastal Forces training establishment teaching the Channel techniques to the newcomers, I was diverted to the planning side before the invasion of Normandy—the D-day of history. Before and during it I worked in a tunnel in Portsdown Hill. Occasionally I could get to sea with the boats whose operations I planned, and there were short and interesting spells in France during the critical tanks battles round Caen.

At the beginning of August 1944 it was arranged that I should go to Cherbourg to help to operate the U.S. P.T. boats—the American M.T.B.s—and set up an operational 'Plot' at the U.S. Headquarters of the Commander Task Force 125. In Cherbourg, the Chief of Staff, Captain Clarke, gave me a most satisfying brief. 'We want,' he said, 'to lay on some operations against the shipping in the Channel Islands. I want you to get together with the P.T. boys, get the operation orders all set and then go out and do it.' Did ever a staff officer have a more admirable prospect? Battles to be thought out and planned and then carried out—and I was to do it all myself. No Admiral could have wished for better.

We used to take the P.T. boats to sea nearly every night. The Chief of Staff had conceived the idea that a Destroyer Escort—the American equivalent of a frigate—should be made available to mother them, and I was greatly in favour of this. The only trouble was that the P.T. boats and the D.E. (U.S.S. *Maloy*) were completely untrained, and the only training we could give them was harbour discussion and practice in action.

During my early days in Cherbourg I wrote an appreciation of the situation in the Channel Islands. I collected what intelligence was available and drew up a table of enemy forces. I worked out a plan to take advantage of any move which they might make among the islands, and put up a number of ambitious schemes involving the use of four British Fleet destroyers then in Cherbourg. Greatly to my surprise this appreciation was extremely well received and was used as a basis for all our operations. In accordance with it, our nightly patrols continued. I arranged them usually to cover any shipping which might pass between Guernsey and Jersey, so that we used to spend the night a few miles west of La Corbière—the south-westernmost headland of Jersey.

On the first night that we did it, we had two units of P.T. boats from Squadron 34, whose squadron commander—Jack Scherertz—was with us. We had been on patrol since dusk, but it was not until about four-thirty in the morning that our radar first detected enemy ships coming from St Peter Port in Guernsey and evidently bound for St Helier in Jersey. There appeared to be at least five ships in the convoy and intelligence led us to believe that two would probably be 'M' class Minesweepers, more dangerous customers than the trawlers which probably made up the rest of the escort. Somewhere in the middle would be the escorted ship, a smallish coaster, or perhaps two. Coasters were all that was left to the enemy in the Channel Islands, in the way of merchant-ships, in those days.

From the dark plotting room of the *Maloy*, gazing at my cathode-ray tube and its little blips of light, I vectored one unit of three P.T.s on to the target, but they missed the interception astern. Then I moved in the second unit of two P.T.s The sea was flat calm at the time and there was a fog. They all got in among the enemy and the two boats became separated.

The second lost his head and fired his torpedoes blind into the fog ahead. Needless to say they missed.

At about this time I made a bad slip; I told the unit which had missed the interception what the enemy bore from him, but I used the wrong call sign, so that it went out as if addressed to the unit which was in action. This called forth a plaintive cry on R/T: 'Hell, I'm in the middle of them.' It was the last we ever heard from that boat. Some of the enemy appeared from the Plot to be slowing up, while the rest went on into St Helier. It was now full daylight, but it was still foggy. We ourselves were about four miles from the shore, and we vectored the rest of the P.T. boats to join us. There was still no word from the 509 boat. When the others were alongside, we had a quick conference down on the iron deck of the *Maloy*. They were all anxious to go and look for the 509 boat, but I knew that two echoes remained on our scan, in the roadstead outside St Helier. There was still fog although it was now nearly eight o'clock, and three boats still had torpedoes. By the first principle of war the object must be relentlessly pursued—and the object was the destruction of enemy ships, not the rescue of the 509 boat. I put this point of view to Jack Daniel, who was Officer in Tactical Command of the unit, and he saw it at once. I was much tempted to go with him, but Jack Scherertz pointed out that the vectoring would be complicated in the fog and that I ought to stay in the *Maloy* to do it. Scherertz himself decided to lead the party, and it was agreed that after the attack they should search to the westward for the 509 boat. Only two of the three boats were to take part, as the remaining one had developed a defect of some kind.

It was an extraordinary scene as the P.T. boats pushed off from the D.E. in the bright light of day to attack a target only four miles away in the fog. I rushed up to the Plot and watched them closing in on the radar scan. Scherertz came to the edge of the fog and 300 yards beyond it was a trawler lying bows on. He fired his torpedoes—though with a head-on target they had little chance of hitting, and disengaged at once, coming under heavy fire as he did so—fire which both his boats returned. On the radar scan we could see him coming away at speed with the shells splashing around him. He told us on R/T that he had casualties and he came straight alongside us to transfer them. Again, not more than twenty minutes since they had left, we had the P.T. boats alongside, as we lay stopped four miles south of St Helier; and then the fog began to lift. We got the wounded safely across to the *Maloy*, and then moved off as fast as possible to the westward. Soon, however, we ran into another patch of fog and this gave us our chance to turn north again in search of the 509 boat. We had no idea at all where she might be. If she was sunk we had little or no chance of finding the survivors in the fog; if she was only disabled we expected to find her by radar. Perhaps the enemy had stopped to pick up the crew—we had seen them split up and the echoes which Scherertz attacked had been well astern of the others. Perhaps she had gone ashore in the fog on disengaging, for the battle had been less than a mile from the Jersey coast. With the fog so patchy it would have been wrong to take the *Maloy* any closer to the shore, and there was no sign of an echo on the radar scan. The P.T.s were about to make a cast across the scene of the battle when the fog began to clear altogether and we had to withdraw at best speed, out of range of the shore batteries. We could only hope that the crew of the 509 boat had been, or would be, picked up and taken prisoner. There was nothing more that we could do to rescue them; and as the mist cleared and the islands came into sight, we set course sadly for Cherbourg, west about round Guernsey and the Casquets.

Jack Scherertz had been slightly wounded in the battle and his face was covered with blood. The C.O. of the boat had a lucky escape, for the back of his tin hat had a large dent in it from a splinter, but he was unscathed. Several of the crew had been wounded and I went to the sick bay aft to see how they were getting on.

That was the P.T. boats' first blooding in the Channel Islands. We sent aircraft to search for the 509 boat and we swept the area with P.T. boats the next night, but without success. Meanwhile the German broadcasts claimed to have sunk two, one after being rammed by one of the escorts.

Two days later Wattie (the Coastal Command Liaison Officer) and Sherwood, ex-C.O. of one of the P.T. boats and now Flotilla Operations Officer, went up in a Walrus to look for survivors. They saw a body in the sea off La Corbière and landed to identify it. It was one of the 509 boat crew, though they could find no identity disc. Sherwood recognised it, and later identified it from photographs of the crew. A week, or more, later, part of the 509 boat, badly burned, was salvaged by another P.T. boat. Those were the only clues that we ever had to the nature of her fate.

It was bad luck that we should lose a boat in the very first action, and, with her, one of the best officers in the flotilla, but the operations went on, with occasional breaks for a night of bad weather.

My time at Cherbourg came to a rather sudden close when I was summoned to return at once to Portsmouth to complete the report on our part in the invasion.

At this time I was full of schemes for intensifying the war against the Germans in the Channel Islands, but I found that there were more urgent commitments.

A few days later the Captain Coastal Forces, Channel (C.C.F.) my immediate boss, decided to pay a lightning visit to the Continent to clear up a number of minor problems, both at Cherbourg and at Courseulles, where I had been posted immediately after the invasion, and I accompanied him. Our flagship for the journey was S.G.B. *Grey Shark* and this was the first time I had been to sea in an S.G.B. since relinquishing command of the flotilla. In many ways I wished that I were still leading the S.G.B. flotilla. But then I wondered whether in fact it would have been as interesting as what I had been doing, and came to the firm conclusion that it would not.

After our routine business I accompanied my boss on a visit to Monty's headquarters where we stayed the night, but I never saw the great man himself.

Two days later I summoned S.G.B. *Grey Shark* to Arromanches from Cherbourg, to take us back to England. We crossed on a calm evening of exceptional visibility so that we had scarcely lost sight of the French coast, it seemed, before St Catherine's Point on the Isle of Wight came up ahead. For the next week or two I remained working in my old job with Christopher Dreyer on C.C.F.'s staff in the Tunnel in Portsdown Hill. The Coastal Forces which we were operating were embarking upon their most productive period of the war, the evacuation of the Germans from Le Havre. Each morning we laid on the operations at Fort Southwick and each afternoon we went down to H.M.S. *Dolphin* to do the briefing. Here, just as they had done before I went to France, the Destroyer and Frigate C.O.s whose ships because of their tall masts were being used as mobile radar stations, met the Senior Officers of the M.T.B. units and the Coastal Forces Control Officers who would conduct the battle on the cathode-ray tube. Together they worked out the tactics which proved to be the most highly specialised co-operative technique for night fighting in small ships to be developed in the Second World War.

The evacuation of Le Havre and its attempted reinforcement lasted from 23rd until 30th August, 1944. During that time the enemy is believed to have suffered the following losses and damage: nine tank landing craft, two trawlers, four coasters, one E-boat, two R-boats, all sunk; one T.L.C., one coaster and one R-boat driven ashore; one trawler, one T.L.C., two coasters, five E-boats and four R-boats damaged. This was achieved without loss to ourselves and with only very light casualties.

By 1st September the enemy ships had been drummed up the Channel. With the exception of the few that remained in the Channel Isles, still harassed by the destroyers and P.T. boats I had trained, and what shipping attempted to move along the French coast south of Brest, no targets remained for Coastal Forces west of the Straits of Dover. Suddenly, overnight, we at Portsmouth found ourselves with nothing to do but write the reports and wind up our affairs.

It was then that I started my flying lessons in a Tiger Moth from Gosport. My instructor was Tim King, a Squadron Leader in Coastal Command and, in peace-time, a flying instructor. I managed to get in about seven or eight hours flying so that I would have been able to go solo had it not been that we were flying a borrowed aircraft and dreadful trouble would have come to Tim if I had broken it!

We used to fly from Gosport aerodrome to Appledram—a disused airfield on which I could practise 'circuits and bumps' without getting in anyone's way. Tim bought me a book which I swotted up before each lesson. At one point I read farther ahead than I should have done and on the following day as we ambled over to our practice field I put the nose down to gain speed and pulled the stick back into a quick loop. It was almost a flick manoeuvre and Tim was rightly cross. That was not what he had given me the book for. But secretly I think he was quite pleased at my progress.

One day in the first week of September we were flying at 2,000 feet along Portsdown Hill when I suddenly saw a single goose flying parallel to us at the same height. As he came closer I saw to my amazement that it was a Brent Goose of the Light-bellied form. It was incredibly early in the year for such a record. This same day was extremely bumpy and turbulent, and I remember hoping that these conditions were not too common, else maybe I should not take to flying in light aircraft! Little did I realise then that thirteen years later I should be impatiently awaiting the bumpy days in order to get good lift for soaring in my glider.

Karl Müller

Kapitänleutnant

P.O.W. Camp 7.

28. CHARLIE

I was soon moved to Great Yarmouth, to join the staff of Captain Coastal Forces, The Nore. Off the Dutch coast the M.T.B.s continued to operate against evacuation convoys, but as usual the winter campaign was fought more against the weather than the enemy.

On the night of 18th September, 1944, two M.T.B.s led by Lieutenant J. F. Humphreys, D.S.C., R.N.V.R., and controlled from the frigate *Stayner* engaged three E-boats off the coast of Belgium and all three enemy vessels were sunk. British casualties were three killed and one wounded. A collision between two of the E-boats largely contributed to this startling result. The M.T.B.s picked up a number of survivors—among them Kapitän-Leutnant Karl Müller, Senior Officer of the Tenth Schnellboot Flotilla, known to his friends as 'Charlie'. The name of 'Charlie' Müller, one of the few E-boat Commanders to hold the Ritterkreuz, was well known among the officers of the Coastal Forces. I knew, for example, that I myself had met and engaged him at least once in my Steam Gunboat, in the action off Start Point.

Early in October I was instructed to go to a prisoner of war camp in the Home Counties in order to interview Charlie on technical matters relating to E-boats and Coastal Forces. I found a pleasant-faced young man about twenty-eight years old, and his English was better than my German.

I found that his attitude was quite definite, and perfectly

realistic. The war was lost to Germany and the quicker it was brought to an end the better for all concerned, particularly the Germans. To this end he was prepared to help so long as he did not disclose details which might threaten the lives of his colleagues in the Schnellboot Service. All of them, he said, recognised that the war was lost when the first break-out from the Normandy Bridgehead took place. They had come to accept that they were weaker at sea and in the air, but until then they had imagined that they were still stronger on land. Charlie kept repeating that the war must be made to end quickly.

About a week after this first talk, my colleague, Christopher Dreyer, Staff Officer Operations to C.C.F., joined me for a second visit to the P.O.W. camp, and we spent four and a half hours in conversation with Charlie. He talked in general about the superiority of the E-boats as warships over our Coastal Forces. All E-boat personnel were quite satisfied that they had greatly superior craft. This was said very politely and without arrogance. Charlie told us in detail about a colleague's visit to Hitler at Berchtesgaden in March 1944. His friend had been summoned to give details and advice on E-boat development. He was amazed to find that Hitler knew intimate details of the boats, asking whether the new four-centimetre guns had been a success, and discussing technical features of the new engines. He had also heard Hitler confirming alterations to the *Gneisenau*, and quoting the length of barrel of her guns and other exact figures. Charlie's friend said it was possible to have an ordinary conversation with Hitler without feeling that one was talking to the Fuehrer of the Reich, but that there was something queer about his eyes, which seemed to look through you. He believed him to be remarkable, but definitely mad.

At that time I had almost completed the manuscript of a book on the Coastal Forces in the Channel and North Sea. The typescript of the book had not yet been through the Admiralty censorship, but as I was anxious to achieve the greatest possible accuracy I asked to be allowed to show it to Charlie Müller and permission was given. Charlie evidently enjoyed it, and soon afterwards I received a letter from him, written in English, in which he said that in his opinion the book was 'particularly attractive because of its close resemblance to life'; he said he had taken some notes about the rise of the Coastal Forces during the war.

Here the story might have ended, but for a proposal to send Charlie to a P.O.W. Camp in the southern United States. While he was awaiting passage at a U.S. transit camp, volunteers were hastily sought for an exchange for repatriation by way of the besieged port of St Nazaire which was still in German hands. A well-known politician was to be returned in exchange for a German officer of distinction, at short notice and without consultation with the British authorities. Charlie was selected and a few hours later he was back in Germany. When I heard of it I thought ruefully of the instructions I had received before the interviews: 'Be as frank with him as you like,' they had said, 'he's in for the duration.' And when, a few weeks afterwards, my book went up to the Admiralty for censorship I told them that whatever they decided to cut out of it they could not hope to keep any of it from those Germans who could use it best. Charlie knew all about it.

Later the East Coast Convoy route was simultaneously attacked by a large number of E-boat units—so many that the radar plot was greatly confused. Next morning I rang up Christopher Dreyer, now at H.M.S. *Vernon*, the Torpedo School. 'Did you see the details of last night's E-boat activities?' I asked him.

'Yes.'

'Did anything strike you about it?'

'If you mean did it remind me of how we asked Charlie why the E-boats never tried a mass attack to swamp our radar plots, the answer is it did.'

29. END OF MY WAR

At long last the Admiralty came up with a Command for me, and a choice one it turned out to be—the *Cardigan Bay*, a brand new anti-aircraft frigate building at Leith. To be sure, it was not a destroyer (as originally promised), but it was in many respects better: a really last-word ship. In the early spring of 1945 as the German war was drawing rapidly to its end, my time was divided between various courses and visits to the shipyard to see how the building of my frigate progressed. I went through the famous tactical anti-submarine course run by Captain Gilbert Roberts, C.B.E., R.N., at Liverpool; through the damage-control course at Baron's Court, which taught me how to keep a badly damaged ship afloat; and through an advanced Tactical Course at Greenwich. I went also to see the other ships of the 'Bay' class which were being built, in order to see the snags which arose and how they were dealt with.

At the time of my appointment 'to *Cardigan Bay* in Command', it had been evident that the war in Europe would be over before she was commissioned. There would remain, of course, the war against Japan. At that time a Japanese capitulation seemed very remote. How, one wondered, could unconditional surrender be obtained from a people who by tradition believed in death before dishonour—who were already fighting their naval war with suicide bombers? Could the Allied war aims be achieved short of killing the last Japanese? I had never been to Japan; I simply did not know the answers to these questions, but I foresaw a long continuation of the Pacific War. And it would all be happening a long way away from my wife and child.

Then with mounting speed Germany was overrun and the European War was suddenly at an end. The principal aim of five long years had been won, and yet it was not quite all over. I could not pack up and go back to my family brushing my hands together and saying, '*That's* done.' But a decision had to be made. And by a strange twist of fate, this was made for me.

I was sitting at my desk on the ground-floor room of our London house, when a man knocked on the front door. He told me that his name was Holbrook, and that he was Chairman of the Conservative Association at Rugby. Would I, he asked me, join the short list of their prospective candidates to stand as M.P. for Rugby. Polling day in the General Election of 1945 was then only three weeks away and a quick decision was called for.

Here it was, then—the decision which had been at the back of my mind for so long. Not the Navy *versus* politics, but the War *versus* my family. And for some time I had been worried about my family. All was not well with my marriage. I had subjected it to greater strains than it could stand. My dangerous and distant life in the Coastal Forces had taken me away from my wife Jane, and perhaps this was the time when I could come back to her. When the decision had to be made she was away in the country; but we talked on the telephone and I found that on the whole she wanted me to accept the Rugby offer. There was still my ship, my beautiful new frigate, the Command for which I had waited so long. Was this to be denied me at the last moment? I had one night in which to decide, and on the following day I accepted and was on my way to Rugby. I did not get selected there, but a few days later I became the Conservative candidate for Wembley North.

I failed to get in by 435 votes, and as I had now left the

Navy, I plunged back into ornithology and conservation and began painting hard. I returned to my birds with a new and passionate delight, and in the autumn of 1945 I received two letters from ornithologist friends which were to have a very great effect on my life. Both the letters were from farmers, and both concerned wild geese. The first was from Howard Davis, an experienced observer of birds, living near Bristol, who sent me a copy of a paper he had written on the great flock of White-fronted Geese which has wintered on the Severn Estuary from time immemorial. If I could spare the time to come down, he wrote, he would like to show them to me.

The second letter was from my old and valued Lincolnshire farmer friend, Will Tinsley. At the beginning of the War some of the best birds from my lighthouse collection had been taken over to his farm to live in the orchard and about the farmyard. Among these had been a pair of Lesser White-fronted Geese, perhaps the most beautiful of all the world's grey geese which I had first met in Hungary and later in their thousands on the Caspian shore.

At that time the Lesser Whitefront was the rarest British bird; it had only been recorded once, and on any list you cannot have a rarer bird than that. It shared that distinction with some twenty other species which had only been recorded once in Britain. This single record was in 1886 when an immature Lesser Whitefront was shot in Northumberland by Alfred Crawhall Chapman, brother of Abel Chapman, the famous wildfowler and author. The Lesser White-fronted Goose breeds as far west as Scandinavia and from there eastwards across sub-arctic Europe and Asia almost to the Pacific. Those Lesser Whitefronts which breed in Lapland fly southeastwards on their winter migrations, through Hungary to Macedonia and the Mediterranean.

I had brought some slightly wounded Kis Lilliks (the first word, pronounced Kish, means small in Hungarian) back with me from the plains of the Hortobagy to my lighthouse home. When the War came and my collection of live waterfowl was disbanded, a pair of Kis Lilliks was taken over to join Will

Tinsley's collection. Now in his letter Will reported an extraordinary occurrence; he said that in 1943 a wild Lesser White-fronted Goose had come down one day out of the sky and landed beside his tame pair and had stayed there in the orchard for several days. There was little chance that the bird could have escaped from any other collection, but was a truly wild bird. 'No doubt about the identification,' I remember saying to myself. 'If Will says it was a Lesser, then a Lesser it most certainly was.' From this I fell to wondering how many people there were in the whole country who would know the difference between a Lesser Whitefront and an ordinary Whitefront.

It is, to be sure, a little smaller, but not much; its bill is a good deal smaller, and rather pinker, but the only definite distinguishing character is the golden yellow eyelid which encircles the eye of the Lesser Whitefront. How often, in the field, can a wild goose's eyelids be critically examined? Supposing, I thought, these Lesser Whitefronts came regularly to the British Isles, who would recognise them? Of course, Will Tinsley would, but I could not think of very many others. And if they came, where should one look for them? It seemed to me that they would be most likely to mix accidentally with those species of geese which migrated to Britain from breeding grounds farther to the east. Two species of grey geese do this—the Bean Goose and the Common or Russian Whitefront, and the largest flock of Russian Whitefronts in Britain in winter was to be found on the Severn Estuary. Here, then, was the chance of putting my theory to the test. If it was correct I might expect to find a stray Lesser Whitefront among the larger geese if I could only get close enough to see their eyelids.

A few weeks later I was staying in Stafford, and suggested to my friends John Winter and Clive Wilson that we might take up Howard Davis's invitation; on the following day, after a telephone arrangement, we met him at Slimbridge. We walked from the bridge over the canal and down to the end of the lane, after which he led us out towards a war-time pillbox commanding a view of the saltings upon which the geese were feeding. Bent double, we crept across the field, behind the low sea-wall and into the dank concrete box. From the embrasures we had a most wonderful view of a great flock of 2,000 wild geese. Among them we saw, quite near by, a young Bean Goose, then a Barnacle, and a Brent and later a Greylag. There were also a few Pinkfeet, but the majority were, as they should have been, Russian-bred Whitefronts. That evening we went back to stay with Howard Davis at his farm near Bristol. As he drove me back I outlined my wild idea about the Lesser Whitefronts and was rash enough to suggest that it was for this very purpose that we had come down to the Severn. On the following day we were back in the pillbox overlooking the green Dumbles and the grey carpet of wild geese. Again the young Bean Goose was close in front of us.

We had been in the pillbox, I suppose, for a little over half an hour when Howard Davis said quietly, 'There's a bird here which interests me. Would you have a look at it?' In a few moments he had directed me to the goose in question among the tight mass of geese in front of us, and the instant my binoculars lit upon it I realised that it was a Lesser Whitefront. My spine tingled. Here almost too easily was proof of my far-fetched theory. It was no doubt, a small discovery, but for me it was a moment of unforgettable triumph, a turning-point; or is it only in looking back on it that I have invested it with so much significance because it changed the course of my life?

From the pillbox we watched the little Lesser Whitefront for half an hour or more, satisfying ourselves that the eyelids were in fact golden yellow, that the bill was small and extra-pink, and that the white forehead patch rose high on to the crown of the head. The bird had that smooth, dark, perfect look, almost as if there was a bloom on the feathers, which is so characteristic of the Lesser Whitefront.

Later in the afternoon we moved farther down the seawall to get a better view of a part of the flock which was beyond the fence that crosses the Dumbles at the half-way mark. Here among 200 or 300 more Whitefronts was a second Lesser

Whitefront. To make certain, we went back and found our original bird still almost in the position in which we had left it. Here, then, undoubtedly were two Lesser Whitefronts; if Will Tinsley's war-time bird was to be accepted, as I felt sure it should be, these were the third and fourth specimens of their kind ever to be officially recorded in Britain.

In the following year we saw three Lesser Whitefronts, and in most of the succeeding years in this Severn flock there have been at least one, sometimes as many as six of them, appearing as strays among the Russian White-fronted Geese.

On that day in December 1945 the third and fourth Lesser Whitefronts had brought the total number of kinds of wild geese we had seen together on that marsh to seven, and as we walked back from the pillbox I came to the conclusion that this was the place in which anyone who loved wild geese must live. Here were two empty cottages which might become the headquarters of the research organisation which had been taking shape in my mind over the war years, the headquarters of a new collection of waterfowl, of the scientific and educational effort which I believed was so badly needed for the conservation of wild fowl. As we squelched up the track, past the 100-year-old duck decoy, into the yard and back along the muddy lane towards the canal, I looked at my surroundings with a new eye, an eye to the future, for this was the beginning of the Wildfowl Trust.

30. THE WILDFOWL TRUST IS FORMED

IN 1945 there were four other possible areas in which my new collection and research station might have been started. One of them was an old familiar place—Brogden—on the north side of the Kent Estuary in Westmorland, scene of our earlier wildfowling adventures. But during the War its grass fields had come under cultivation and the geese had largely given up going there. Another possible place was an old Keep overlooking a marshy valley in Wigtownshire. Two others had the advantage of being nearer to London: Amberley Wildbrooks in Sussex and the High Halstow marshes in Kent, where there was a fine old red brick farmhouse called Swig's Hole, an ancient and derelict decoy and a flock of several hundred White-fronted Geese. At Slimbridge the geese were in thousands, rather than hundreds, and the decoy was less derelict, though the house was no more than a cottage: and besides, Slimbridge had its Lesser Whitefronts.

The last bridge over the Severn is the now damaged and disused railway viaduct at Sharpness where the river narrows. Immediately above this the estuary is much wider, with an expanse of water at high tide which is three miles long and a mile wide. Farther upstream the river gets gradually narrower round a series of great bends. At low water many hundreds of acres of sand are exposed—an ideal roosting place for wild geese and ducks. Over this part of the river the tidal range is more than thirty feet and the spring tides produce a wave over the sand which builds up as the river narrows, into the famous Severn Bore—a breaking wave five or six feet high which sweeps up the river at about twelve miles an hour.

Between Gloucester and Sharpness the tides make the river virtually unnavigable, and for more than 100 years sea-going ships have reached the deeper water above Gloucester by way of the Gloucester and Berkeley Canal. Near Slimbridge the canal runs through flat meadows which have been progressively reclaimed from the Severn tide over four centuries. The pushing out of successive sea-walls to strengthen the natural silting of the river mouth and make it permanent has created an area of 1,000 acres known as the New Grounds.

The main feeding grounds of the geese lie between the canal and the tidal shore. Early in the winter the birds feed largely on the 200 acres of grassy salt-marsh known as the Dumbles, which lie outside the sea-wall; and it was here from one of the four pillboxes built during the Second World War that we saw the first Lesser Whitefront. Later in the season the Dumbles become almost bare of grass, and the geese move into the fields inside the bank.

The first, and perhaps most important advantage of this area over almost all other wild goose resorts in Britain was the Manorial Right of the Berkeley family over the foreshore to the centre of the river channel at low water.

On this right the continued existence of this large flock of Whitefronts mainly depended (and still depends). The geese were preserved for shooting, but the numbers of geese shot and the amount of disturbance caused by the shooting were very small. The Berkeley Goose Shoot had been conducted in a reasonable and moderate manner ever since guns were invented; the geese owed their long and continuing sanctuary to this sporting interest.

The second advantage of this area for the purposes of studying wild geese was the sea-wall itself—the high bank which keeps the spring tides out of the low-lying fields and runs along the back of the Dumbles. Watchers can move freely behind it without disturbing the geese, and by happy chance it lies to the south of the birds so that the sunlight illuminates them throughout the day, without ever shining in the eyes of the watcher.

In most places the second-hand value of a war-time pillbox is strictly limited, but the four on the sea-wall, built when Hitler's invasion seemed inevitable could be well enough adapted to their new purpose. It was possible to enter them from behind, unseen by the birds on the Dumbles, and the view could be improved quite simply by opening out the embrasures. We also needed a number of new observation posts to be spaced between the pillboxes, so that wherever the geese might be feeding on the marsh we could safely peep over the bank opposite them without being seen. In this way it seemed that the wonder of watching the wildest of wild birds at really close range could be enjoyed by many people who might never otherwise have had the chance.

The first of the new huts was built by German prisoners during the summer of 1946. They were of wood, thatched with straw, and were fitted with hinged shutters, so that if the geese were close they could be watched through a narrow slit, which could be opened wider if they were farther away. They were also fitted with benches to sit on, with an arm-rest for steadying binoculars and even a foot-rest. It was my theory that intensive observation and study would be much better carried out if the observer was reasonably comfortable. One of the most important features of these hides was the covered approach to them from behind the sea-wall, but although they were frequently copied elsewhere during the next few years, they were always so sited that they could only be entered by first driving the birds from the area after which the observer hoped they would return. The whole secret of the observation huts at Slimbridge is that they can be entered by a party of twenty or thirty people when the geese are within ten yards on the other side, and provided that no one sneezes or coughs loudly the party can watch them and leave the hide again without the birds knowing anything about it.

On Sunday, 10th November, 1946, a meeting was held at

the Patch Bridge Guest House, Slimbridge, and it was agreed that a Society be formed with the name of 'The Severn Wildfowl Trust'.

So the new organisation which I had been planning for so long was officially formed, for the scientific study and conservation of wildfowl.

I had more or less given up shooting. My personal doubts had increased and been finally crystallised by a particular incident. During a goose-shoot the six or seven 'guns' were standing in a cluster when a single goose flew over. Each man (and I was one) raised his gun and fired two barrels. Twelve shots went off at the goose, which staggered in the air, flew on and then began to lose height. It came down far out on the mud flats in a place quite inaccessible because of the soft mud which in parts of that estuary amounts almost to quicksand. As it landed, I watched with my glasses, and saw that both legs were broken. It crashlanded, come to rest quivering on its belly and put its head up. There was nothing that any of us could do. It was 500 yards away and out of reach. We went later to the hotel for lunch, and in the afternoon we went shooting again, and as we passed the sea-wall I saw with binoculars that the bird still sat out on the mud, its neck still raised. At dusk we went back to tea. On the following day I came out again to watch the geese. The shooting was over and many of the geese were feeding in the fields as if nothing had happened. But out on the mud, in exactly the same place sat the goose with the broken legs. 'What right,' I said to myself, 'have we men to do this to a bird for our fun—to impose that kind of suffering? I should not want this for a sworn enemy and that goose was not my enemy when I shot at him—although I was his.'

'That kind of suffering,' I had said—but what kind of suffering was it, for without being a bird how could one know what pain they felt? It has been held that pain in birds is something quite different from, and much less than, pain in humans. But in spite of all this the goose with the broken legs was upsetting.

236

I thought, too, that in the past I had derived enormous pleasure, good health and interest from being out on the marshes at dawn and dusk. The birds with their beauty and wildness had been an endless source of delight. The difficulty of outwitting them, the discomforts and occasional dangers—these, and not the killing made the sport of wildfowling one of the most exciting in the world. I was not interested in killing the birds. I would have given anything for a handy portable device which for the same output of knowledge, skill and manual dexterity would bring a bird to hand alive and unharmed. It seemed likely that, had I never been interested in wildfowling, my enjoyment and my knowledge of the birds would have been less. Perhaps so long as a man is deriving so much good as to offset the bad, the balance might still fall in favour of the wildfowler. If I were advising a young boy I would say to him: 'Of course you will enjoy wildfowling; it will bring you unequalled thrills, and if you never experience those thrills you will probably never enjoy the birds themselves to quite the same extent, for you will not learn the subtle Goose/Rook, Wigeon/Starling distinction, the subtle difference between man's attitude to his traditional quarry and his attitude to all other birds.'

I am doubtful whether this argument that I might offer is sound, but I am quite sure that as soon as the doubts and the disquiet prevent one from enjoying shooting there can no longer be any reason for going on doing it oneself. So I have sold my guns, and I no longer shoot.

Besides the wild geese there was, of course, the decoy, which lay in the little wood close beside the headquarters cottages. Berkeley New Decoy was its full title, but it had not been effectively worked for about thirty years, although it had been repaired with the intention of working it in 1937. There was stout string netting still on the pipes which needed only a small amount of patching. Only two of the four pipes were usable, the other two having at some time or other been filled with mud from the pond and blanked off. When we got it going again, the first season's catch was only six ducks, but although they were so few and only Mallards, they were, to us, six very important birds—our first. They were duly ringed and released.

We fed the decoy to attract the ducks and I remember watching an evening flight in that first season and counting twenty-nine Mallards as they splashed down with a ring of bright water on the twilit pool. Since then we have counted well over 1,000 birds coming in to the half-acre of open water, but in those days twenty-nine seemed a lot.

It gave me great pleasure to have a duck decoy to develop which could be compared with Borough Fen Decoy where I had learned the decoyman's art. How we built up the lead and the catches from year to year is shown by this table:

Total ducks caught

1946/7	.	.	.	.	6
1947/8	.	.	.	.	133
1948/9	.	.	.	.	269
1949/50	.	.	.	.	609
1950/1	.	.	.	.	1,203

Since then a record catch of 2,237 was made in the winter of 1957/8.

Around the new headquarters—the three cottages at the end of the lane—were some marshy fields, where we began to dig out ponds and to build fences to enclose a new collection of live waterfowl.

The collection was to be started from a nucleus of birds brought together by Gavin Maxwell, a friend from lighthouse days, at his home in Wigtownshire. To look after these birds I had engaged John Yealland (later Curator of Birds at the London Zoo), whom I met near Brussels in 1938 when he was curator of an excellent waterfowl collection there.

John Yealland and I went up to collect and bring back about fifty geese from Gavin's home at Monreith. It would be touch and go whether the new pen would be completed in time for the arrival of these birds. We brought them down hopefully, only to find at the last minute that it was not.

The birds were in crates and could not remain in them over-night. The only place in which they could be released was in the rooms of the empty bungalow beside the Decoy. The quarrelsome Upland Geese had the larder to themselves, the Snow Geese were in one bedroom, the little Ross's Geese in another; the Emperors had the kitchen. They emerged from their boxes in the dim light of torches, and we watered and fed them. By noon on the following day the pen was completed and the birds were herded out of the house, through the yard and down the lane to the gate of their new home. To this nucleus of a collection were added a few pairs of birds which had been at the lighthouse before the war; the Lesser White-fronts which had spent the war at Will Tinsley's farm, a pair of Red-breasted Geese which had been kept for me by Rick Pilcher, a surgeon in Boston; and there was a Spur-winged Goose which was said to be thirty years old. These were all under the care of John Yealland, and later his two assistants, Eunice Overend and Tommy Johnstone. So once more I found myself occupied with the delights and disappointments of a collection of waterfowl. Some of the magic of my old light-house had been recaptured. I was keeping birds again.

But at that time the wild geese were to me the most marvel-lous aspect of the Wildfowl Trust, and the observation huts worked better than I had ever dreamed they could. In the win-ter of 1946 my mother came down to see the geese, and pro-nounced herself enthralled by them. Early the next year she fell ill of leukemia and died on July 24th. She was full of courage, and gay and cheerful to the end. Wayland and I motored with my stepfather to Sandwich and spread her ashes along the beach she had known and loved.

31. AN IMPORTANT DECISION

My marriage had gone wrong and Jane left the London house, happily without lasting bitterness. All my thoughts and energies went towards the development of the Severn Wildfowl Trust. It was necessary to have a small secretariat to look after my activities, and an organiser to manage the secretariat. Such an organiser was Elizabeth Adams, who ran this for me for eight months before leaving to marry my brother Wayland. The last thing she did before she left was to make arrangements for her successor. Thus it was that I came to interview a shy, quiet girl called Philippa Talbot-Ponsonby who sat before me looking small and neat and serious. She got the job, and thus I made the most important personal decision of my life. For this decision led to my second marriage, and many years of great happiness.

Having almost been taught to fly at the end of the War, I decided that the job should be completed. Philippa and I both trained at the same time at Kidlington near Oxford. I found flying a Tiger Moth again immensely stimulating and at the same time 're-creating'. With goggles and helmet in the windswept open cockpit, my noisy and rather smelly flying machine took me into a new world of three dimensional freedom. There was manual dexterity to be mastered and scenic railway sensations in the aerobatics, and below, the living map of familiar

241

England. It was a first step towards the much greater enjoyment when I later took up gliding.

On occasions I was commissioned by the B.B.C. to do commentaries. The first had been the Victory Procession, during which I became lost for words when called upon to describe the curious pagoda-like structure that had been set up in the middle of Parliament Square. Later I was one of the commentators at the wedding of Princess Elizabeth and the Duke of Edinburgh.

I was drawing and painting hard, too. In 1947 I was granted permission to make portrait drawings of Princess Elizabeth and Princess Margaret, which I did straight on to plastic as lithographs. I was alarmed that the drawings would not justify the time given by the sitters, so much so that it became an obsession with me. But the Queen seemed pleased, and the Princesses were patient and charming. These were my first meetings with Queen Elizabeth II, who was later to become Patron of the Wildfowl Trust and a regular visitor to Slimbridge.

Before the War I had been on the brink of branching out into new fields in painting. After the War, all I wanted to do was to go back to the old life and try and recapture it. I wanted to paint birds exactly as I had done before, as a manifestation of my safe return. Sailing reflected this return, too. Although John Winter and I felt we should now be outclassed by the younger generation we had entered for the Prince of Wales's cup in 1946. To our delighted surprise we won comfortably by about three minutes.

I had joined the Council of the Yacht Racing Association, and found myself Chairman of their Olympic Committee with the job of organising the yachting events in Tor Bay for the Olympic games.

It was at this time, too, that I concluded a piece of scientific research that had begun before the War. It was a part of my great interest in and reverence for the processes of evolution. Before the War David Haig Thomas had returned from West Greenland with a pair of White-fronted Geese. When I saw

242

them I was immediately struck by the fact that their plumage seemed very dark and that their bills seemed to be yellow instead of the usual milky pink. This could have been due to the conditions under which they travelled, but it crossed my mind then that Whitefronts from Greenland might always be of this kind.

Two years later, in 1937, David went to Greenland again, and I had some of these birds sent back to me. They were identical with the two I had seen before. Next we had to find out where they spent the winter. I remembered that Sir Ralph Payne Gallwey, in his famous book *Letters to Young Shooters*, published in 1896, had described Whitefronts as having yellow bills. I had always thought this to be a mistake, for all the Whitefronts that I had seen up till then had had pink bills. But then it occurred to me that Sir Ralph was not only a very careful observer, but that he had done most of his wildfowling in Ireland. This seemed to call for a visit to Ireland, and so in January 1939 John Winter and I had set out for Londonderry. The expedition was a success; we shot three Whitefronts and brought one back with us alive. All four had yellow bills. By now, too, there were a number of recoveries in Ireland of geese ringed in Greenland.

And so, on 17th March, 1948, Christopher Dalgety (my old wildfowling colleague of university days) and I presented a paper to the British Ornithologists Club describing the type specimen of a new sub-species to be formally designated the Greenland White-fronted Goose, *Anser albifrons flavirostris*, Dalgety and Scott.

In this way, slowly and sometimes ponderously, small details are added to the sum of human knowledge.

In October 1948 I paid my first visit to the Delta Waterfowl Research Station near Winnipeg in Canada. If the Wildfowl Trust has an opposite number anywhere in the world, it is at Delta, at the southern end of Lake Manitoba.

The Lake shore is a narrow tree-grown sand-bar which divides the open water from a vast wilderness of marsh three or four miles wide and forty miles long. This is the summer home and breeding ground of great numbers of ducks—a sea of reeds and bulrushes with pools and bays and channels, bounded by the wheatfields to the south. Al Hochbaum, the Director of the Station, is a big, gentle, friendly man and I have only a very few times been so certain I should like a man at the moment I first saw him. We had many things in common, for we had both reached our scientific interest in wildfowl from the sport of wildfowling and Al enjoyed drawing and painting them as much as I did. Already when I first met him his famous book, *The Canvasback on a Prairie Marsh*, with his own illustrations had been published.

The research station was the last group of houses at the eastern end of the village of Delta, a village standing on the sand-bar between the lake and the marsh. In front of it was an artificial two-acre pond excavated by bulldozer and beyond it the reed beds stretching away into the distance. Living on the pond were about sixty Canada Geese, a Whistling Swan and a Richardson's Goose, and beside the pond was a large aviary made of telegraph poles with wire stretched between and wire-netting over the top. In this was another little pool and about thirty more Canadas, which were being kept full-winged and would be released the next spring. Also on the pond were some Canvasbacks and a few Pintails, Shovelers and Gadwall, which had been reared by hand for subsequent release. All these birds attracted a good many wild ones and there were about seventy or eighty on the main pond on the morning I arrived, most of them Greenwinged Teal. Al told me that a few weeks earlier 700 or 800 wild birds were to be seen daily on the pools and that he had caught and ringed about 700 in lobster-pot type traps each about the size of a motor-car.

Al was very keen to build a decoy pipe on to this pond so that he could catch at his convenience; he recognised that the great advantage of a pipe over a trap is that if untended for a few days its efficiency improves, whereas it is essential to visit traps daily without fail. I was equally anxious that he should build the first American duck decoy and drew out for him the design of a pipe. Later I pegged out the exact positions on the ground where it was to be built. In the following year I watched ducks being caught in it, and it has been operated successfully ever since.

I found that the research station consisted of a range of indoor pens, large rooms where the ducklings were reared, an incubator house where 900 eggs could be hatched and a large laboratory where the birds were examined, weighed, measured, studied, skinned and so on. In summer there were between twenty and thirty students always working there from universities, game departments and other organisations. The main researches were in game management using ducks as game birds, and the finances were largely derived from the Wildlife Management Institute, a body financed by the firearms and ammunition industry.

If this kind of fascinating work was being done in North America, why not in Europe, and who better to do it, I thought, than the Severn Wildfowl Trust? It was at Delta that I first heard about the X-ray examination of ducks and geese to discover how many of them carried lead pellets in their bodies, either from eating them or from being wounded. The proportion of wounded birds seemed surprisingly high. I decided that similar samples of European ducks and geese should be examined. I saw the tail and wing feathers of individual ducks being painted for field identification, and heard how dyes were injected into the eggs just before hatching so that the ducklings came out a bright colour and were thereafter identifiable.

From the Delta station I went on to see the vast concentrations of ducks and geese on the famous Bear River Marshes in Utah and on again to see even larger flocks in the Sacramento Valley in California where I had been in 1938. Here I saw in its winter quarters that neatest and most elegant of the snow geese—Ross's Goose. I spent two days watching them feeding in the stubble fields and returning at night to the refuge at Willows.

The next thing was to follow them to their almost unexplored Arctic breeding grounds in the middle of the north shore of the Canadian mainland.

Thus one day at the end of May 1949, with two American companions, Paul Quenean and Harold Hanson, I was on my way to spend the summer in the Perry River region of the North-West territories.

This was my first experience of exploration. Up till now my father's Polar travels had inhibited me, but this seemed absurd when my knowledge of a rare goose could only be completed by spending a summer in the Arctic. It was a summer of unusually bad weather and we were often confined to camp. But in spite of the late snowstorms the expedition was entirely successful. We found and studied the colonies of Ross's Geese, we explored and named new lakes and rivers, and made friends with the Kogmuit Eskimos—a cheerful, friendly tribe. We mapped, listened to the ticking of our Geiger counter (which was never quite fast enough), collected specimens of mammals and birds and rocks, took films and stills, rechecked the position of the Perry River from sun sights and found it was in the District of Keewatin and not in the District of Mackenzie as shown on the map, counted the brood sizes of six kinds of geese and, finally in August brought back ten live Ross's and two Whitefronts in the Fairchild Husky float-plane which had flown in to collect us.

The following winter I was commanded to show the film I had made to the Royal Family at Sandringham. It was a week-end invitation and on the Saturday I was to shoot pheasants. Michael Adeane, an old Cambridge friend, who was then Assistant Private Secretary to King George VI lent me his guns, and fortunately, though I did not shoot especially well, I did not disgrace myself. In the afternoon we were joined by the ladies, who stood beside a different gun at each drive. The Queen stood by me at one and Princess Margaret at another. Once the Princess urged me to shoot at a Woodcock which was heading for my neighbour, but as my neighbour was the King I refrained from poaching his bird! Surprisingly, the Woodcock sailed over unhit by the King's four barrels.

During this visit to Sandringham I outlined to the King a proposal which had been in the back of my mind for some time for the establishment of a new Yacht Racing Trophy. For a good many years there had been no challenge for the America's Cup, and it seemed then that with the disappearance of the big J-class yachts the famous jug would pass into history and never be raced for again. My idea was that the old J-class *Britannia*, which had been sunk at sea at the end of her long racing career, should be commemorated by a Britannia's Cup. For some reason the King did not like the idea of linking the cup to the old and famous sloop. He was, however, prepared to present a Britannia Cup, and soon after he wrote in his own hand as follows:

Buckingham Palace,
26th March, 1950.

'Dear Scott,

'Many thanks for your letter giving me the particulars of the 1851 Cup presented by Queen Victoria. I will now discuss the matter with Sir Ralph Gore who happens to be both the President of the Yacht Racing Association and the Commodore of the Royal Yacht Squadron. I am very glad you mentioned this matter to me privately as it makes all further conversation so much easier. I was so sorry that my daughter's visit to you was spoiled by a too ardent well-wisher!

I am,

Yours very sincerely,
George R.'

The last sentence referred to the first time that Princess Elizabeth came to the Wildfowl Trust, when the papers had run the headline 'Mystery Woman in Blue Spoils Royal Visit'. It was early in March and the wild geese, 2,000 strong, were feeding that morning in the Tack Piece immediately opposite to the Rushy Pen. They could not have been better placed in front of the observation huts, but by ill-luck a young girl who wanted to catch a closer glimpse of the Princess decided to come in by way of the sea-wall and the fields. In doing so, of course, she put the geese out of the Tack Piece and far out on to the mud banks about ten minutes before the arrival of the Royal Party. The poor girl wrote afterwards saying, 'Please I am not a Mystery Woman in Blue; I am a sixteen-year-old girl and I am very sorry to have upset the geese and the Princess.'

32. ROCKET NETTING

In the course of our studies at the Wildfowl Trust (the word Severn had been dropped from our title because of the world-wide nature of our research) it became necessary to ring massive numbers of wild geese. We were studying the Pink-footed Goose and a team headed for Scotland each year in October equipped with rocket nets. The invention and development of these nets followed on from my efforts with springs many years earlier. But whereas the original object had been to catch a few geese for the collection at the lighthouse, the new object was to catch them in bulk for ringing. If we could catch enough, not only should we find out more about their movements and migrations and about their expectation of life, but we might even be able to use a sampling method to measure their populations.

We decided to try pulling out a net with the Schermuly Pistol Rocket Apparatus, as used for saving life at sea, and in the summer of 1947 I went to the proofing ground of Messrs Schermuly Brothers, of the S.P.R.A. works at Newdigate, Sussex.

It was not until the following February that we had the first chance to try out the complete equipment on the White-fronted Geese at the New Grounds. Mr A. J. Schermuly came down especially for the attempt, and so did Keith Shackleton, and a photographer from *Country Life*. There were only about 1,300 geese on the estuary at the time, and on the afternoon before the attempt we made a reconnaissance of the feeding grounds.

The geese were no longer to be found in the three small fields into which they had flown at dawn, but we came upon them at last much farther away round the edges of a 100-acre field at the Frampton end of the New Grounds. Here, however, the wheat in the centre of the field had been grazed almost bare, and the geese had congregated in a thick swathe along two edges of the field. One of these edges was formed by a barbed-wire fence, and the other by a shallow creek or 'flash', no more than a few yards wide. Along the top of the slope leading up from the flash the geese were sitting most thickly; indeed, we could not remember having seen Whitefronts more tightly packed.

We flushed them gently from the field, and walked over to examine the area and select the most suitable spot on which to set the net in the darkness before tomorrow's dawn. In view of the north wind, we thought that it should lie along the drills of the wheat at the edge of the field where the shoots were longer because the geese had not grazed there so much. We then explored the nearest available cover, which was an old disused sea-wall some 100 yards away across the flash. All this decided, we returned in the dusk, feeling that our chances were reasonably good if only the geese would come again to the area in which we had last seen them. That night great preparations were made. We rose at four next morning and set off in two parties, one by car with the heavy gear, the other to walk the mile and a half, planting 'scare geese' in the small fields on the way (to prevent the geese from landing there), and soon after five-fifteen a.m. we met on the old sea-wall and went out together, all seven of us, across the flash at its lowest crossable point, and down the edge of the wheat to the corner of the fence. There we laid out all the equipment we had brought in a small heap so that nothing should be overlooked and be left to frighten the geese when daylight came.

The patch we had chosen for the net was about ten yards from the fence, and, like the rest of the field, it was covered with small lumps of clay which were frozen solid. We found, as we laid out the thirty-yard length of net, that the meshes caught frequently on these lumps and were held firm. The chances that it would fly out freely, however neatly we folded it, seemed very small. But we could not do more than lay it carefully and hope for the best.

As soon as the net had been furled the party divided and some went off to fetch the portable hide which had been left beside the car. Three of us stayed behind to set out the rockets and lay the firing wires. It was getting late. Already the eastern sky was bright and we knew that we had a bare twenty minutes before the arrival of the geese. We stretched out the wire, slid the rockets into their pistols and attached the head string of the net.

Twenty yards ahead of the net, five yards less than the net should, in theory, be able to throw (for its overall dimensions were thirty by twenty-five yards), I made two tiny cairns of lumps of frozen clay, one opposite each end of the net. These were to be the markers, to show when the geese were within the 'catching area'.

When we got back to the old sea-wall we found that the rest of the party had just finished erecting the portable hide. The flex, however, had not been laid the full distance and the roll of it still lay twenty yards away along the barbed-wire fence. At this critical stage a large skein of geese came up to the field and it looked as if they would settle. But by great good luck they swept back to circle over the small fields, and while they did it I rushed down and collected the coil of flex, spreading it as I returned. It reached the portable hide with exactly two feet to spare and was laid under one corner to the battery. We went to collect grass with which to decorate the hide, and the party was split up when the geese returned. Five of us flopped down into the three-sided square of wire-netting and barrage balloon fabric, while the other two hid themselves in the ditch about fifty yards away.

About 300 geese came straight for the 100-acre and settled in the middle of the bare part of the wheat field. This was excellent, we thought, for they were directly down wind of our net and seemed likely in a few hours to feed up to it. Meanwhile more geese came slipping in over the belt of trees in the background—skein after skein in an almost unbroken stream. They came with great confidence, flying low and setting their wings as soon as they reached the edge of the field. By the time that the sun rose, oval and orange-red behind us, there were over 1,000 geese feeding in a tight pack in front. Then came a startling development. A family party of geese rose from the great crowd and flew towards the corner of the field—our corner. They settled about forty yards in front of the net. They were followed by others, until a regular flight began. Bunch after bunch swept in and pitched in the ever-thickening crowd in front of our net. So far everything had gone unbelievably right. For the next hour we lay breathlessly in the hide as the geese advanced into the 'catching area'. They were ten yards from the little clay cairns—five yards, two yards, passing between them, and then the cairns were swallowed up in the milling crowd of geese which advanced still closer to the net. Was all in readiness? The battery, the leads—the leads, where were they? They were nowhere to be seen. Two feet of the end of the flex had been pulled under the edge of the hide in that hurried last minute, but it was not there now. We peered out through the observation slit in the front of the hide. The black shiny insulated wire led towards us, but just outside the hide it turned off at right angles. While we had been camouflaging the hide someone must have kicked away the end of the lead; it was outside the hide, on the same side of it as the geese. What were we to do? Slowly and dexterously we lifted a corner of the hide and reached out towards the lead. My fingers closed over grass stems, over a bramble, but not over the missing flex. One of my companions squinted down through the observation slit. 'Another four inches and you'll reach it.' At last I felt the flex and pulled it into the hide. The crisis was over, and the geese were another five yards closer to the net.

The slit in the hide was at a very awkward height, so that one could only use glasses through it by supporting oneself on the other arm, and then only for short periods. During one of these quick looks, however, I noticed a Pinkfoot, no doubt one of the three young birds which we had observed scattered among the Whitefronts all through the winter. As usual he was at the edge of the flock and in the forefront of those which crowded in towards the net.

Now was the critical time. At what distance would the geese first see and keep away from the net? Would they turn about and walk quickly away from it once they had detected its presence? We watched anxiously. A feature of the advance of a flock of wild geese when feeding is that from time to time the more powerful and influential geese drive others away from them; and so the leading edge of the flock keeps bulging where a bird or a family has run a few paces forward at the close approach of a quarrelsome gander. At length there came a time when the fugitive birds would no longer run forward. If pursued they turned and threaded their way back through the flock. They would not come nearer to the net than about four yards from it. The crowd in the 'catching area' could not get any thicker. It had reached saturation point. It was now or never. Mr Harris got ready with his camera and Mr Scher-muly with the ends of his flex.

'All right, let her go!' The circuit was made and the rockets fired; simultaneously the whole flock of 1,300 geese rose into the air with the combined roar of wings and of voices. We all jumped up to watch. As the cloud rose we could see that a small patch of flapping geese remained on the wheatfield. We had made a catch. We set off to run towards the net, and I think the geese were more alarmed by the sudden appearance of seven people careering across the field in scattered forma-tion than they were by the discharge of the rockets themselves, and on any future occasion we have planned to remain hidden until the uncaught birds are well clear.

As I came to the net I made a quick count, thirty-two geese. We had succeeded. We had made the first substantial catch of geese alive for ringing. It was a satisfying moment. Then be-gan the laborious task of extricating the birds from the net.

Almost before we had started one bird, however, extricated itself and flew off. But we lost no more. Among those remaining was the Pinkfoot which we had seen advancing into the 'catching area'. He was ringed and released. Some of the birds were released one by one, but sometimes they were released in couples, which we thought to be the better way, as the two then flew off together. Fairly soon it became apparent that many of them could not be extricated from the net without cutting some of the meshes. It was astonishing to what extent the birds had become ravelled up in so short a time. It was astonishing, too, how docile and resigned the geese seemed to be, and how little they struggled while being extricated. One old gander was full of spirit and continuously pecked my knee while I was disentangling his neighbour and finally himself. We ringed several young birds including a family of five with their parents.

We had pulled the net at eight-forty a.m. and it was half past nine by the time we had finished.

As we walked back to the hide some of the geese were returning to the fields, and a large skein circled low over the 100-acre. They did not settle, but, on the other hand, it was evident that they had not been disastrously frightened by the discharge of the rockets.

We returned home greatly elated with our success which, in spite of the net's bad throw, was much greater than any of us had really been expecting.

The next catch at the New Grounds in February 1950, using two nets, yielded seventy-one Whitefronts. Big numbers seemed to be on, so in March we took the nets to Scotland and tried them on Pinkfeet and Greylags, and although our hopes were often high, twenty-five Greylags was our best catch.

But I realised more than ever that rocket netting was a thrilling pastime. We might have invented a useful technique for the scientific study of birds, but we had also invented a first-class sport, and we did not have to kill the geese to show we had outwitted them; we had to do something much more difficult—to catch them unharmed.

Since those days the equipment and the techniques have greatly changed. The record catch is 490 Pinkfeet, and a month of netting may yield a catch of over 3,000. We are more sure of our success than we were in those early days; and yet it is still possible to sit fruitlessly over a net from dawn till dusk for three days running and have to retire empty-handed at the end of it.

For the Pinkfeet and Greylags and Barnacles that we have been studying by this means, we set out two nets facing each other in the middle of the chosen field. The nets are sixty yards long and furled on a great drum from which they are unwound into position. When spread the nets stretch out twenty yards, and as they are to be thrown towards each other they are laid forty yards apart. Spaced along each net, and half buried in the ground at an angle of about forty-five degrees are six rockets loaded with cordite, and wires which will fire all twelve rockets simultaneously are led away to a camouflaged trailer 'hide', parked inconspicuously beside the hedge. The nets and rockets are hidden by straw in the stubble fields in which we usually set for Pinkfeet. The space sixty by forty yards between the nets is the catching area and in this not only must the geese be persuaded to land, but to concentrate.

The nets are most often set the night before. Often the first geese come to the field before it is light enough for them to see the stuffed decoys. Geese have surprisingly poor eyesight in twilight. They probably settle elsewhere in the field and must then be driven away, otherwise the later arrivals will go to them in preference to the stuffed ones. But in due course, if all has been done well, the first party of live geese settles with the decoys (which are stuffed in a sleeping position so that the lack of movement does not raise suspicion). We call these first geese 'live decoys' and if they are well placed we have then only to wait while the skeins come streaming from the roosting place and pour down into the catching area.

The suspense is almost unbearable as the last birds flap down and fold their wings. A pause till all are feeding, a ten-second count down and . . . 'Sheeee . . .', the nets are out and over the

255

geese. There is a moment of surprised silence as the great birds leap into the air, followed by the clamour of the un-caught part of the flock. More than 1,000 geese may be circling round uncaught. Many begin to land again, some of them on top of the net. After the second circle the bulk of the flock heads off to settle three fields away. A few small parties are still circling low and trying to settle again with the birds under the net.

The Land-Rover with the ringing and weighing equipment and the 'keeping-cages' drives down on to the field and the long scientific job begins.

First the keeping-cages have to be set up at one end of the nets—small rolls of hessian which when stretched on stakes form a row of small compartments each to contain a single goose sitting on the ground and covered by four walls and a roof of stretched hessian. Each cage has twenty-five such com-partments and for a good catch of say 300 plus, thirteen cages will be needed, so that the whole flock can be held and released simultaneously. This is important because geese are family birds, parents and young normally remaining together during the winter. Were they to be released one at a time, the families would be broken up. Not only would this be bad for the geese but it would make the caught birds abnormal and spoil the experiment.

It takes nearly three hours to clear 300 geese from the two nets. When all the work has been done and all the geese are ringed, the keeping-cages are lifted off in quick succession so that the whole great flock flies off together. Then the nets must be cleaned of every stick of straw and refurled on their drums, the rockets must be recharged, the electric leads reeled in, and all must be repacked in the van, and trailer in readiness per-haps for a set the same evening, if a new field of adequate promise has been located. An essential feature of the popula-tion measurement study is that the samples must be taken from as many of the Pinkfoot's winter haunts as possible. This means that we seldom fire the nets more than two, or at the most three, times in the same locality each year.

Sometimes we have reset the net in the same field, and once we caught a bird in the second catch which had been ringed in exactly the same spot on the day before.

By the spring of 1951 we had marked no more than 600 Pink-footed Geese, using our nets mostly in Scotland, and although they were scarce on the Severn estuary, they were evidently going to be easier to study than our Whitefronts. They decoyed better and were therefore easier to catch with rocket nets; the bulk of the world population was in Scotland and England during the winter; and their breeding grounds in Iceland and Greenland were a great deal more accessible than those of the Whitefronts in Arctic Russia.

Our expedition, it seemed, should be to Central Iceland to study the Pinkfeet in the summer and perhaps to find some of the 600 we had ringed. So on sure-footed Iceland ponies we rode with James Fisher, an old friend, Finnur Gudmundsson, head of the Museum in Reykjavik, Philippa Talbot-Ponsonby and I, with an Icelandic farmer, Valentinus Jonson, as guide; up the River Thjorsa to the Hofsjokul ice-cap and camped for the summer at the edge of a great breeding colony of Pink-footed Geese. It was during this expedition that Philippa and I were married.

Only in the last few days of this expedition did we learn the proper technique for herding the flightless geese into nets at the tops of the hills to which they habitually run. For most of the month of July when the goslings are still too young to fly the adult geese are also flightless, having moulted their wing feathers.

We decided that our new-found technique should be given a better trial and that we should make a second expedition. So in the summer of 1953 an expedition of five Englishmen and three Icelanders returned to the meadows of the Thjorsa below the Hofsjokul ice-cap. Whereas in 1951 we had caught and marked 1,100 Pink-footed Geese, now in this 1953 expedition we marked over 9,000. Two of the roundups enclosed more than 3,000 geese each.

It was a brilliantly simple technique which we now perfected. Several square miles of the marsh were surrounded by horsemen moving the geese very slowly and gently towards a prearranged hillock. Once the mass had assembled on the summit they were held there while a horseshoe of small-mesh nylon netting was set up on stakes near by, forming a corral into which they could gently be driven.

With the drives in Iceland and the rocket nets in Scotland and England, we have marked more than 25,000 Pinkfeet in ten years, during which it seems that the population breeding in Iceland and Greenland and wintering in Britain has fluctuated between about 40,000 and 70,000. One individual bird was caught four times—first in Iceland in 1951, then the following year in Scotland, then in Iceland again in 1953 and, finally, a second time in Scotland. Many more have been handled three times by our team. When you find a bird that was ringed as gosling it is agreeable to be able to say to it, 'I've known you since you were so high.' Our Pinkfoot study with the rocket nets and the round-ups in Iceland made a good subject for a lecture.

One day I was lunching with a television producer friend, Desmond Hawkins, who asked me to do my lecture with film at his son's school, so that he could think of it in terms of television.

Fortunately for me the schoolboys seemed to enjoy it and chortled away at my drawing of Finnur, the largest ornithologist in the world, on his little Icelandic pony. Thus began my version of the television lecture with film.

For my first few television pieces I used my own film, but it soon ran out. Either I had to give up TV or find new film. Desmond suggested that I might be chairman of a series, and introduce other people who had natural history film to show. The recipe was moderately successful and the new pattern appeared once a month, though it was still difficult to find enough good film.

In the summer of 1955 I attended the International Ornithological Congress at Basle, Switzerland, and there saw a startling film of woodpeckers taken by a brilliant young Ger-

258

man cinematographer called Heinz Sielmann. It had been taken inside the woodpeckers' nests by cutting into the back of the tree, setting up the hide behind it and finally accustoming the woodpeckers to sufficient light for photography. By any standards it was one of the most remarkable achievements of wild life photography ever screened. That evening Heinz agreed to bring his film to England and show it in my TV programme. His woodpeckers got a listener research appreciation figure that was second only to the Coronation.

'Our series,' said Desmond Hawkins soon after the woodpecker success, 'should have a title and a signature tune. Do you like *Look?*'

'Not very much; it's the title of an American magazine which is about quite different things.'

Desmond said, 'But it's a good title.'

'Well,' I said, 'if you say so. . . .' And so *Look* it became, and a signature tune was commissioned. At first it had been monthly, but now it became fortnightly, and later weekly for a series of six or seven.

For some years after the end of the War my main home and headquarters had been in London, and I had travelled each week-end by car to the New Grounds to watch the growth of the Wildfowl Trust. But it soon became apparent that this constant shuttle service between London and Gloucestershire should be reduced to a minimum, and that maintaining two homes was not only expensive but very inconvenient. Gradually my main centre of activity changed from London to the New Grounds, to the little eighteenth-century farm cottage which was to be my principal home for six years. It was in the old coach-house of this cottage that I installed a picture window and the room became part sitting-room and part studio.

In 1952 our daughter Dafila was born, and two years later our son, Richard Falcon. The two children were christened on board my father's old ship *Discovery* just as Nicola had been ten years before. In accordance with nautical tradition the ship's bell was the font.

With an increasing family our cottage was now bursting at

the seams. We had decided to build a new house next door to it, and overlooking the birds in the Rushy Pen.

The building of the new house was to be accompanied by the conversion of an L-shaped cow-byre behind the old cottage into a staff hostel and laboratory wing. Beyond it, and connected by a passage, was to be our private house, and beyond that again my studio.

There are few things more enjoyable than planning a new house and its surroundings. In this case the surroundings were of especial importance because the great picture window of the studio was dependent on the landscape design of the new duck-ponds to be excavated in front of it. Over my bed in our tiny attic room in the old cottage I had fitted a sheet of glass. Above it I could slide any drawings, maps or plans about which I wanted to think carefully. The plans of the new house were put up there and I was often late for breakfast as I lay in bed building in my mind the picture of our home on that seemingly far-off day when it would be finished.

My year-old daughter Dafila tapped down the foundation stone with the handle of the trowel, and at long last the house was finished. My son was born three months after we moved in. Were I to have the opportunity of building the same house again there is hardly anything that I would change. As a home for our family it still seems to me almost perfect.

33. THE RAREST GOOSE

My interest in the processes of evolution has produced in me a kind of reverence for every living species. Many people, I know, share this feeling. The prospect of the extinction of any existing species then appears as a potential disaster which man's conscience should urge him to prevent.

It was in the 1930s that I first became aware of the danger which threatened the Ne-ne or Hawaiian Goose, and in those days I wrote to Mr Herbert Shipman of Hilo in the big island of Hawaii, who, I had read, kept in his garden a small flock of live Ne-ne. In the wild state the bird seemed to be becoming rapidly rarer. Mr Shipman undertook to give me a pair of these geese on condition that I would go out to Hawaii to fetch them, and this I might well have done had it not been for the intervention of the Second World War.

After the War I learned from various sources that no more than thirty-two Ne-ne were known to exist and that the world population of the species was almost certainly less than fifty.

In the early days of the Wildfowl Trust, a letter was sent to the Government of the Territory of Hawaii asking what steps they were proposing to take to save this last remnant from extinction, but the interventions of a well-meaning society on the opposite side of the globe are unlikely to be well received by Government officials in any part of the world. Our letter remained unanswered. A little later I was in correspondence on some other subject with an American scientist, Dr Charles Schwartz, who mentioned that he had recently been invited to visit Hawaii in order to advise the Board of Agriculture on the management of its game birds. He added that he was very uncertain whether he would be taking the job. I wrote immediately imploring him to accept on the grounds that this was perhaps the only opportunity of saving the Hawaiian Goose. Whether my letter had any effect I do not know, but Dr Schwartz took the job and focused the attention of the Department on this tiny remnant population so successfully that a new project was planned for the breeding of Hawaiian Geese in captivity. In charge of this project was an ornithologist, Don Smith, who had studied for some time at the Delta Waterfowl Research Station. When he sought advice from Delta, Al Hochbaum in turn suggested that he might consult the Wildfowl Trust, and in this way we found ourselves invited to help with the Pohakuloa Propagation Project.

It was not until the following year that this help took the form of sending to Hawaii our then curator, John Yealland. John started out there our standard rearing programme by which each female can be persuaded to lay at least two clutches of eggs each year, thus greatly increasing the potential annual production. Before he returned after his breeding season in Hawaii John Yealland went to see Mr Shipman, who had provided the original four birds for the breeding project at Pohakuloa. Was the offer he had made to me before the war still open? Mr Shipman said that it was, and John returned to England with two beautiful Ne-nes.

This was in 1950 and in the following spring the two birds made nests and each began to lay eggs in them. Clearly there was something wrong somewhere. We sent an urgent cable to Hawaii for a gander, and meanwhile took away the infertile eggs, blew them, ate the contents in an omelette and preserved the shells. A week after the despatch of the cable a fine male Hawaiian Goose arrived at Slimbridge. He was called Kamehameha after the greatest King of Hawaii, and his two wives were called Kaiulani and Emma after a famous Princess and a famous Queen of the islands. In the following year both these two females nested and nine young were successfully reared. From that time onward the world stock has steadily increased until in 1966 there were believed to be over 500 Ne-ne in the world—better than ten times as many as fifteen years before—of the 220 reared at the Wildfowl Trust ninety-six had been sent to Hawaii to re-establish the species on the island of Mani.

But many other species are in desperate straits. The Ivory-billed Woodpecker has probably gone, and so too, I fear, has the Pink-headed Duck of India and perhaps the Golden-backed Hanging Parakeet of the Philippines, but the Japanese Crested Ibis with eleven individuals and the great Whooping Crane of North America with just fifty, the California Condor with about the same number, the large flightless ground parrot of New Zealand called the Ka-ka-po and the Eskimo Curlew with unknown but tiny populations, these and many other species are hanging on by the narrowest margins. Controversy rages on whether the last remaining individuals should be taken into captivity and reared artificially. This was successfully done with Père David's Deer and the European Bison, and when the prospect seems otherwise hopeless I have no hesitation in saying that it should be tried. Extinction is final. No technique to avert it should be overlooked.

Among the bird species less heavily threatened but still very rare is the Trumpeter Swan of North America. It is the largest of the world's swans and the 1,500 individuals which remain live in the Rocky Mountains and Alaska, except for a very few in captivity.

One day when the Queen, then Princess Elizabeth, was walking round the Wildfowl Trust she told us that she was shortly to make a Royal Tour of Canada and asked if there were any birds she might bring back for us. I murmured that we had for some time been trying to acquire some Trumpeter Swans. A couple of months later came a cable from Canada which said that three pairs of Trumpeter Swans had been presented to Her Royal Highness and asked whether the Trust would be willing to look after them for her. In due course five of the six swans were caught. The sixth pushed open the door of the trap and escaped. The five were sent to England, and Her Majesty came down to see them only a few weeks after her accession.

Wild-caught swans do not normally breed until they have been some years in captivity. After two years one of the female swans died. This left us with three cobs and a pen. We wrote to British Columbia reminding them that the sixth swan was still to come, and asking whether they could send two pens while they were about it. Not long after, two beautiful young females arrived, and in 1959 one of them nested, but she only laid two eggs and neither hatched. In 1960 she laid five eggs, of which two were fertile, but again neither hatched. We have often noticed that the first attempts of young birds to breed are unsuccessful, but that the chances of success improve with time. By 1965 we had successfully raised only four.

All the species of swans in the world are represented in the enclosures at Slimbridge, and many of them breed. One pair of Australian Black Swans regularly rears two broods each year. The cob was lent to us by Sir Winston Churchill 'until such time,' as he put it, 'as I may need him again'; he is a splendid bird and must have sired more than thirty cygnets since he has been at Slimbridge.

As President of the International Yacht Racing Union I had been invited to preside over the International Jury at the Olympic Games in Melbourne in 1956. This seemed to be the opportunity for filming a series of programmes on Australian wild life and we planned a round the world tour to include New Guinea, New Zealand, Fiji and Hawaii on the way home. With Philippa and me came Charles Lagus as cameraman.

On our way from New Guinea to New Zealand we spent three days at Cairns on the Queensland Coast, going out each day to swim with face mask and snorkel over the coral gardens of the Great Barrier Reef. For part of these three days I was in a new world. Nothing I had ever done in Natural History stirred me quite so sharply as my first experience of skin-diving on a coral reef. The dramatic threshold which is crossed as soon as one put one's mask below the surface is, to a natural-ist, nothing less than miraculous. Much has been written already about the scarcely explored new 'continent' of the ocean. I had read these descriptions in books and yet I was unprepared for the visionary revelation when I first saw the real thing.

My diary is full of drawings of fish—the common fishes of the coral reef. I drew the marvellous yellow-and-black striped and barred Butterfly Fish of the genus Chaetodon. I drew the black-and-white Damsel Fish, the superb Anemone Fish which are golden-red and pale-blue bands, and the ridiculous Razor Fish which swim perpetually standing on their heads. But to begin with I did not know their names.

The first two dives I made were in rather murky water at a place called Double Island near the mainland shore. There was a great profusion and variety of fishes, but it was on the second dive in the afternoon that I came upon a shoal of about twenty round fish like vertical dinner-plates, about eight or ten inches across, which stayed in a cluster just above the rocks. They were brown and marbled and it was this shoal that sud-denly showed me the immense possibilities of all these fish in terms of comparative ethology—the comparative study of animal behaviour.

Next day we were taken to Michaelmas Cay, a small islet thirty miles from the mainland where the water is crystal clear. I noticed at once that most of the fish were different from those at Double Island. There were two kinds of bright-blue Damsel Fishes, one about four inches long in which the male has an orange and yellow tail and the female is all blue. They live in pairs and their blue was of such brilliance that it appeared iridescent like a butterfly's wing. The other kind lived in shoals and were smaller with no orange tail and of a slightly different shape. The blue was paler though no less brilliant.

The following day, Christmas Day, found us at Green Island, also out on the Barrier, about thirty miles from Cairns, and here there is an underwater observatory—a large tank sunk in twenty feet of water, accessible by stairway from a pier above and fitted with port-holes through which the fishes can be seen and photographed. This observatory, from which I distinguished no less than fifty-two different fish species swimming freely in the sea outside, provided the appendix to our new discovery. Once again most of the fishes were new, and one of the most colourful and amusing looked rather like a pig with prominent blue stripes between its eyes and across the tip of its snout, with a sharp radial pattern of black and white and yellow on its sides (identified long after as *Rhinacanthus aouleatus*, the Pig-snout Trigger Fish). They ran up to ten inches long and were quite charming in their manner. Once again the loveliest sight was the shoals of blue fish—a soft blue species in big shoals always near coral, the tips of which were just the same colour.

I found a pair of Razor Fish floating with heads vertically downward. I chased them to see if I could scare them into any other swimming posture, but they kept easily ahead of me, still vertical. Crawling slowly up and down over the ripples on a patch of white sandy bottom was a hermit crab in a tall shell and about five inches long. At the edge of the coral were shoals of large Parrot Fish—one or two rainbow-coloured males among a dozen or so drabber females. Everywhere we met saucer-shaped *Chaetodonts* or Butterfly Fish always in pairs which were identical, but each pair were of a different species.

Then and since I have pondered on how all these different species of Butterfly Fish can live on the same reefs, at the same depths, apparently with much the same feeding habits, and yet each with a different bold pattern of spots or stripes to assert his specific identity.

I have watched fishes through a face mask in Hawaii, the West Indies, the Panama Canal, the Galapagos Islands and East Africa. My knowledge of birds has helped me to understand them, and they in turn have clarified for me many problems in ornithology. But for me, as a painter and a naturalist, those first dives on the Barrier Reef were the revelation. The wonder of it seemed appropriate to that hot Australian Christmas Day.

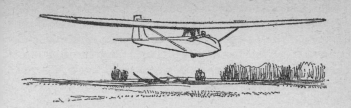

34. THE SILENT SKY

Gliding had always sounded an adventurous business. It evidently had much in common with sailing, and it was one of those things I had been meaning to try one day, but so far the chance had never come my way. And then one day my neighbour rang me up:

'Have you been to see the gliders yet?'

'What gliders; where?'

'Look out of your window and you'll probably see one flying along the Cotswold edge. They belong to the Bristol Gliding Club which has just moved to Nympsfield.'

Half an hour later I was on the new gliding field being offered a flight by the Chief Flying Instructor, John Parry Jones, in a side-by-side two-seater. As we waited for the cable to be towed out from the winch at the far end of the field, John told me what to expect. There was a quick cockpit check, a shout of 'Take up slack' followed by 'All out' and our glider was pulled violently forward. Almost at once it was airborne and heading steeply into the sky like a kite while John prattled away, and I gripped the bottom of the instrument panel and wondered how he would know when he had got to the top.

What would the downward swoop be like? Unexpectedly it was far nicer than the climb. John released the cable with a click and we floated out over the valley below. There we sat 1,000 feet above the airfield, peacefully admiring the view. At

first the air was quite smooth, but as we flew over the Cotswolds it became bubbly and buoyant. John tipped our wings
sharply into a bank and we went round in tight circles. We had
found a thermal—one of the up-currents for which the glider
pilot is always looking. Our flight lasted nineteen minutes, and
as we swept in to land at an increased speed and trundled to a
standstill I realised that it was not the last flight I would make
in a glider.

I decided to take up gliding and a whole new field of enjoyment opened up before me, a new and satisfying outlet for
my occasional restlessness. To go sailing meant a long car
journey from my home, but directly above it was an ocean of
sky waiting to be explored!

Perhaps the greatest appeal of gliding is the simplicity of its
basic concepts. In a glider you are competing against gravity.
When you are going up you are winning, when you are coming
down you are losing. There is something satisfyingly direct
about it. As the glider is always sinking, the pilot's skill is in
finding air which is rising faster. In the early days the easiest
up-going air to find was the wind hitting a hill face and being
deflected upwards. The glider's scope is limited by the length
of the hill and the height of 1,000 or 2,000 feet to which the
up-draught extends. But the time a glider can fly in hill lift is
limited only by the pilot's endurance. It becomes comparable
with pole-squatting. With the exception of the five-hour requirement for the Silver C badge, duration is no longer a
measure of gliding prowess. The discovery that thermal up-
currents could be used opened up a whole new field of long-
distance flying. By finding thermals—the bubbles of hot air
which rise from some part of the ground that has become hotter in the sun than its surroundings—and circling tightly in the
up-going column, the glider gains enough height to set off in
search of the next thermal, and so on across country until the
sun gets too low to set off any more of them. The little white
bun-shaped *cumulus* clouds of a summer's day are the tops of
these thermals, and the pilot goes from cloud to cloud knowing, if the day is good, that there will be lift under each. In

this country the record distance in 360 miles, and the world record—flown in the United States—is 550.

Cumulus clouds are not always small and bun-shaped. Sometimes they become vast thunderheads or *cumulo-nimbus* clouds (*cunims* for short) and these have very powerful up-currents. In this country such clouds have taken gliders to more than 30,000 feet—for which, of course, oxygen is necessary.

Still only half-explored is a third kind of lift called 'wave'. When water pours over a weir or a hidden stone in a stream there often arises downstream a series of standing waves which remain more or less stationary. The same thing happens when an air mass flows over a mountain range. In the upward part of such a wave a glider has been carried up to 46,000 feet.

All these things I read about and heard about in the talk that went on at the Gliding Club as I learned my new technique. I learned, too, about launching methods. At Nympsfield we used a winch with about 1,000 yards of cable which pulled the gliders up like a kite to about 1,000 feet—or a third of the cable length; but there were other methods. Auto-towing involved a fixed length of wire and a motor-car on a runway. This is even more like running with the string of a kite. Aero-towing—being tugged into the sky by a light aeroplane—is the most efficient way of all because the glider can release at an adequate height to be fairly sure of finding a first thermal. From 600 feet up the pilot should be planning his approach to land. A launch to 1,000 feet gives him only a very short time to look for thermals, whereas with a launch to 2,000 feet (the standard height for aero-tows) he has more than three times as long. For this reason in competition, flying aero-tows are almost invariably used.

At the opposite end of the scale there is bunjy launching. In this the glider is catapulted off the top of a ridge into hill lift. The power is supplied by half a dozen people running down-hill to stretch the bunjy. But the Bristol Gliding Club's new field was not a bunjy-site.

I flew solo for the first time in a Slingsby Tutor and to begin with I thought this might be the limit of my ambition.

Beginning at the age of forty-six it was absurd to think of doing much more. But I should have known myself better, or perhaps I had not reckoned with the cunningly devised carrots which hang before the aspiring pilot—the 'Certificates' of the International Aeronautical Federation, designed expressly to lead ever onwards. There are to begin with, A, B and C certificates which are likely to be achieved fairly quickly with modern gliders and teaching methods, but after that come the Silver C, the Gold C and, most difficult of all, the three Diamonds. When I first learned of these things back in 1956 only one British pilot had all three Diamonds and even today there are only a handful. Maybe, I said to myself, it would be fun to have a Silver C, and from then onwards I was committed.

For the Silver C I would be required to stay airborne for five hours, to fly across the country for fifty kilometres, and to climb 1,000 metres (3,281 feet) above the height of launch or any subsequent lower point before the climb. It would, no doubt, be some long time before these three could be achieved, I thought.

By now I had learned enough to have a glider of my own and was flying in my very own two-seater T42B Eagle, which I called *Sea Eagle*, and in it one blustery day at Nympsfield the Duke of Edinburgh made his first flight in a glider, with Peter Collier who had been my instructor in the back seat. By the following year I had gained my Silver C badge. Somehow, it could not be left there. The Gold C badge loomed up ahead. For this I must fly 300 kilometres (187 miles) and climb 3,000 metres or 9,843 feet from the lowest point of free flight.

On 1st July, 1957, the clouds were gangling and loose-limbed like rather bedraggled chickens. Their feathery flanks trailed away to a damp and ragged fringe at the bottom. Twice I tried to get up to them, flying alone in the *Sea Eagle*, but each time I scraped in weak thermals for little more than twenty minutes. My third launch was at four p.m. and for half an hour I struggled to keep up. A thermal off the spur on the ridge took me very slowly to 1,500 feet, but an excursion under the most promising cloud out in the vale drew a complete blank. Back at the ridge another weak thermal suggested that it was better to look down to the most likely thermal sources for lift than to look up to the clouds. I drifted back over Stroud, scarcely climbing above my glide-path home, until at 2,000 feet I suddenly noticed a slight improvement and at 2,800 feet I was among the trailing wisps of a small cloud. So far I had flown about four times in cloud, and on one proud occasion had climbed over 1,000 feet on turn-and-slip indicator—no Artificial Horizon was fitted at that time—before using the air-brakes to check excessive speed. Here, I thought, was an opportunity for some much-needed practice. So, with the green ball of the variometer standing at a fairly steady five feet per second up I wandered into the murk. After a while my circles emerged on one side, so I moved farther into the cloud and the lift fell away to nothing. I turned north flying through patchy cloud with glimpses of the ground. The cloud looked darker ahead—much darker. Almost at once I was in much stronger lift, with the variometer standing at ten green all the way round. I settled down to the routine I had read about not long before in an article in the magazine *Sailplane and Gliding*. Let the eyes rotate round the three main instrument readings and say them out loud. 'Turn and slip and speed and turn and slip and speed . . .' I said to myself out loud and unceasingly, breaking the monotony occasionally when the speed approached sixty m.p.h. to say (also out loud) 'get that bank off—too much turn', for a colleague had recently suggested that too much bank was probably the cause of my earlier zoomings.

After a while the green ball went even higher up the tube and the altimeter ploughed round in the most purposeful manner. 'Turn and slip and speed . . .' I kept saying, while I wondered how long it could last—6,700 feet was my previous highest: the Club record was eight and a half: it would be nice to get to nine . . . The green ball stayed mostly at twenty. A little tuft of water appeared at the front of the canopy by the ventilator, then the canopy began to mist over, and there was an icicle on the pitot-head mounted on the nose; then it began to get lighter and much rougher. I pulled down my loosened straps and gripped the stick more firmly. With my other hand I held on tight to the connecting bar of the air-brakes (a safe hand-hold which cannot jerk them open in a bump). 'Turn and slip and speed . . .' came from a very dry mouth. 'Turn and slip and speed and turn and . . . get that bank off . . . and slip and speed and . . .' The hand of the altimeter wound on past 9,000 feet. I'm not quite certain at what stage the idea of a 'nice little exercise in cloud-flying' changed into an attempt at Gold C height.

A lot of things were happening now. It became very turbulent indeed; the *Eagle* had no oxygen; and then I could not remember how many feet there were in 3,000 metres, but I was too fully occupied to work it out. The speed became erratic, the sailplane was tossed about like an autumn leaf and then suddenly there was silence and the air-speed indicator swung down to nought; we were in a spin. Now, I felt, was quite a good time to pull out the air-brakes and when a suitable air-speed had been restored I glanced across to the altimeter—10,800 feet. With the air-brakes out I was trying rather unsuccessfully to fly straight and level in a south-westerly direction and a few seconds later, just twenty minutes after I had gone into it, I burst out of the side of the cloud. It was dazzlingly bright and supremely beautiful; immediately below me was the cauliflower top of one of the foothills of my cloud; and far, far below that again were the straggly wispy *strato-cu* fragments which had been covering four-eighths of the sky all day. I made a 360° turn to look at the cloud behind me, and only then realised that it was a solitary giant—the only big cloud within twenty miles. From below I had had no idea it would be so big.

There did not seem to be very much more above, but I was so close to it that perhaps, as with a mountain peak, the summit was hidden by the closest bastion. Most striking of all was the colour—a brilliant golden-yellow in the evening light. The grandeur of the scene was breathtaking, and I was still under the influence of the glorious relief that the sailplane was under control again. At the same time I was desperately trying to do mental arithmetic and to establish my whereabouts. 'A thousand metres is 3,281 feet, so what is 3,000 metres? Three ones are three, three eights are twenty-four, four and carry two ... ah! that must be Aston Down, and there's the green reservoir on Minchinhampton Common ... and carry two, three twos are six and two is eight, three threes are nine—9,843 plus 1,000 for the launch ... Golly, aren't those clouds beautiful over there under the sun. Well, 10,843, but ... but ... I only went to 10,800. I've missed my Gold C height by forty-three feet!' Except, of course, that I must have lost at least that after the launch and before my first thermal. But supposing the barograph did not agree with the altimeter. Obviously I had cut it dangerously fine. Incidentally, from that height if I had set off straight away I could have made one glide to Lasham in Hampshire (sixty-five miles from Nympsfield) and we wanted the *Sea Eagle* at Lasham for a TV programme three days later, so that's another opportunity missed. Bother!

By now I was half-way home and down to 7,500 feet, with plenty of sink about. What should I do? If I went back to Nympsfield maybe Peter Collier my instructor could cap in and get *his* Gold C height, but that was rather unlikely as the cloud was now far downwind and no other clouds looked at all promising.

Very gradually it became more and more clear that there was only one sensible thing to do—to turn back, re-enter the cloud, make certain of Gold C height and then head for Lasham. Even after this conclusion became inescapable I found I was still pointing towards Nympsfield. I took a final screw on my courage and swung into a steep 180° turn. The die was cast. I was committed to a further 'short exercise in cloud-flying'.

Five miles to the eastward my cloud still brooded over its own dark shadow lying across the valley at Chalford. It was a bigger cloud now, and it seemed to be higher—a towering giant more frightening than ever now that it had come to manhood. Its top was apricot-coloured and crisp, with purple shadows; its foot was murky blue almost merging with the darkness of the Cotswolds below. My first climb had been made in ignorance of the size and quality of the cloud I had been sucked up into, but this time I could see my opponent only too well. I would dearly have liked a really good reason for staying out in the friendly sunshine.

I must have been flying in some fairly strong down-draughts, because I only got back to the cloud at about 4,000 feet—a few hundred feet above its base. I switched on the turn-and-slip and plunged into the side having made a mental note that south would be the quickest way out. At once I found lift and began to circle, but it was not very good, and in searching around to improve it I burst out into the clear air to the north-west. Back inside again I ran straight into steady ten green, which soon improved to about twenty. 'Turn and slip and speed . . .' From the beginning the climb was more turbulent than the first. I kept trying to get into the darkest part, in the hope that it would be smoother away from the edge, but it was a vain hope. There was a patter of rain, and later a patter of hail; and there was icing at the front of the canopy as before. Did the hail make it a *cunim*, I wondered? It was not very loud hail, and there was no lightning. But, *cu* or *cunim*, I was steaming up at twenty feet per second and bouncing about like a pea in a pod the while: '. . .and turn and slip and speed . . . hold off that bank . . . and slip and speed . . .' The altimeter crept past my previous best and up to 11,000, and now the turbulence increased sharply. With no oxygen I had no par-ticular wish to go much higher, but the attempt to straighten up on a southerly course proved disastrous; a few moments later rapid fluctuations of the air-speed persuaded me to pull out the air-brakes. Until then I was still going up and the alti-meter needle now stood at 11,500. I was holding on tight to the air-brake control with one hand, gripping the stick grimly with the other, and occasionally pulling down my shoulder-straps which kept working loose. Still attempting to fly straight and level I found that the air-speed continued to fluctuate disconcertingly; and then suddenly it increased very sharply so that the indicator read eighty m.p.h. The brakes were out, and at this speed we should have been losing height fast, but instead the green ball was at twenty and the altimeter needle was surging round clockwise. Fascinated and seriously worried, I watched it go up 700 feet in about thirty seconds before, with a frightful bump, we flew into a violent down. A few moments later the air-speed shot up again, and once more with full brakes out and eighty m.p.h. on the clock we climbed 700 feet; again there was a violent jerk and we were going down; and then suddenly we were out in the blessed evening sunshine. The panic was over. I tried to shut the brakes, but they were frozen open. Ahead two great walls of cloud were closing together and I aimed at the gap. The *Sea Eagle* just squeezed through and I could almost hear the clang as they met behind me. I tried the brakes again, and they closed half-way but no more. And so my hard-won height fell away in a miserable glide with the red ball steadily at ten feet per second down or worse.

Nevertheless I headed for Lasham. The total distance from Nympsfield was sixty-five miles, but already my cloud had taken me fifteen miles to the eastward, so that I had barely fifty-five miles to glide. From 11,000 feet in still air, with the air-brakes in, Lasham should have been in the bag with a little to spare. But with the air-brakes out and the sky full of sink it was quite another kettle of fish.

I flew out over the Cerney gravel pits half hidden by wispy cloud and headed for Swindon. Every minute or so I tried the air-brakes again and managed to get them a little more shut, but I was down to 7,000 before they finally clicked home. To get to Lasham now I must obviously find some more lift. Over Marlborough was another big cloud, and beyond this and to the east were a couple more. I headed out west of my course to the Marlborough cloud. I was a few hundred feet below cloud base when I got to it ... and found nothing. A bonfire was burning at the edge of Savernake forest and the smoke came up towards my cloud. There was even a tuft of slightly lighter

277

cloud at the point where the bonfire's hot air appeared to enter the darkness of the decaying giant. Round and round I went muttering the familiar sailplane pilot's *cri de cœur*—'There must be something here somewhere.' But the best I could find brought the red ball down to one for part of the circle. At a quarter past six in the evening it was perhaps only to be expected.

I headed on, working desperately at my gliding-angle graph, and soon saw that Lasham was just beyond my grasp. Clearly there would be no more lift so I had the choice of landing in a field a few miles short of turning off to the nearest aerodrome. Andover seemed to be within reach and from there I could be aero-towed to Lasham; so to Andover I went—forty-eight miles from Nympsfield.

I landed safely at a quarter to seven among gliding friends at Andover and the Barograph had duly recorded a climb to Gold C height.

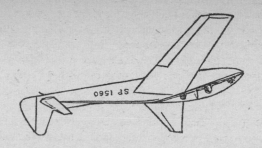

35. STRAIGHT AND LEVEL

Most of us who glide say that we do so because it stimulates us. What we mean is that it frightens us. The question is: 'How much?' If it frightens us too much we no longer enjoy it; if it does not frighten us enough we become bored. Somewhere between the two, we think, lies the special appeal of our sport, and it leaves a fairly wide scope for individual variation.

Ever since I took up gliding I have always been a member of the Straight and Level Club. Aerobatics are only enjoyable to me in their mildest forms. Chandelles are all right, loops are my limit and anything which disturbs the dust from the cock-pit floor is well beyond it. Thus when I arrived to watch the World Gliding Championships at Leszno in Poland in the summer of 1958 I was astonished, as I got down from the taxi which had brought me from the station, to see a two-seater Bocian glider circling at 500 feet over the middle of the aero-drome *upside-down*. It was not until the following day that two of my friends from the Midland Gliding Club told me that they had both been indulging in this doubtful entertain-ment and one of them—a Pole named Teddy Proll—said that if I wanted to fly during my short four days at Leszno he could arrange it. At this point I thought I made myself clear that although there was nothing I should like to do more than to sample the Polish thermals, there was nothing I wished to do *less* than to fly upside-down. An hour or so later Teddy Proll approached me excitedly and said he had arranged it all and that in a few moments I could have a flight in the Bocian.

Soon afterwards, at the launch point, I was introduced to the charming young man who was to fly with me. He spoke a very few words of English and a very few words of German, and to make quite sure I explained to him at some length in both languages that the limit of my ambition was perhaps an hour of comfortable thermal soaring after which I hoped to return equally comfortably to earth. He seemed an intelligent young man and appeared to understand me perfectly. There was some delay because on the previous landing the air-brakes had become inexplicably jammed. When the seats were removed a screwdriver was found wedged behind the air-brake control. Apparently during inverted flight it had slipped out of a pocket. At least this particular hazard would not come my way. No inverted flight for me!

We were launched by aero-tow with a sixty-foot tow rope—half the length of the tow ropes I was used to. It was of a suitable thickness for towing a motor-car and wholly innocent of any 'weak link' arrangements which would be obligatory in England. I found that the climb to 500 metres required all my attention, for the tug—a low-wing monoplane—was terribly close in front of us. At 500 metres we released in an indifferent thermal and I started to turn. My companion shouted 'No, no! Not yet!' and seized the controls. We flew farther into the thermal, which then admittedly improved, and was of such enormous dimensions that the straight period did not carry us through to the other side as it would have done in an English thermal. As we began to gain height I found that my companion was a confirmed 'pudding-stirrer'; the control column was in constant motion and as a result (so it seemed) we had quite a rough ride. After a while the thermal grew weaker and I asked if I could fly again. Here I was lucky, for I decided to move over to another thermal underneath a cloud which was just forming and this was so much stronger that we roared up at about 500 feet a minute. And so we wound our way to cloud base (but not into cloud because the turn-and-slip indicator batteries were flat). From 5,000 feet we headed back towards the aerodrome. 'Now . . . aerobatic!' said my friend. Could it be that he had misunderstood me? Well, there was no harm in the simple ones. I performed a couple of fairly mild chandelles followed by a loop. 'Is very nice,' said my friend, 'now I show you.' He took over the controls and in a second we had half-rolled and were flying upside-down. A number of unfortunate circumstances dominated the next few moments. First I had not taken the elementary precaution of tightening the lower pair of straps. Tightly though my shoulders were held, my midriff was only loosely supported. In order to offset this disadvantage I had found a convenient hand-grip for my left hand under the seat. Everything seemed under control, although I was hanging rather far away from the seat itself. A few moments later my companion began an inverted turn. At this point the seat, unaccustomed to an 'upward' pull of one and a half times my weight, gave way with a splintering crash. This was greeted by a loud guffaw from behind me. I wonder whether you can remember as a child lying belly downwards in your bath? I was in just such a position, only the bath was the perspex canopy. It was at this stage, to my undying shame, that I could no longer withhold a stifled cry for mercy. With a flip back of the stick positive G was restored as we half-looped out. Hastily I tightened the straps, for clearly we had not seen the end of this business. In a few seconds we were involved in two consecutive slow rolls. But with the straps tighter I felt slightly more secure, although my toes were curled around something—perhaps the variometer bottle—which was quite certainly not designed to take the strain now bearing upon it.

The next thing was a half-loop to inverted-flight and at that precise moment we hit the edges of a thermal. 'Ah-ha,' said my companion and we began to circle upside-down. It was only when he started to tighten the turns and we had already gone up fifty metres that I allowed a further expression of dismay to escape my lips. This time, in what I hoped was a firm voice, I followed it with 'right way up now, please'. A few seconds later a more normal world was restored to me. We were still regrettably high. 'Now Immelmann,' said my companion, and in quick succession we performed two half-loops, rolling off the top. After what I had already suffered these were, it must be admitted, comparatively mild and I even made so bold as to try one myself, but it was executed at too slow a speed, and my companion demonstrated with two more. As we now approached the lower limit of what in this country would be regarded as aerobatic height I began to breathe again, but my relief was premature. First came two rather charming little flick-stall turns, a manoeuvre which only leaves you on the straps for a second or so. It is not unpleasant as a sensation and is quite spectacular in appearance, for the glider seems to cartwheel in the sky. We were now down to 500 feet. Down went the nose yet again. 'What now?' I thought. At the edge of the aerodrome our Bocian half-rolled on to its back and we made a run across the whole width of the field upside-down. Surely there could not be much more. We half-rolled out, went up into a chandelle, round, out brakes and a spot landing which trickled us up to the hangar door. An enthusiastic Teddy Proll rushed up to take a snapshot and to ask the inevitable question: 'Did you enjoy it?'

Back in England I was glad enough to return to my beautiful *Sea Eagle* whose Certificate of Airworthiness specifically excluded inverted flight. That spring she had done me proud by taking me from Nympsfield to Penzance—a flight of 305 kilometres which completed my Gold C. It was the thirty-fourth Gold C to be issued to a British pilot.

Olympia 419

36. DIAMONDS AND BEYOND

By the summer of 1959 I had been launched 550 times and had flown in gliders for 300 hours with only one mishap. One day in the previous summer the winch had failed during a launch; I had wallowed on the wire and allowed the speed to fall off too much; so that the *Sea Eagle* landed heavily and the little wheel was pushed up through the bottom of the fuselage.

Then came the disastrous 31st May, 1959. I had been soaring with a passenger on the west ridge at Nympsfield and was returning to land, a little lower than usual. It might have been prudent to turn in early and land at the upwind end of the field, but the hay had not yet been cut at that end, so it would be slightly better to go on to the downwind end. Then I saw that the T21—the side-by-side trainer—was also coming in to land. I felt that I could not cross ahead of him. So I swept out to turn behind him. I should have known—indeed, I did know—that there would be a down-draught curling over the hangar and down the ridge behind it, but the T21 was in front of me. I was committed to going astern of him. Then the 'curl-over' took charge. In gliding circles it is sometimes known as 'the clutching hand'. As I turned in, the trees in front rose up to meet us. We were evidently not going to make it. The only thing to do was to increase the speed by lowering the nose and trying to dive through the topmost branches. We were still turning slightly and the low wing broke the telephone wires; the Eagle slewed round a little and the bushy top of the tree

283

pulled down the speed, so that she stalled. There was a nasty splintering crash and we were on the ground, still sitting in the glider, neither of us hurt, but under my feet I could see the grass covered with little broken bits of plywood.

Half an hour after the prang I was sent round on a circuit in another Eagle, though I have since been told that the wisdom of this time-honoured practice, which is supposed to restore the nerve, is now regarded as very doubtful.

The Eagle was going to take not less than two months to repair. I considered carefully what I should do. The accident had been caused by an accumulation of misjudgements. I had left the ridge too low, I had been unduly influenced by the insignificant factor of the uncut hay, I had failed to realise that I could safely have turned in ahead of the T21, I had underestimated the curl-over. Did all these mistakes amount to a conclusion that I was accident-prone? Or did they alternatively reduce the chance that I would ever make those particular errors again?

For a day or two my morale was at a low ebb. But then determination returned. I was not going to give up gliding. After all, there were still the three Diamonds to be added to my Gold C badge.

I had had a trial flight in a single-seater Olympia 419X and had been so impressed that I now ordered one immediately. The new machine—a sixty-two-foot span world-beater at that time, and perhaps still—was ready on the afternoon of 18th July, and I went to fetch her from Newbury, trailed her to Nympsfield and flew her for two hours in the evening. She was a honey. The weather forecast for the morrow was good and if the day fulfilled its promise I was going to try for the first of the Diamonds—a goal flight from Gloucestershire to Great Yarmouth. Of the three requirements perhaps the easiest is Diamond Goal: this involves a flight of not less than 300 kilometres (the Gold C distance), but to a declared landplace. The other two are Diamond Distance—a flight of 500 kilometres, and Diamond Height—a climb of 5,000 metres or about 16,400 feet.

My Diamond Goal was achieved on that first cross-country flight in the new machine, but no chances arose in the summer of 1959 to try for the other two diamonds. Suitable days to fly 500 kilometres (312 miles) for Diamond Distance are very rare in this country. In Britain, in most wind directions you get to the sea too soon. I had no illusions about it; I knew that Diamond Distance was very difficult indeed, but on 14th May, 1960, with a rather rare south-south-westerly unstable airstream the thing seemed worth trying.

The wind was strong though the lift was patchy. But it meant that while I struggled to gain height, circling in the thermals, I was being blown up England at an encouraging speed. Twice in the Midlands I was convinced that the flight would end, but each time I managed to creep back up again. By Durham big storms had spread cloud over most of the sky. I was down to 800 feet, but I was shown a weak thermal over a junk yard by two gulls and circling continuously though scarcely rising at all, I drifted with the wind towards Newcastle. Laboriously I crept back up to 4,000 feet and circled into the bottom of a little grey patch of cumulus. Then a remarkable thing happened. The lift suddenly and startlingly increased. From 100 feet per minute my rate of climb had increased to more than 1,500 feet per minute. At about 9,000 feet I put on my oxygen mask, and as the altimeter passed 10,000 I turned the oxygen to low. Still the altimeter needle went round half as fast again as the second hand of a watch. But at 13,500 it became lighter and turbulent and the lift fell off, so I turned to the north-west and flew straight and level.

From a bright white mist I flew with absolute suddenness into almost twilight darkness, the glider dropped like a down-going lift and a hideous roar broke out as hail bombarded my perspex canopy. A moment later lightning began to flash, but so deafening was the roar of the hail that I heard no thunder. I was now back in lift again, and going up fast though not quite so fast as before.

Diamond Height had suddenly become a possibility. My low point of 800 feet immediately before this climb meant that the 5,000 metres need only have 800 feet added to achieve the necessary height—16,405 plus 800 equals 17,205—call it 17,500 for luck! Ice crystals were penetrating into my cockpit from the cracks round the canopy. Already there was a thin coating over my knees. The inside of the perspex was entirely frosted over, and so were the faces of the instruments.

At 17,600 the lift began to fall off again and as my second diamond should be safely on the barograph trace, I turned on to a north-westerly course to concentrate on the third—the magic 500 kilometres. Although I did not know it till later my altimeter had lagged behind the barograph, which, after being checked, dutifully recorded that I had reached a height of 18,300 feet.

By now I had a serious problem on my hands. The great anvil of ice crystals had spread out from the top of the thunderstorm, and joined the overcast from earlier ones. I was flying in cloud which was probably unbroken ahead of me. Theoretically, from this altitude at Newcastle I should have been able to reach my declared goal at Portmoak, fifteen miles north of Edinburgh, but the 419's wings were covered with ice, and her rate of sink was greatly increased. I could not expect the ice to melt until I was down to 5,000 or 6,000 feet. But there was worse than this. I had little idea of the direction and strength of the wind, and I was probably not going to see the ground till I was down to cloud base. This had been 4,000 feet before the storm, but behind the rain there had been cloud almost down to the ground. If the wind up here was stronger or more westerly than I calculated, I might well come out of cloud over the sea and too low to get back to shore. I turned a little bit more to the westward and soldiered on through the grey blanket of cloud, while the hum of the Artificial Horizon began to fall in pitch as the battery ran down.

After about half an hour there was an irregularity in the grey and then a sudden break. In the open patch still 10,000 feet below, I could see the coastline and the unmistakable outline of Budle Bay. A moment later it was swallowed up in the cloud again. I adjusted the course accordingly and flew on through the clouds. When I next emerged, Berwick and the Tweed were just ahead, and still at 4,000 feet I crossed the border into Scotland. But unless I found more lift I had no hope of getting across the Firth of Forth to Portmoak, and it was now late in the evening. I was flying almost at right-angles to the wind by this time as I crept along the coastal plain near St Abbs Head, slowly but steadily sinking. At last I picked a field near the village of Cockburnspath and landed. It was six-forty-five p.m. and I was 298 miles from my starting-point—14 miles short of the 500 kilometres. It chanced that no one in Britain flew farther than 298 miles during 1960, so the flight qualified me for the Wakefield Trophy. It was not until March 1962 when I went with Phil to S. Africa that I was lent a Skylark 3 glider by Boet Domisse on the day after my arrival in Johannesburg and sent off to fly a 500-kilometre dog-leg which I duly completed to become at last holder of all three diamond badges.

In May 1963 I entered for the British Gliding Championships at Lasham in Hampshire. The holder, Nick Goodhart, who had been competing in the World Championships in the Argentine in February was unable to take more time off from the Navy. John Williamson, another of our world championship pilots, a former British champion and son of the author Henry Williamson, remained to be beaten. He won the first day of the competition—an out and return race—and I was tenth, which was not a very promising start. But I won the second day—another out and return race—though John was second, which left him still leading handsomely in the competition. During the next three contest days I managed to close the gap. By the last day John was still leading with 3,711 points, but I was only sixteen points behind him, and the task was a goal race of 136 miles from Lasham to Chivenor Aerodrome, just beyond Barnstaple in Devon. There was a tail wind of thirty knots and the thermals were quite strong, though broken and difficult to circle in, and there were big distances between them. I was lucky and never got low. But one and a half hours out and about twenty-five miles from the goal, with the Devon

287

coastline to the north doing strange things to the air, I needed another 500 feet for a final glide in to the finishing line. There was a weak rather turbulent thermal which gave me lift halfway round each circle and almost as much sink in the other half. But this might well be the last thermal I would get because of the stable air blowing in from the sea, unless, of course, I were to find the elusive lift which comes from a seabreeze front. However, the sky was clear ahead, and the only prudent thing was to work up those last 500 feet which took about four minutes. Then I was away on course down the wind to Chivenor. I had not gone half a mile before I ran into rising air. This *was* the sea-breeze front, and I was going up when I did not need the height. I put the nose down until I was flying at 90 knots, then 100. Faster I must not go for the air was turbulent—yet for part of the journey I was still rising. This did not matter as you can cross the finishing line at any height below a kilometer, but it meant that my four minutes thermalclimbing had been wasted, though I could recoup a little by flying in faster. As I came within sight of the airfield, still at nearly 3,000 feet (of which more than half were unnecessary), I could see that several gliders had arrived before me; but, then, many had started before me—success is measured by time over the course. I knew that John Williamson had crossed the starting line a few minutes before me. Had he arrived? I scanned the five gliders on the ground ahead. One was a red Olympia with white wings and dayglow strips on the tips. This was certainly the pattern of John's glider, but there was something wrong about the red tail with its white number. Surely his had a white panel on the rudder with the number in black. So this was *not* John Williamson's glider. Even at the time, I recognised the discovery as one of the golden moments of my life. In a deliciously satisfying tingle of excitement I crossed the finishing line at 100 knots, 1,600 redundant but now insignificant feet up, to become 1963's British Gliding Champion.

37. A TERRIBLE FAILURE

In the following year I did not defend my title; I was too busy learning how to sail a twelve-metre yacht. Tony Boyden commissioned the *Sovereign* from a design by David Boyd who had designed *Sceptre*, a previously unsuccessful challenger for the America's Cup. According to the tank tests *Sovereign* would have a five per cent better performance than *Sceptre*. A second twelve-metre called *Kurrewa V*, financed by the Australian brothers Livingstone and campaigned by Owen Aisher, was to fight it out with *Sovereign* for the honour of challenging. *Kurrewa V*, also from the board of David Boyd, scarcely differed at all from *Sovereign*.

Sovereign had been sailing during the previous summer, when I had taken her for a race in Cowes Week, which we had won by an unspectacular margin. Later in the year Tony Boyden invited me to join his team, as a candidate for helmsman, to start the intensive preparation on 1st April, 1964, that would culminate in the America's Cup series—the best of seven races—in September of that year.

For me, virtually without twelve-metre experience (I had sailed *Sceptre* in three races and *Sovereign* in one), there were three objectives. The first was to learn to steer the boat well enough to be selected as helmsman, rather than the other two candidates—Eric Maxwell or Bruce Banks who had much more experience. The second was to beat *Kurrewa V*, so as to be selected by the Royal Thames Yacht Club to make the challenge. The third was to win the America's Cup.

During the first part of the season we sailed against *Sceptre* in Weymouth Bay, and found the old boat unaccountably difficult to beat. Later we raced against *Kurrewa V* in the far too sheltered waters off Portsmouth. Her helmsman was 'Stug' Perry, Olympic Silver medallist and yachtsman of much wider experience in keel boats than I had ever had. On a day when she tried out a new and evidently unsuitable mainsail, we beat *Kurrewa* by twelve minutes, but for the most part the racing was close and exciting, and one race ended in our favour by half a boat's length. When the time came to take the boats over to the United States, Tony had decided to select me as helmsman, but *Kurrewa* had beaten us one more time than we had beaten her, and she was currently regarded as favourite for selection.

On arrival at Newport, Rhode Island, we saw the American boats for the first time. If the difficulty in beating *Sceptre* had been the first intimation of impending disaster, here was the second. In sheer refinement of detail both *American Eagle* and *Constellation*, which was finally selected to defend, were in quite a different class to *Sovereign* and *Kurrewa V*.

The final selection trials of both defender and challenger were very closely fought exciting races. In one Paul Anderson, our fore-deck hand, was knocked overboard by an unwinding winch-handle when we were leading. We described a quick circle and were lucky enough to snatch him out of the water at the first attempt. The whole operation cost us about two minutes, but we lost the race.

This was a happy period; the team worked in remarkable harmony with a crew of eleven and a dozen more who included spare crew, technicians and devoted group wives who kept house for us in a huge faded mansion on a hilltop overlooking the sea. And gradually we gained the ascendancy over our rival *Kurrewa*, until finally *Sovereign* was selected.

I doubt if any of us had any illusions about our chances of beating *Constellation*. The moment of truth would come after the two boats had settled down to the first beat of the first race. Either *Constellation* would eat out to windward of us, or, an exciting possibility, she would not. The idea that we might eat out to windward of her was scarcely considered as a possibility by any of us. That moment of truth would come between about twelve-five and twelve-fifteen on Tuesday, 15th September, 1964.

The techniques of starting a match race between two boats are capable of great elaboration. It does not matter when you start so long as you start before the other boat, and within the rules there are ways and means of preventing the other from getting to the starting line. The result can be much circling and follow-my-leader during the ten minutes before the starting signal.

We practised starts intensively against Lord Craigmyle's old twelve-metre *Norsaga*, so that when it came to the America's Cup races we were at least as good and perhaps a little better than our opponent at the curious waltzing manoeuvres during those ten minutes, though in the first race my old friend Bob Bavier escaped from us and made as good a start as we, perhaps a fraction better. Nevertheless we had our wind clear, and we settled down to sail the boat to windward.

By now I felt that I had become used to steering-wheel instead of the more familiar tiller. *Sovereign* was a responsive boat to sail, and two minutes after the gun she was going beautifully, spinning along at seven and a half knots and high on the wind. After three or four minutes I had a look at *Constellation*. We might have been going well, but she was going a great deal better. It was the moment we had been waiting for and she was holding a course from three to five degrees closer to the wind than us, and going just as fast. It was to be as we had feared it might be. *Constellation* was unbelievably good to windward.

The results of the 19th Challenge for the America's Cup are yachting history. *Constellation* won in four straight races, by large margins—in one case twenty minutes. We need not have been so far behind, but when we could not keep up by using normal methods we felt forced to try something different—like sailing faster through the water by accepting a broader angle on the wind. Desperate measures of this kind usually put you farther astern, and this accounts in part for the extent of our defeat. Running before the wind we were beaten for quite another reason—for bad sail selection. The spinnakers we used each day except the last were far too big. On the last day when we set the small one we kept up with *Constellation* on the run. But on the wind, as ever, she ate out to windward of us devastatingly.

The result was a foregone conclusion from that moment ten minutes after the start of the first race, yet we had to go through with it. We could win the start (and we did so on the second and third days and on another when the race was cancelled for lack of wind, though not on the last day when we were over the line before the gun), but we could not win a race, and yet the *morale* of *Sovereign*'s crew remained astonishingly high and cheerful. We would go out each day and do our best. We could do no more.

What was wrong? The hull? Well, I do not think it was as good a hull for the broken sea set up by the spectator fleet as *Constellation*'s. The sails? They were better than *Kurrewa*'s, but they were not as good as *Constellation*'s. The spars? The mast was bulkier and stiffer than *Constellation*'s and we did not have the bending boom which automatically flattened the mainsail in a breeze. The helmsman? He was probably not as good at sailing a twelve-metre to windward as *Constellation*'s. The crew? Here I yield nothing to the American boat. We may have had a little more bad luck with gear in the Cup Races than in the selection series, but *Sovereign*'s crew was every bit as efficient as *Constellation*'s.

We returned somewhat dejectedly from the United States. We had made a disastrous showing, we were simply no match for the combination of skills brought together by the defence. We had fallen flat on our faces, but as Uffa Fox

292

remarked, what really matters is to be able to get up again and go on.

Fortunately for me there was not long in which to ponder our failure. I was soon off to Japan to preside over the International Jury at the Olympic Games.

38. A NEW ARK

A different kind of ship had been launched and entrusted to
my care three years earlier—a kind of Noah's Ark. In September 1961 we had started the World Wildlife Fund to raise
on a professional scale the money needed for the conservation
of nature, for saving the world's wildlife and wild places. This
was to be the fund raising and campaigning arm, while the
International Union for the Conservation of Nature, of which
I was a Vice President, continued as the scientific and technical arm.

I was fortunate in persuading the Duke of Edinburgh to
take an active part as President of the British National Appeal
and later as an International Trustee. Prince Philip engaged
the interest of Prince Bernhard and he became President of the
International Fund, which had its headquarters at Morges in
Switzerland.

W.W.F. moved forward rather slowly at first (except for
one anonymous donation of £100,000). But by 1966 nearly £1
million had been channelled into conservation as a direct result
of the Fund's initiative.

It was during three trips to Africa, and two to South
America that I had awoken to the desperate urgency of
world conservation, and further journeys to the Far East,
to India and to the Caribbean have reinforced my con-
victions.

I have tried to condense my thoughts on man's basic responsibilities into a single page which could be called my Conservation Creed. The argument runs as follows:

What man did to the Dodo, and has since been doing to the Blue Whale, and about 1,000 other kinds of animals, may or may not be morally wrong. But the conservation of nature is most important because of what nature does for man.

I believe something goes wrong with man when he cuts himself off from the natural world. I think he knows it, and this is why he keeps gardens and window-boxes and house plants, and dogs and cats and budgerigars. Man does not live by bread alone. I believe he should take just as great pains to look after the natural treasures which inspire him as he does to preserve his man-made treasures in art galleries and museums. This is a responsibility we have to future generations, just as we are responsible for the safeguarding of Westminster Abbey or the Mona Lisa.

It has been argued that if the human population of the world continues to increase at its present rate, there will soon be no room for either wildlife or wild places, so why waste time, effort and money trying to conserve them now? But I believe that sooner or later man will learn to limit his own over-population. Then he will become much more widely concerned with optimum rather than maximum, quality rather than quantity, and will rediscover the need within himself for contact with wilderness and wild nature.

No one can tell when this will happen. I am concerned that when it does, breeding stocks of wild animals and plants should still exist, preserved perhaps mainly in nature reserves and national parks, even in zoos and botanical gardens, from which to re-populate the natural environment man will then wish to recreate and rehabilitate.

These are my reasons for believing passionately in the conservation of nature.

All this calls for action of three kinds: more research in ecology, the setting aside of more land as effectively inviolate strongholds, and above all education. By calling attention to the plight of the world's wildlife, and by encouraging people to enrich their lives by the enjoyment of nature, it may be possible to accelerate both the change in outlook and the necessary action.

It has been estimated that conservation all over the world needs each year £2 million. This is no astronomical figure. It is half the price of a V-bomber, less than one-twelfth the price of the new Cunard liner, or the price of, say, three or four world-famous paintings.

Much money is needed for relieving human suffering, but some is also needed for human fulfilment and inspiration. Conservation, like education and art, claims some proportion of the money we give to help others, including the as yet unborn.

Even if I am wrong about the long-term prospects—if man were to fail to solve his own over-population problem, and reaches the stage 530 years hence when there will be standing room only on this earth—even then the conservation effort will have been worth while. It will have retained at least for a time, some of the natural wonders. Measured in man-hours of enjoyment and inspiration this alone would be worth the effort. Many will have enjoyed the pictures even if the gallery is burnt down in the end.

The community chest which seeks to make the gallery representative and maintains the fire-alarm system is the World Wildlife Fund.

With so much of my time spent forwarding the cause of the World Wildlife Fund, I had to be careful not to neglect my earlier creation—the Wildfowl Trust. Fortunately its splendid team of Curator (Tommy Johnstone), Controller (Tim Sparrow) and Director of Research (Geoffrey Matthews), kept it running very smoothly, and a major step forward was the building of a new research centre with exhibition space, a lecture hall, work rooms for our eight resident scientists, a new shop and an improved main entrance to the grounds. It was inaugurated by Her Majesty the Queen with Prince Philip on 23rd April, 1966.

This new building gave me the chance to put together a permanent exhibition—'This Man and This Earth'—relating conservation to the most pressing problems facing mankind. It begins with a mirror carrying the legend above: 'You are looking at a specimen of the most dangerous and destructive animal the world has ever known', and underneath: 'He is also the most imaginative and creative animal, and has evolved a conscience—keep it with you as you go round this exhibition'. Scales hold the balance between two headings: 'Man Creates' and 'Man Destroys'. Then come what I believe to be the three greatest dangers to man—nuclear war, over-population and boredom in the Age of Leisure.

We try to show man's inheritance of natural treasures and our responsibility to conserve them for future generations and this leads on to the Wildfowl Trust's own part, small, perhaps but not insignificant, in the overall effort to change the outlook of a generation to the natural world in which we were evolved. The exhibition is designed to show that an enlightened attitude to nature is an integral part of civilisation, that it is not 'kids'-stuff' nor the province of cranks and crackpots, but rather that it is in the main stream of human progress.

39. SWAN LAKE

In 1964 I became a grandfather with the birth of Daniel Asquith, and in 1965 my first grand-daughter Emily was born. Nicola had married Kip Asquith, a great-grandson of the Liberal politician who was my mother's great friend—the first Earl of Oxford and Asquith. As a grandfather I did not feel substantially different or more grown up. It will be an effort in my case for the process of growing old to be graceful. I intend, for example, to be the first octogenarian on the moon.

It was in February 1964 that a new development took place on the pond outside my studio window which was the beginning of a very special pleasure; at that time I first became 'Swan happy'. Since then our daily life at Slimbridge during the winter months has largely revolved around the wild swans.

Bewick's Swans (called after the eighteenth-century wood-engraver and ornithologist) had been coming each winter from breeding grounds in Arctic Russia to the ponds of the Wildfowl Trust in twos and threes for ten years or more, and the numbers had been slowly increasing. By the winter of 1963–4 there were over twenty, but they never came to the pond in front of my big window. To persuade them to do so we moved our four tame pinioned Bewick's and the five related North American Whistling Swans over into the Rushy Pen and began to feed additional wheat. Within a week all twenty-four wild swans were coming regularly to feed in front of my window. At once we noticed that the black and yellow pattern on the bill

299

was different on every swan, so that each could be immediately recognised, and soon they all had names. Among them were the Major and Ethel (with one cygnet Rudi), the Owl and the Pussy Cat, Lancelot and Victoria, Pop and Mom (with four cygnets) ... In March they went north-east to their Arctic breeding grounds, and it was not until 4th December that the first ones returned—a pair called Pink (because he showed a lot of pink at the gape of his bill) and Rebecca with their two cygnets, Reuben and Rachel. I was rather surprised by this, because I had known the parents before they were married, and indeed had thought Pink more likely to select Amber as his mate. However, here he was with Rebecca, and it was not until February 1965 that Amber arrived with her mate, new to us, called Pepper. During that winter the numbers of swans built up impressively to a total of fifty-six at the peak time, and altogether seventy-five different swans accepted our hospitality. We had extended the pond during the previous summer and the swans found it very much to their liking. In the following summer we extended it still farther to lengthen the runway for them and increase the holding capacity of what was now inevitably called Swan Lake. We also cut back many trees so as to improve the approaches for the heavily wing-loaded swans, whose aeronautical skill, we found, varies almost as much as their bill-patterns.

We shall never know whether it was an unusually early onset of winter in the Arctic or the memory of Utopian conditions at Slimbridge that brought the first swans back on 21st October, 1965. Pink and Rebecca arrived with three cygnets, Pepper and Amber with two, Kon and Tiki with three. What was of even greater interest was that the Pink family always came and went between the estuary and the Rushy Pen as a family of seven, which included Reuben and Rachel, their young of the previous year. The thrill of watching Pink and Rebecca arrive with their family was only to be compared with the arrival of Anabel, the Pink-footed Goose which spent two winters at my lighthouse before the war. But this was much more so; it was their third year, and for the second time they brought their young. No doubt the lure was mundane enough, a plentiful supply of food. Yet somehow the link which I had developed with these magnificent birds gave me as much pleasure as any ornithological experience I can remember. That these birds should be drawn back after their 5,000 mile round trip to this tiny pond, seventy yards long by forty yards wide, lying close under the walls of my house, gives me a feeling of wonder and delight that is hard to describe.

By November when Phil and I set off for wildlife conferences in Delhi and Bangkok, sixty-five swans had assembled on Swan Lake. When we got back the numbers had risen to eighty-seven.

40. ANTARCTIC EXCURSION

My first visit to the Antarctic began early in January 1966.
Polar regions had been left out of my plans ever since I had
decided in early days that I must stand on my own feet. Parts
of five summers spent studying nesting wild geese in Lapland,
Iceland and Arctic Canada were the only exceptions I had
allowed myself and they scarcely qualified as 'polar travel'.
But at the age of fifty-six this particular vanity seemed rather
empty and pointless. So when the B.B.C. invited me to join a
three-man filming team they were sending to Antarctica, I
accepted with the hope that the Press would not put out the
headline 'Following in his fathers footsteps'. (In the event, this
was the exact headline that all but a very few newspapers
used.)

On the way to New Zealand—the jumping-off point—I decided to break the journey in Fiji to look once more at the
fishes on the coral reefs, last seen there nine years before.
Knowing more of ichthyology than I had done then, it was a
most rewarding venture. I was delighted to find colonial
anemones with their attendant anemone fish in exactly the
same place as before, and young Platax at the foot of the
Korolevu beach exactly where they had been last time. I spent
forty-eight hours in Fiji, twelve of them in the water with a
mask on. The rest of the Antarctic team met me at Christchurch. It consisted of Christopher Ralling, as producer, and
Charles Lagus, the cameraman who had accompanied Phil and

me on the round-the-world trip filming wildlife for the *Far Away Look* television series which had taken us to Fiji nine years before. We were to be the guests of the U.S. Navy for a short trip of less than three weeks 'down to the ice', and magnificent hosts they turned out to be—from Fred Bakutis, Admiral Commanding Operation Deep Freeze and Mike Goodwin, the Commander in charge of the arrangements for us, down to Charlie Brown, the naval rating attached to our party as assistant cameraman and sound engineer.

Antarctica is nearly as big as North America. It is mostly covered with snow compressed into ice by its own weight into an ice-cap which is 11,000 feet thick in places and 9,000 feet at the South Pole, and that is 9,000 feet above sea level. It has noble mountain ranges rising to 13,000 and 15,000 feet, no vegetation, perpetual daylight in summer and perpetual night in winter. It may have between 2,000 and 3,000 people living there in summer—a tenth of that number in winter. They come from seventeen nations who have agreed by Treaty to forget about territorial claims for thirty years and to co-operate in a comprehensive programme of scientific research. It is an enlightened and imaginative concept which is working well and could perhaps contain the seeds of international agreement and co-operation in other fields as well. About half the people live in one town—the U.S.'s McMurdo Base on Ross Island where my father's hut, built at the time of his *Discovery* Expedition in 1901, still stands overlooking the little harbour. McMurdo 'City' has a church, a post office, a bowling alley, a hospital, well-equipped scientific laboratories and a nuclear power station. It lacks one essential ingredient of civilised life. There are no women.

We flew to Antartica in a C130-Hercules transport plane from Christchurch, in about eight hours. The first view of Antarctica—the incredibly beautiful coastal mountains of Victoria Land from 28,000 feet make a perfect introduction to the continent.

We touched down on skis at Williams Field, the U.S. airport on the Ross Ice-shelf which serves McMurdo Base four miles away and the New Zealand 'Scott Base' about two miles away. A helicopter took us to the helopad in McMurdo City and we were soon installed in a comfortable, overheated hut labelled Press, which was to be our operating base.

The next two and a half weeks were memorable for the lack of cold and wind, two ingredients of the Antarctic environment which we had expected, for the over-abundance of good food, for the good company of the international scientists working on the U.S. Antarctic Research Programme and for the half-dozen excursions we made during the period to various places—including the South Pole.

I think my most vivid memories will always be of my father's hut at Cape Evans, the base for his journey to the Pole in 1911–12. The infinitely beautiful backcloth of Mt Erebus— the 13,000-foot active volcano—hangs behind it, as it does behind most of the places on Ross Island (except sadly McMurdo Base itself, where the surrounding foothills shut it out). The Hut at Cape Evans stands on a relatively snow-free point jutting out from the snow-clad petticoats of the volcano. There is quite extraordinary beauty and perfection in the setting, with icebergs stranded in the bay and the sea ice heaving in the wave motion along the shore. The Hut itself stands only twenty yards from the sea. It has been cleared of snow and put into perfect order (restored would be the wrong word) by a party of dedicated New Zealanders led by L.B. Quartermain. The last people who lived there and used it as a base were the members of the Ross Sea party of Shackleton's unsuccessful Trans-Antarctic attempt between 1915 and 1917. But if some of the provisions which crowd the shelves come from the later expedition, many more date from my father's last winter there in 1911.

To walk along the snow-covered shore line among penguin and seal tracks, to look at the old hut, still in perfect repair, nestling almost at the foot, so it seems, of Mt Erebus, to imagine my father's first selection of the site, as the *Terra Nova* lay at anchor among the ice floes—this was the first thrill of our wonderful eight-hour visit to Cape Evans. The next was to sit in the alcove where my father sat writing his diary in the famous photograph by Ponting. I was brought up with that photograph. A huge enlargement of it hung on the staircase at Leinster Corner, and now hangs in my house at Slimbridge. In it the photographs he had put on his wall included a photograph of me as a small child. The photographs had been taken down when the party left the hut, and the table had been replaced in 1915 by a larger one. But the place was the same place, and here I sat down to write up my own diary, while the camera and lights were set up for filming our 'B.B.C. documentary'. The hut was cold, in contrast to the warmth and good cheer which it always provided in my father's time, and yet I felt a warm feeling of contentment as I sat there bringing my journal up to date. Few places in the world have had for me a more powerful aura of happiness than that cold deserted hut. The Discovery Hut at McMurdo (The Hut at Hut Point) had seemed to have a sad menacing feeling about it, which had made me wonder whether the preservation of these historic huts was even justified, so different must they inevitably be from the days when they were acting as home to an expedition. Perhaps, I thought then, it would be better to burn them down rather than leave a dead, cold, dirty museum piece. But at Cape Evans (and again when I went to Shackleton's old hut at Cape Royds, beside the Southernmost Adelie Penguin Rookery in the world), I felt quite differently about it. Here was the closest contact in actuality that the present generation of Antarctic travellers could have with the pioneer explorers. Films and books told much, but the huts themselves, still standing, their contents preserved by the low temperatures, were the only tangible links with the past. The fifty or sixty years since they were built was not very long, but they remained a significant part of the short history of Antarctica, and as such they deserved the efforts being made to preserve them.

In the late evening, with the sun still high in the sky, our scarlet helicopter created its own small blizzard of whirling snow as it landed beside the Hut to ferry us back to McMurdo and 'civilisation'.

Most of the travel and supply in the Antarctic is by sea and by air, in C130s for the long haul and in helicopters for the short. But there is still some cause to travel overland, and tracked vehicles more or less directly descended from the motor-sledges tried out by my father are used extensively today. In this sector (the Ross Sea Dependency) only the New Zealanders use dog-teams, and we went over to Scott Base for a few days to see and to make comparative films of the various travel methods. Mike Prebble, leader of the New Zealand team of forty-five, kindly arranged for us to go out over the ice-shelf—and it was here that I learned the gentle art of driving a motor-toboggan with its central caterpillar track.

We camped out one night on the shelf, in tents that hardly differed at all from the tents my father used, and on the way back I rode on a sledge behind one of the dog-teams. Dogs, it seems, are on the way out, but in the mild weather that we had while we were there it was still the most enjoyable by far of the available transport methods.

While at Scott Base I put through a telephone call to my home in England. It was half past one in the afternoon Ross Island time and half past one in the morning at Slimbridge. The line was adequate (with its essential radio links) and for five minutes I talked to my wife and my son Falcon. They told me that the Bewick's Swans in front of the studio window had increased from eighty-seven to over a hundred.

To get to Cape Crozier at the other end of Ross Island where my old friend Bill Sladen has been studying penguins for a number of summers, we took a helicopter and were there in three-quarters of an hour. This was the journey which Cherry Garrard described as the Worst Journey in the World when made on foot in winter to bring back eggs of the Emperor Penguin for embryological study. Unfortunately the last Emperors had gone out with the sea ice a fortnight before we arrived in Antarctica, but the huge Adelie Penguin Rookery was packed with nearly full-grown chocolate-coloured downy young. A hundred and fifty thousand pairs nest on the slopes just north of the Cape. Here is a remarkable chance to study a species with a rather simple ecology based upon the pelagic shrimp Euphausia—known as Krill—which are its food, and Leopard Seals and Killer Whales and Antarctic Skuas which are its predators. Because of their extreme tameness, these penguins are especially easy to study. Their behaviour patterns are of particular interest to the psychologist, their physiology (and especially their temperature control mechanisms) to the physiologist, their population dynamics to the demographer . . .

It was stimulating to spend a day with Bill Sladen and his team hearing about all this work, just as I enjoyed my discussions at McMurdo with Carleton Ray who has been swimming under the sea ice with Weddell Seals. Carleton and I had swum together with aqualungs in the Bahamas many times, and I had hoped to swim with him in McMurdo Sound, but unfortunately the sea ice had become too rotten for these operations some time before we arrived, and in any event Carleton had been concentrating this year on hydrophone work in his study of sound communication in marine mammals.

He showed me some of the local fishes which were being kept alive in the biological laboratory, and I made paintings of several species which had only previously been drawn from dead specimens (when the colours are quite different).

We spent a day on board the icebreaker *Glacier* in McMurdo Sound, clearing the approach channel and pushing icebergs out of the way. For sheer beauty this was one of the most memorable days—for the beauty of the table berg which towered seventy feet above the sea, with seven or eight times that depth below the water, and of the patterns of the cracks which shot out from the ship as we crunched our way into the sea ice, and of magnificent Erebus, towering smoke-plumed above the blue-black open water of the Sound, where the Minke whales lazily broke surface, head and spout first, dorsal fin later.

41. ONE END OF THE EARTH'S ROTATIONAL AXIS

It takes under three hours in a Hercules to fly the 800 miles from McMurdo Base to the South Pole. We went a longer way round over the Pole of Inaccessibility (the part of the continent farthest from any open sea) in order to land supplies at the newly established Plateau Station. Thus we arrived at the South Pole at ten p.m. on 20th January, 1966, fifty-four years and three days after my father. We could have arrived on the anniversary, but I am glad we did not; this was no sentimental journey, and the timetable of our work was more important.

There was a thin patchy mist of ice crystals as we approached flying low over the featureless expanse of white snow. Suddenly the station appeared three or four miles ahead, a few dark dots on the snow. These consisted of half a dozen huts of strange and specialised shapes, a large number of radio masts, some chimneys belching steam and an ice runway on which, after a couple of circuits for filming, we landed on our skis. What a way to arrive at the South Pole—sweaty-hot in an overheated giant aircraft! Yet even the great change was itself stimulating. We were met by the commander of the station—Amundsen—Scott Station is its official title—and as soon as the Hercules had taxied away again for its take-off he led us from the bright sunshine down some steps into the bowels of the snow, into a network of tunnels and caverns.

The temperature above had been minus 33°F or 65° of frost, but with little wind and warm sun on one's face, it did

not seem very cold. In the tunnels under the snow it was colder
—about minus 40°. Set in the rabbit warren of cold tunnels
are the well-heated rooms of the research station, the laboratories with the sophisticated machinery of physics (including a
computer), the living accommodation, the mess, the sick bay
with its operating theatre, the wash-room with its flush lava-
tories, the gymnasium, the night club which, being at 90°
South, is called Club 90 with its bar, its soft lights and its pin-
up girls.

There were forty-five men living and working at the South
Pole, nineteen of whom would be spending the winter there,
studying cosmic rays, the ionosphere, the aurora, seismology,
geomagnetism and meteorology.

I did not sleep very well that night—in a double-decker cot
in the sick bay with the top storey occupied as well. The principal reason was the altitude, for the Pole is believed to be
9,180 feet above sea level (9,000 feet of it being compressed
snow) and because of the centrifugal effect of the earth's rota-
tion on the atmosphere, the air is even more rarified so that it
is the equivalent of about 11,000 feet in other latitudes. On the
following morning we put on layer after layer of our thick
clothing—itself an exhausting business at that altitude—and
the U.S. Navy's excellent thermal boots which are rather like
a rubber vacuum flask round each foot. Protected like knights
in armour, we came up into the sunshine again, where there
was still 65° of frost.

The exact site of the South Pole is a matter of some controversy. Sun observations give a point about 400 yards from
the entrance to the station, but star sights give a point in among
the handful of small buildings which rise above the snow
(the aurora lab, the radar sphere, the meteorologist's balloon
house). A third position at the top of the steps up from the
station has been selected for the 'tourist Pole' with its ball
mirror on top and its neighbouring signpost giving details of
the distances to the home town of various past inhabitants of
the station. But the point derived from the sun observations is
generally known as the Geographical South Pole.

The commander of the station (who was also the Medical Officer) embarked us in his small-tracked vehicle. 'And now, if you all are ready,' he said in a southern drawl, 'we'll go out to the Pole and I can show you that area . . .' So in the little Nodwell we trundled out to the Pole, where a guyed mast about twenty feet high was flying the U.S. flag. As the Station is operated by the U.S. Navy it is natural that the stars and stripes should fly highest there, but I was sorry that the Norwegian and British flags could not have been *somewhere* in evidence at the Geographical Pole itself, which would have demonstrated an appropriate sense of history.

The next two hours were spent in making films and photographs at the South Pole. I shook hands with the commander, I looked up at the American flag, I walked towards the Pole not once but a dozen times, I stood in front of it in various groups and the cameras whirred and clicked—it was a photographic bonanza. I remembered, though, that fifty-four years ago my father was also involved in photography at the Pole, and the thought made the whole distasteful business a fraction more bearable.

Standing at the Pole one is far enough away from the station to feel the emptiness of the snowfield all round. Away to the horizon in every direction the rough windswept snow surface is unbroken, but for the few excrescences above the underground station.

'Great God, this is an awful place,' my father had written, and awful it must have been with Amundsen's tent already there and the prospect of 800 miles to walk back against time and the onset of winter . . . awful for its monotonous flat immensity, awful for the cold and the wind. For us, with 400 yards to walk back to a hot lunch in the snug overheated camp under the snow, it was not quite so awful, even in the literal sense in which my father used the word. But it was still one of the most isolated places in the world. During the last month eighty-six plane landings had been made here—and indeed a Hercules came in while we were filming out at the Pole—but in another few weeks all physical contact would be cut off for

311

six months of darkness, and the over-wintering party would have to be wholly self-sufficient. The South Pole was still, we felt, 'frontier country'. I found it stirring to think that people should have come in the first place, through all those fearful hardships, and that they should still come, to this one particular spot on the limitless expanse of flat snow because of its quite intangible significance as one end of the earth's rotational axis. I found it exciting that they should have made a scientific station here, supplied exclusively by air, and that they should choose to spend a whole year—some of them—in the middle of this featureless plateau. But as I looked out to that indistinct horizon I wondered whether anyone here would ever again know the desolation of spirit that my father and his comrades must have felt when they arrived in 1912, and during the desperate two months of their unsuccessful return journey.

We spent two days at the Pole and then flew in two and three-quarter hours to McMurdo Base. Cloud hid the Beardmore Glacier which I should have liked to see, but farther on the route was clear, so clear indeed that the peaks of Mt Erebus and Mt Terror came into view more than 140 miles away. Far to the right was the open sea, and we could follow the edge of the ice-shelf to the Bay of Whales where Amundsen set out for his dash to the Pole. As we approached Ross Island our pilot maintained his altitude so that we could circle the crater of Erebus before landing. This was another unforgettable sight, another of the scenic marvels of Antarctica. We flew through the smoke plume of the volcano—with a substantial bump as we hit the warm rising air—then circled one way, turned and circled back. In the foreground below us was the steaming crater, beyond the smooth white slopes of Terror, and beyond again the ice fingers of Cape Crozier where the ice barrier perpetually calves into the open sea. The majesty of it was suddenly overwhelming. I turned to look the other way and there under the sun, black in the shining silver of the sea was Inaccessible Island, off the little point of Cape Evans, where I could just pick out the old hut. Ahead as we began to lose height was McMurdo City with Nukipoo—its pale-green nuclear power station—showing clearly against the black of Observation Hill from whose peak they kept watch for the returning Polar Party which never came, and where the great cross was put up in the following summer inscribed with Tennyson's line from Ulysses: 'To strive, to seek, to find, and not to yield.'

I found myself thinking how pleased my father would be if he could know what was going on in Antarctica today . . . how he would approve of the developments, of the International Treaty, of the vast scientific programme, of the new techniques in polar travel, of the potential future of the Antarctic.

Most of the things which bring people to 'the ice' nowadays were quite unknown in my father's day. Cosmic Rays and the Ionosphere had not been discovered. Flying was in its infancy and he could not have foretold the importance of meteorology; nuclear power and satellite tracking had not been thought of. So many new things in fifty years . . . who can doubt that even more new reasons for coming to the Antarctic will emerge in the next fifty. I wondered how long they would keep women out of the Antarctic and wished they had allowed my Philippa to come with me. Already the reasons they gave were rather unconvincing.

A few days later I was taking a last look at Mt Erebus and Mt Terror as the Hercules headed northward gaining height over McMurdo Sound on its way to Christchurch, New Zealand.

42. THE WINDOW

I am back in the window where this book was begun—the window of my studio overlooking the Rushy Pen at Slimbridge. Outside the pond is white with swans. For the last two weeks, since I came back from the Antarctic, there have been 118 wild Bewick's Swans coming in each day from the estuary —the migratory swans which breed 2,500 miles away in Arctic Russia. Today there are seven new ones, making 125 and thirty-five local Mute Swans add to the whiteness of our Swan Lake.

I have been trying to learn the names Philippa has given to the thirty odd new Bewick's Swans which have come since I went away. What particularly delights me about these swans is that we have persuaded them to come by a conscious effort on our part to which they have so spectacularly responded. As I watch dusk is falling and the first swans are beginning to leave for the estuary where most of them will roost. They take off past the window, brilliantly illuminated by the golden floodlights against the deep ultramarine of the dusk. The foreground of this magical scene is occupied by a mass of floodlit swans upending within a few yards of the window.

As I sit gazing entranced at this scene, I think of all the things I ought to be doing ... of the commissioned picture seven by four and a half feet, just behind me which must be finished, of the commentary for one of my *Look* series television programmes which must be finally polished before to-

morrow when it is to be recorded in Bristol, of the fish identification paintings I must complete for my Fishwatcher's Guide
to the Caribbean coral reefs, of the work I must do on the
Agenda for the next meeting of my Survival Service Com-
mission—the part of the International Union for Conservation
of Nature which deals with species of animals and plants
threatened with extinction. Then I think of the mountain of
correspondence which has accumulated during my Antarctic
trip—much of it to do with the World Wildlife Fund where
constant hard work is necessary to keep up the flow of money
so desperately needed.

I think of all these things and I go on watching the swans.
When they have gone out to the river I shall get down to work.
As I sit here with my wife I am more than ever convinced that
I am the luckiest man I know. I say this not with smugness or
self-satisfaction but because I can think of nothing sadder than
to live a happy and interesting life without recognising it.
Maybe I am an ostrich with my head in the sand. Maybe Fate
or my own or other men's folly has all kinds of disasters in
store for me, but they cannot take away these exciting and
happy years. Not to acknowledge such good fortune would be
inexcusable.

THE PATH OF THE KING
by John Buchan

John Buchan, with the consummate art of a great story-teller, traces through the pageant of history the fortunes of successive members of a line destined one day to give the world a master. It was a line of men and women set apart from their contemporaries by a strength and nobility of spirit, a quality that found its last fulfilment and its final flowering in the leader that the New World has been waiting for.

FLIGHT OF THE BAT
by Donald Gordon

A Russian missile lands in Hyde Park. It brings a challenge to the leaders of the West: can they within the next seven days land a reply in Red Square, Moscow? Unless they succeed the Western World must face obliteration or servitude.

As conventional methods fail, hope centres on a secret low-level bomber – but can it penetrate the Russian defences, navigate accurately when flying over unknown country faster than sound and at tree-top height and launch its stand-off bomb with absolute precision? And can the crew survive?

THIS ROUGH MAGIC

by Mary Stewart

The tranquillity of an Ionian island is shattered by fear, danger and death – and a man to whom murder is no more than a game.

'There will be few books published this year which will give more enjoyment to more people.'

The Scotsman

This Rough Magic – Mary Stewart's greatest seller, which spent eight months on the American best-seller lists.

THE IVY TREE

by Mary Stewart

In the shadow of Hadrian's wall a house is gripped by terror and hatred when a girl who died four years ago, comes home.

'*The Ivy Tree* has the ideal thriller blend of plot, suspense, character drawing and good writing . . . it opens with the impact of a rifle report on a calm summer's day and drives to its climax of action with compelling urgency.'

Daily Express

MADAM, WILL YOU TALK?

by Mary Stewart

Charity's gay Provençal holiday turned into something very different, something both terrifying and precious, after her first memorable visit to Nîmes. The peacefulness of that golden afternoon was the last brief lull before the thunder.

'There are few to equal Mary Stewart as an entertainer.'
The Daily Telegraph

THE MOON-SPINNERS

by Mary Stewart

'*The Moon-spinners* is a story of private vengeance, of a hunt through the savage countryside of Crete and of a girl who for the first time meets a situation – and a man – she cannot deal with.

'I cannot think of anyone who tells such stories quite so well.'

Anthony Boucher, *New York Times*

'In a class of her own.'

Bristol Evening Post